Black

Update and corrections

brought into force at short notice on April 3rd 2017.

Editors' Notes

We were delighted to be invited to be Consultant Editors for *Blackstone's Handbook of Cyber Crime Investigation*. This excellent Handbook serves to address the increasing rise and sophistication of contemporary cyber crime by providing practical guidance to law enforcement officers who are responsible for tackling cyber crime.

This unique work brings together the diverse range of cyber threats and required investigative expertise into one volume to support the training needs of law enforcement practitioners. Designed as an investigative introduction to cyber crime, this volume juxtaposes practical experience, policy guidance and the law, clearly interpreting and illustrating the complexity of contemporary cyber investigative techniques.

The authors have expertly compiled a valuable Handbook which provides investigators with a much needed resource, directly responding to their training needs by defining cyber crime, accurately describing the threat to communities from online hazards and explaining the actions required by frontline police officers to help effectively to prevent, detect and investigate cyber crime.

This Handbook navigates a clear course through cyber security strategies for law enforcement officers by explaining the local, regional and national cyber crime policing frameworks, underpinned by explanations and practical interpretations so that all police practitioners are better informed to carry out their cyber crime responsibilities.

This work will not only appeal to cyber crime investigators for whom it has been written but will also be a welcome introduction to the resource library of prosecutors, policymakers, security professionals, academics and students.

Babak Akhgar FBCS
Professor of Informatics
Director of the Centre of Excellence for Terrorism, Resilience,
Intelligence & Organised Crime Research (CENTRIC)

Francesca Bosco
Project Officer
Emerging Crimes Unit, United Nations
Inter-regional Justice & Crime Research Institute (UNICRI)

Acknowledgements

This Handbook would not have been created without the creativity, commitment and collaboration between Andrew Staniforth, Research Fellow at Trends Research & Advisory, and Nigel Hughes, Head of the Police National Legal Database.

The authors wish to acknowledge the support of Babak Akhgar, Professor of Informatics and Director of the Centre of Excellence for Terrorism, Resilience, Intelligence & Organised Crime Research (CENTRIC) as Consultant Editor alongside Francesca Bosco, Project Officer, Emerging Crimes Unit, United Nations Inter-regional Justice & Crime Research Institute (UNICRI). Thanks are also extended to Lord Carlile of Berriew CBE QC for supporting this new volume and for providing the Foreword.

The creation of this volume could not have been completed without a multi-disciplinary approach, and the authors wish to acknowledge the support and contributions made by colleagues of the CENTRIC Board, PNLD and also Professor David Wall of the University of Leeds, Dr Richard Burchill, Timothy Ingle, Benn Kemp and Sina Pournouri.

And finally, thanks are also extended to the team at Oxford University Press, especially Commissioning Editor Peter Daniell and Assistant Commissioning Editor Lucy Alexander for their patience and for sharing their expertise.

Contents

Contents

Contents

Abbreviations

ACPO	Association of Chief Police Officers
AFP	Australian Federal Police
AG	Attorney General
APT	Advanced Persistent Threat
BBS	Bulletin Board System
BCU	Basic Command Unit
BIS	Department for Business, Innovation & Skills (now the Department for Business, Energy & Industrial Strategy)
BNP	British National Party
BPC	Border Policing Command
BSC	British Society of Computing
CCU	Cyber Crime Unit
CEOP	Child Exploitation and Online Protection Centre
CERT	Computer Emergency Response Team
CESG	Communications-Electronics Security Department
CFC	Cyber Fusion Centre
CIA	Central Intelligence Agency
CII	Covert Internet Investigator
CIT	Cyber Intelligence Team
CNP	Card-Not-Present
CoE	Council of Europe
CONTEST	COuNter-TErrorism STrategy
CPIA	Criminal Procedure and Investigations Act 1996
CPNI	Centre for the Protection of National Infrastructure
CPS	Crown Prosecution Service
CSOC	Cyber Security Operations Centre
CSP	Communications Service Provider
CSU	Child Sexual Exploitation
CTELO	Counter Terrorism and Extremism Liaison Officer
CTIRU	Counter Terrorism Internet Referral Unit
CTU	Counter Terrorism Unit
DDoS	Distributed Denial of Service
DERO	Digital Evidence Recovery Officer
DFU	Digital Forensic Unit
DoS	Denial of Service
DPP	Director of Public Prosecutions
DRDO	Defence Research and Development Organisation
EC3	Europol Cybercrime Centre
ECC	Economic Crime Command

Abbreviations

EDT	Electronic Disturbance Theatre
EEA	European Economic Area
EEA state	EU states, plus Iceland, Lichtenstein and Norway
ETA	Euskadi Ta Askatasuna
FBI	Federal Bureau of Investigation
FCO	Foreign & Commonwealth Office
FP	Focal Points
GCHQ	Government Communications Headquarters
GPMS	Government Protective Marking Scheme
HIDS	Host Intrusion Detection Systems
HIPS	Host Intrusion Prevention Systems
HOCR	Home Office Counting Rules
HPP	Hackers Profiling Project
IA	Information Assurance
ICC	Interception of Communications Commissioner
ICI	Imperial Chemical Industries
ICSR	International Centre for the Study of Radicalisation
ICT	Information Communications Technology
IDCC	INTERPOL Digital Crime Centre
IDS	Intrusion Detection System
IED	Improvised Explosive Device
IGCEG	INTERPOL Global Cybercrime Expert Group
IGCI	INTERPOL Global Complex for Innovation
IoE	Internet of Everything
IoT	Internet of Things
IPCC	Independent Police Complaints Commission
IPT	Investigatory Powers Tribunal
IRA	Irish Republican Army
IS	Islamic State (Daesh)
ISP	Internet Service Provider
IT	Information Technology
ITBP	Indo-Tibetan Border Police
IWF	Internet Watch Foundation
J-CAT	Joint Cybercrime Action Taskforce
KVM	Keyboard Video Mouse
M2M	Machine-to-Machine
MOD	Ministry of Defence
NCA	National Crime Agency
NCCU	National Cyber Crime Unit
NCIS	National Criminal Intelligence Service
NCR	National Crime Review
NDM	National Decision Model
NFIB	National Fraud Intelligence Bureau
NIDS	Network Intrusion Detection Systems
NIM	National Intelligence Model

NIPS	Network Intrusion Prevention Systems
NPCC	National Police Chiefs' Council
NSA	National Security Agency
NSC	National Security Council
NSRA	National Security Risk Assessment
NTAIA	National Technical Authority for Information Assurance
OCC	Organised Crime Command
OCG	Organised Crime Group
OCSIA	Office of Cyber Security & Information Assurance
OCTA	Organised Crime Threat Assessment
OFT	Office of Fair Trading
OGSIRO	Office of the Government Senior Information Risk Owner
OSC	Office of Surveillance Commissioners
PACE	Police and Criminal Evidence Act 1984
PCC	Police and Crime Commissioner
PCSO	Police Community Support Officer
PDA	Personal Digital Assistant
POS	Point of Sale
PSD	Professional Standards Directorate
PSN	Public Sector Network
RAT	Remote Access Tool
RCCU	Regional Cyber Crime Unit
RFID	Radio Frequency Identification
RIPA	Regulation of Investigatory Powers Act 2000
ROCU	Regional Organised Crime Unit
SARA	Scanning, Analysis, Response and Assessment
SCADA	Supervisory Control and Data Acquisition
SGII	Self-Generated Indecent Imagery
SME	Small and Medium-sized Enterprise
SPOC	Single Point of Contact
SPRs	Strategic Policing Requirements
ST&CG	Strategic Tasking and Co-ordinating Group
TAM	Terrorism & Allied Matters
TT&CG	Tactical Tasking and Co-ordinating Group
UNICRI	United Nations Inter-regional Justice & Crime Research Institute
VPN	Virtual Private Network

Part I

Understanding the Threat from Cyber Crime

Chapter 1

Cyber Threats

1.1 Introduction

The development of the internet and digital technologies represent a major opportunity for the UK, transforming businesses and providing new tools for everyday communication. More than 80 per cent of households in the UK now have an internet connection and internet users are spending increasing amounts of time online, undertaking a greater range of online and social networking activities. In terms of business, online retail spending accounts for approximately 15 per cent of all retail spend each month, an approximate average weekly online spend of £600 million and growing. The internet and online activities have now become central to the very way in which people live their lives in modern society.

While the internet has positively enriched societal communications and economic opportunities, these technological advancements have changed—and continue to change—the very nature of crime, serving to breed a new sophisticated and technically capable criminal. The nature of some 'traditional' crime types have been transformed by the use of computers and information communications technology (ICT) in terms of its scale and reach, with threats and risks extending to many aspects of social life. New forms of criminal activity have also been developed, targeting the integrity of computers and computer networks. Threats exist not just to individuals and businesses, but to national security and infrastructure. Furthermore, the borderless nature of the phenomenon of cyber crime means that the UK can be targeted from jurisdictions across the world, making law enforcement particularly challenging. The new features of crime brought about as a result of the development of cyberspace have become known as cyber crime.

The purpose of this opening chapter is to communicate the definition of cyber crime, to provide clarity as to the categories and classification of cyber crime and to understand more about the threat of cyber crime. It is essential for all cyber crime practitioners, policymakers and professionals to understand what cyber crime is and what it is not, as well as understanding more about the scale, scope and seriousness of the threats from cyber criminals whose activities are serving to damage online safety and threaten national security.

1.2 **The Rise of Cyber-Related Crime**

Cyber crime is nothing new, its origins can be traced back decades. The first piece of criminal legislation to address the use—or rather misuse—of computers in the UK was enacted in 1990. The Computer Misuse Act 1990 made provision for securing computer material against unauthorised access or modification. Although the Act addressed unauthorised access, the concept of causing a computer (or network of computers) to perform a function in furtherance of other crimes was also a central part of this new legislation which, for the first time in the UK, sought to catch up with computer technology that was becoming part of people's everyday lives. While the enactment of laws by UK authorities recognised the threats from criminals harnessing the power of computers, it was somewhat late to arrive on the statute books as criminal computer-based activities were already well advanced, based on the lessons learned from more than 20 years of committing crime with the use of computers. Table 1.1 provides a short history of the key milestones in the rise of cyber crime, providing evidence that cyber-related crime has a rich and recent history.

1.3 **Defining Cyber Crime**

When defining cyber crime, and specifically the key characteristics and classification of the phenomenon, cyber investigators need to understand the impact of ICT on society and how they have transformed the world. Cyberspace creates new opportunities for criminals to commit crimes through its unique features. These features, according to Professor David Wall, an academic expert in the

Table 1.1 Key milestones in the rise of cyber crime

Date	Event
1970	Over the course of three years, the chief teller at the Park Avenue branch of New York's Union Dime Savings bank manipulated the account information on the bank's computer system to embezzle over $1.5 million from hundreds of customer accounts.
1971	The first computer Creeper virus was developed by BBN Technologies engineer Bob Thomas. The virus proved to be an annoyance which served to infect other computer systems. Creeper was an experimental self-replicating program that was designed not to damage but only to display a message. Being the first virus to self-replicate over a computer network, *Creeper* is also regarded as the first computer worm.
1977	Over the course of a single weekend, a programmer based in the Rotterdam offices of Imperial Chemical Industries (ICI) stole hundreds of original computer tapes and their back-ups. The perpetrator and his accomplice attempted to extort ICI by requesting £275,000 for the return of the stolen files.
1982	During the Cold War, the Central Intelligence Agency (CIA) in the US found a way to disrupt the operation of a Siberian gas pipeline in Russia without using traditional explosive devices such as missiles or bombs. Instead, they caused the Siberian gas pipeline to explode using a portion of a code in the computer system that controlled its operation in what they tagged as a 'logic bomb'. The chaos that ensued was so monumental that the resulting fire could be seen from space.
1988	Robert Morris released the first intentional hostile computer worm on the internet which infected thousands of systems. Morris was arrested by US authorities and sentenced to three years' probation, 400 hours of community service and a fine of $10,000.
1994	Russian-based hackers made 40 transfers totalling $10 million from Citibank to bank accounts in Finland, Russia, Germany, the Netherlands, the US, Israel and Switzerland. All but $400,000 was recovered.
1997	The Electronic Disturbance Theatre (EDT) was formed, an activist network which created tools to establish an electronic version of protest sit-ins on the internet. Their Floodnet tool would later be used by protesters from several nations to perform DoS attacks on the website of the president of Mexico and the White House.

(*continued*)

Table 1.1 Continued

Date	Event
1998	A disgruntled system operator remotely manipulated the Supervisory Control and Data Acquisition (SCADA) system of a coal-fired power plant putting it in emergency mode and removing the SCADA system software.
2005	Hackers successfully attacked the air conditioning system of a European bank's computer centre which served to slowly increase the temperature of the computer room causing a shutdown of all computer service systems.
2006	During December 2006, WikiLeaks (an international, non-profit journalistic organisation that publishes secret information, news leaks and classified media from anonymous sources) published its first document on the website http://www.wikileaks.org. WikiLeaks has been predominantly represented in public since January 2007 by Julian Assange, who is generally recognised as the 'founder of WikiLeaks'. Assange, a former hacker, formed a hacking group called the International Subversives who hacked into the Pentagon and other US Department of Defense facilities, the US Navy, NASA; Australia's Overseas Telecommunications Commission; Citibank, Lockheed Martin, Motorola, Panasonic and Xerox.
2009	A series of coordinated attacks against major government, financial websites and news agencies of both the US and South Korea involved the activation of a 'botnet', a compromised computer that can be controlled remotely by a third party. This attack involved a number of hijacked computers that caused servers to overload due to the flooding of traffic from a distributed denial of service (DDoS) attack. The number of hijacked computers varied depending on the source and included 50,000 from the Symantec's Security Technology Response Group, 20,000 from the National Intelligence Service of South Korea and more than 166,000 from Vietnamese computer security researchers as they analysed the two servers used by the invaders.
2010	Iran was subjected to cyber attacks when its nuclear facility in Natanz was infected by Stuxnet, a cyber worm that was believed to be a combined effort of Israel and the US, though no one claimed responsibility for its inception. The worm destroyed Tehran's 1,000 nuclear centrifuges and set back the country's atomic programme by at least two years, as it spread beyond the plant and infected over 60,000 computers.

Table 1.1 Continued

Date	Event
2013	Edward Joseph Snowden, described as an American privacy activist, computer professional, former CIA employee and former government contractor, leaked classified information from the NSA. The information revealed numerous global surveillance programmes, many run by the NSA with the cooperation of telecommunication companies and European governments. During 2013, Snowden flew to Hong Kong after leaving his job at an NSA facility in Hawaii where he then revealed thousands of classified NSA documents to journalists who published stories based on the material which appeared in the *Guardian* and the *Washington Post*. Further disclosures were made by other newspapers including *Der Spiegel* and the *New York Times*. The US Department of Justice unsealed charges against Snowden of two counts of violating the Espionage Act and theft of government property. Snowden flew to Moscow, Russia, where he reportedly remained for over a month and where Russian authorities granted him a one-year temporary asylum which was later extended to three years.
2015	On 31 July 2015, WikiLeaks published 'Target Tokyo', the 35 Top Secret National Security Agency (NSA) targets in Japan including the Japanese cabinet and Japanese companies such as Mitsubishi, together with intercepts relating to US–Japan relations, trade negotiations and sensitive climate change strategies. The list indicated that NSA spying on Japanese conglomerates, government officials, ministries, and senior advisors extended back at least as far as 2006.
2015	During October 2015, hackers attacked TalkTalk, a phone and broadband provider which had more than four million UK customers, accessing 1.2 million email addresses, names and phone numbers and 21,000 unique bank account numbers and sort codes. TalkTalk revealed that hackers had gained access to a maximum of 28,000 obscured credit and debit card details, with the middle six digits removed, and 15,000 customer dates of birth, stating that any stolen credit or debit card details were incomplete and therefore could not be used for financial transactions but advised customers to remain vigilant against fraud. TalkTalk chief executive Dido Harding said the scale of attack was 'much smaller than we originally suspected', but that did not detract from the seriousness of the incident. As a result of the security breach, Members of Parliament launched an inquiry into the attack, with senior ministers stating that the government would not be against compulsory encryption for companies holding customer data.

(continued)

Table 1.1 Continued

Date	Event
2016	Tesco Bank stopped all online transactions for 140,000 current account customers during November 2016 after it discovered that 40,000 customers had been targeted by an online attack. Unprecedented in its scale, the attack resulted in the loss of £2.5 million where customers had money taken from their accounts which were operated through an app or online. Customers reported that sums had been transferred to Spain and Brazil. The banking arm of the supermarket chain revealed that 9,000 customer accounts had been attacked. Benny Higgins, the chief executive of Tesco Bank, apologised to customers: 'Our first priority throughout this incident has been protecting and looking after our customers, and we'd again like to apologise for the worry and inconvenience this issue has caused.'

study of cyber crime, are described as 'transformative keys' and are as follows:

- **Globalisation**—providing offenders with new opportunities to exceed conventional boundaries.
- **Distributed networks**—generating new opportunities for victimisation.
- **Data trails**—creating new opportunities for criminals to commit identity theft.

To support further understanding of how the internet has generated opportunities for criminals to commit new cyber-related crimes, Professor Wall has compiled a matrix of cyber crime which illustrates the different levels of opportunity each type of crime involves. Table 1.2 illustrates this matrix showing the impact of the internet on criminal opportunity and criminal behaviour.

The matrix identifies that the internet has created three distinct opportunities for the criminal which include: more opportunities for traditional crime; new opportunities for traditional crime; and new opportunities for new types of crime. These have impacted upon the behaviour of criminals of which there are four themes including those that are integrity-related, those that are computer-related and divided into two categories are those that are content-related (obscene and violent).

Table 1.2 The matrix of cyber crime: level of opportunity by type of crime

Impact on criminal behaviour Impact on criminal opportunity	Integrity-related (harmful trespass)	Computer-related (acquisition theft and deception)	Content-related (obscenity)	Content-related (violence)
More opportunities for traditional crime	Phreaking and chipping	Frauds and pyramid schemes	Trading sexual materials	Stalking and personal harassment
New opportunities for traditional crime	Cracking, hacking, viruses and activism	Multiple large-scale frauds, trade secret theft and identity theft	Online gender trade and webcam sites	General hate speech and organised crime
New opportunities for new types of crime	Spams, DoS attacks, information warfare, parasitic computing	Intellectual property, piracy, online gambling, e-auction scams, small impact bulk fraud	Cyber-sex and cyber-pimping	Online grooming and targeted hate speech

KEY POINT—CRIMINOLOGICAL PERSPECTIVES OF CYBER CRIME

The matrix of cyber crime clearly illustrates the impact of the internet on criminal behaviour and criminal opportunities but it is one such example of numerous academic models established to provide a better understanding of cyber crime. Many criminological perspectives define crime on their social, cultural and material characteristics, and view crimes as taking place at a specific geographic location. This definition of crime has allowed for the characterisation of crime, and the subsequent tailoring of crime prevention, mapping and measurement methods to the specific target audience. However, this characterisation cannot be carried over to cyber crime, because the environment in which cyber crime is committed cannot be pinpointed to a geographic location, or distinctive social or cultural group.

Acknowledging the global reach of cyber crime and the requirement to establish a common understanding of the threat and risks posed to multiple countries, the Council of Europe (CoE) adopted its Convention on Cybercrime Treaty, known as the Budapest Convention, which identified several activities present in offences of cyber crime. These activities served to shape what elements constituted contemporary cyber crime and included:

- Intentional access without right to the whole or part of any computer system.
- Intentional interception, without right, of non-public transmissions of computer data.
- Intentional damage, deletions, deterioration, alteration or suppression of computer data without right.
- Intentional and serious hindering of the function of a computer system by inputting, transmitting, damaging, deleting, deterioration, altering or suppressing computer data.
- Production, sale, procurement for use, importation or distribution of devices designed to commit any of the above crimes, or of passwords or similar data used to access computer systems, with the intent of committing any of the above crimes.

Despite attempts by authorities to define cyber crime, whose efforts commonly sought to construct a definition designed to protect and indicate violations of the confidentiality, integrity and availability of computer systems, a universally recognised definition of cyber crime remained elusive and presented a real challenge to law enforcement agencies across the world. But the sudden and dramatic increase of the sheer volume of varying types of cyber crime served to shape and inform the collective understanding of cyber crime. When discussing cyber-related crime generally today, there are four recognised types of cyber crime which relate to the matrix of cyber crime produced by Professor David Wall and they are as follows:

- **traditional** forms of crime using computers and the tools and services within the cyber domain (i.e. theft and fraud);
- **illegal content** (i.e. pirated music, indecent images and child pornography);
- **crimes unique to electronic networks** (i.e. hacking and denial of service (DoS) attacks);
- **crimes unique to cyberspace** which threaten physical structures, systems and infrastructures (i.e. manipulation of process control systems to damage power stations and their supply).

In the UK, for the police, policymakers and the public, and for the purposes of this Handbook, cyber crime is best described as an umbrella term used to identify two distinct, but closely related, criminal activities which incorporate the four types of cyber crime which are 'cyber-dependent' and 'cyber-enabled' crimes as outlined in Table 1.3.

KEY POINT—CYBER CRIME CATEGORIES

It is absolutely essential that cyber crime investigators can clearly distinguish between the two recognised categories of cyber crime and that they approach their activities within the context of 'what is illegal offline is illegal online'. For the purposes of this Handbook, the term cyber crime refers to both categories of criminal activity now recognised and well established by the police.

1.4 Cyber Crime Classification

There are many different types of cyber crime within the categories of cyber-dependent and cyber-enabled crimes. Table 1.4 provides a

Table 1.3 Categories of cyber crime

Cyber-dependent crimes	Offences that can only be committed by using a computer, computer networks or other form of ICT. These acts include the spread of viruses and other malicious software, hacking and DDoS attacks, i.e. the flooding of internet servers to take down network infrastructure or websites. Cyber-dependent crimes are primarily acts directed against computers or network resources, although there may be secondary outcomes from the attacks, such as fraud.
Cyber-enabled crimes	Traditional crimes that are increased in their scale or reach by the use of computers, computer networks or other ICT. Unlike cyber-dependent crimes, they can still be committed without the use of ICT. These types of cyber-enabled crime include: • fraud (including mass-marketing fraud, 'phishing' emails and other scams; online banking and e-commerce fraud); • theft (including theft of personal information and identification-related data); and • sexual offending against children (including grooming, and the possession, creation and/ or distribution of sexual imagery).

summary of the different types of cyber crime that are prevalent today but this is not an exhaustive list as cybercriminals continue to develop new and ever more sophisticated methods to commit their crimes.

1.5 **Current Cyber Crime Threats**

It is critical for cyber investigators to understand and recognise the scale and nature of cyber crime, how it is changing over time and whether interventions to tackle the problem are having an impact. This will help to drive forward policy decisions with a sound

Table 1.4 Typology of cyber crimes

Phishing	Phishing is a form of fraud in which the attacker tries to learn information such as login credentials or account information by masquerading as a reputable entity or person in an email or other communication channel. Their messages may ask the recipient to 'update', 'validate' or 'confirm' their account information. The term phishing (also known as spoofing) comes from the increasingly sophisticated lures of cybercriminals as they 'fish' for user's financial information and password data.
Spam	Spam is a term used to describe unsolicited emails, electronic junk mail or junk newsgroup postings. Spam is generally email advertising for a product or service sent to a mailing list or newsgroup and can be generally regarded as an annoyance as the emails may be unwanted and can consume network bandwidth impacting upon the speed and efficiency of computers and their wider networks. Spam is used by cybercriminals to deliver viruses, malicious code and phishing emails.
Hacking	Hacking, one of the most widely analysed and debated forms of cybercriminal activity, is defined as any technical effort to manipulate the normal behaviour of a computer, computer network connections and connected systems. A hacker is any person engaged in hacking. Hacking and hackers are most commonly associated with malicious programming attacks on the internet and other networks.
Denial of service	Denial of service (DoS) attacks are aimed at specific websites. The attacker floods the webserver with messages that are endlessly repeated. This ties up the system and denies access to legitimate users. DoS attacks which are carried out by someone attacking from multiple computers are known as distributed denial of service (DDoS) attacks. DoS and DDoS attacks represent major cyber security challenges to both government and private industry.

(continued)

Table 1.4 Continued

Cyber stalking, harassment and bullying	Cyber bullying is the use of electronic information and communication devices such as email, instant messaging, text messages, blogs, mobile phones, pagers, instant messages and defamatory websites to bully or otherwise harass an individual or group through personal attacks or other means. The taunts, insults and harassment of cyber bullying has become rampant amongst young people and has become so prevalent with emerging social media and text messaging that it has affected every school in every community.

Cyber stalking and harassment is defined as:
- having received unwanted emails that were threatening or obscene; or
- respondents having personal, obscene or threatening information posted about them on the internet.

Identity theft	Identity theft represents one of the fastest growing cyber crimes in the UK which is the act of obtaining sensitive information about another person without his or her knowledge, and using that information to commit theft, fraud or other crimes. Identity theft continues to represent a major challenge to law enforcement, made increasingly difficult by a combination of factors including citizens' lax online security measures and cybercriminals escalating and evolving methods of gaining and utilising personal information.
Credit card fraud	Credit card fraud is the unauthorised use of plastic or credit cards, or the theft of a plastic card number to dishonestly obtain money or property. Credit card losses amount to £350 million per year in the UK of which 20 per cent is the result of credit card fraud abroad where criminals use stolen UK credit card details at cash machines and retailers in countries that have yet to upgrade to chip and PIN capabilities. The largest credit card fraud type in the UK is card-not-present (CNP) fraud which encompasses any fraudulent online, telephone or mail order payment. The primary challenge for investigators of CNP offences is identifying the perpetrator(s) as neither the credit card nor the cardholder are physically present in-store at the point of sale.

Table 1.4 Continued

Auction fraud	Auction fraud occurs when items or goods are purchased that are in fact fake or stolen, or when the seller advertises non-existent items for sale receiving payment for goods in advance which are never received by the customer. The most common complaints of auction fraud, which has seen a dramatic rise following the phenomenon of online trading, involve:
	• buyers receiving goods late or not at all;
	• sellers not receiving payment;
	• buyers receiving goods that are either less valuable than those advertised or significantly different from the original description;
	• failure to disclose relevant information about a product or the terms of sale.

evidence base in this area and is vital in the context of emerging forms of cyber crime and technological developments.

1.5.1 Industry estimates of cyber-dependent crimes

Anti-virus providers generally conclude that security 'attacks' globally are in the billions and that these levels are continuously increasing. Industry report detecting 403 million unique variations of computer viruses or other malware globally, providing an insight into the scale and complexity of securing cyberspace. Reports from private industry security providers very often relate to the global levels of threat rather than the UK situation alone, and there are limitations to their estimates. It is important that those engaged in the prevention and detection of cyber crime recognise that there tends to be a lack of transparency in how estimates are produced and figures are often not comparable between anti-virus providers as they use different units of measurement, with different geographical coverage and customer bases. The British Society of Computing (BSC) has recommended 'caution' with the use of industry figures but reports compiled by anti-virus providers are helpful in understanding the nature of various threats, even if they may not accurately measure the scale of cyber-dependent crime in the UK. For example, industry reports have observed an increase in Trojans—a virus that masquerades as a legitimate program, but collects personal data from a user's computer. They have also identified the emergence of fake anti-virus software, which imitates legitimate anti-virus software but is actually a form of malware that can be used to extract users' personal information. Anti-virus providers state that the level of unsolicited emails (or 'spam') received by users, as a proportion of all email, is falling, although spam is still a common experience amongst internet users. Over half of adult internet users report spam as the most common negative experience online. Some of this decline has been attributed to the closure of 'botnets' responsible for driving large amounts of spam. Botnets refer to clusters of computers infected by malicious software that are subsequently used to automatically and repeatedly send out spam or other malicious email traffic to specified targets.

1.5.2 **Police recorded crime**

Police recorded crime does not distinguish between online and offline offences, making it difficult to identify cyber crime. Police record crime in accordance with the provisions of Home Office Counting Rules (HOCR), which set out the crime to be recorded which is determined by the law. Since there is no specific offence (or offences) of cyber crime—aside from those specified in the Computer Misuse Act—police recorded crime does not distinguish between offline and online offences. Whether or not the offence was committed online or offline, is cyber-enabled or cyber-dependent, the offence recorded is on the basis of the offence in law. For example, a fraud committed using a computer would usually be recorded as a fraud under police recorded crime.

Before the national roll-out of Action Fraud, the UK's National Fraud and Cybercrime Reporting Centre, both computer misuse and fraud offences were recorded by individual police forces. Action Fraud completed its roll-out in April 2013 and has since taken responsibility for the recording of all fraud and computer misuse offences. Action Fraud captures reports from the public and businesses on these crimes and classifies them in a way which allows distinctions to be made between computer misuse, online fraud and offline fraud. Action Fraud also assesses them against the provisions of the law and the requirements of HOCR. Where a report falls short of being recorded as a crime under HOCR, Action Fraud has the facility to record it as an incident, for intelligence and information purposes.

1.5.3 **Cyber-enabled crime: fraud and theft**

Victimisation surveys indicate that only a small proportion of internet users report being victims of cyber-enabled fraud and mass-marketing scams. This suggests that the public largely ignore unsolicited communications, although victims may not perceive themselves as 'victims' if a loss is refunded by a bank. On average, just 5 per cent of internet users report experiencing financial loss from credit/debit card misuse online. Surveys generally report low levels of response to both online and offline mass-marketing scams, with 2 per cent overall falling victim according to the Office of Fair Trading (OFT). The OFT also reveals that less than 1 per cent of internet users reported losing money to a romance scam. However, the personal sensitivities of the victim are likely to influence reporting rates in this type of online fraud. In terms of online retail fraud, on average 15–20 per cent of UK internet users have reported the non-arrival of purchased goods, goods being counterfeit or not as advertised.

Industry sources and victimisation surveys suggest that the number of fraudulent emails that attempt to get users to relinquish personal information (so-called 'phishing' emails) are rising in the UK. Only a small proportion of phishing attack victims experience financial losses from phishing attacks and surveys suggest that around 3 per cent of internet users have experienced financial loss from fraudulent messages or have been sent to fake websites. However, since it is challenging for victims to accurately attribute the source of their financial loss to a phishing email, levels of phishing are likely to be under-reported.

Cyber-enabled fraud accounts for around one-third of all reports received by Action Fraud of which shopping and auctions represent the largest proportion of cyber-enabled fraud. As awareness of cyber crimes, the police response and the Action Fraud reporting facility grows amongst the public and businesses, reports of computer misuse and fraud offences are expected to increase.

The costs recorded from online banking fraud have been declining—peaking in 2009 at £60 million and falling to £35 million in 2011. Such estimates, however, only provide a partial picture, representing losses to the banking/payment industry and not to the retail sector or the public. Recent attempts to estimate the loss from cyber crime to the retail sector by the British Retail Consortium reported overall losses of £205 million. The estimate focuses on e-commerce fraud and comprises £77 million in direct losses (most notably, identification-related fraud, card and card-not-present fraud, and refund fraud), £16.5 million in online security measures and £111.6 million in lost revenue from online fraud prevention. However, it is difficult to estimate such losses accurately. Many of the survey-based estimates of loss that have been undertaken are likely to represent just a fraction of the individuals/ organisations surveyed and may be skewed upwards by extreme losses reported by a few respondents.

'Insider threats' are a prominent issue reported in business surveys. However, the limited evidence available is mixed on whether they are a bigger problem than outsider attacks. Insider threats may be malicious or targeted activity, but may also be accidental or negligent. The majority of recent online crime incidents reported by businesses were thought to be external attacks from outside the organisation although it is not possible to verify the accuracy of these reports.

KEY POINT—THE COST OF ONLINE FRAUD AND THEFT

In a specially commissioned survey for Get Safe Online, the UK's leading source of online safety information, over one in five (21 per cent) victims of a cyber crime believed they were specifically targeted by fraudsters and over one-third (37 per cent) had been left feeling vulnerable as a result. Only 38 per cent of the victims believed that the incident was down to bad luck and over half (57 per cent) thought it was becoming much easier to fall victim to an online crime.

The survey went on to show that over a quarter of victims (26 per cent) had been scammed by phishing emails or 'vishing' phone calls. These are a much more targeted type of scam where the fraudster uses data about the victim pieced together from various sources, such as social media and intercepted correspondence, to sound convincing, and manipulates them into sharing confidential information linked to online accounts. Other areas where victims were targeted include:

- fake tax rebate emails (13 per cent);
- phone/tablet/laptop hacking (9 per cent);
- identity theft (5 per cent);
- cyber bullying or harassment (4 per cent);
- personal images stolen via webcam hacking (1 per cent).

41 per cent of people who have been a victim of a cyber crime lost money, with the average person losing £738. Men, however, are likely to lose significantly more, with the average loss being £839 compared to £617 for women. Shockingly, 8 per cent stated that they had lost in excess of £5,000.

Separate figures, prepared by the National Fraud Intelligence Bureau (NFIB), give an indication of the sheer scale of online crime, with over £268 million lost nationwide to the top ten internet-enabled frauds reported between 1 September 2014 and 31 August 2015. The figure of £268 million comes from reports of fraud to Action Fraud, calculated when the first contact with victims was via an online function. However, as a significant number of internet-enabled fraud cases still go unreported, the true economic cost to the UK is likely to be significantly higher. According to the survey, almost one in five (19 per cent) do not bother reporting a cyber crime.

Despite concerns over personal details and online security, and the rise of reported incidents, consumer online confidence appears to be growing and users continue to shop and transact online. The OFT has reported that the proportion of online shoppers with no concerns about their experiences has doubled and an increased proportion feel that online shopping is as safe as shopping in-store.

1.5.4 **Cyber-enabled crime: sexual offending against children**

Few studies distinguish between online and offline forms of sexual offending against children. The National Crime Agency (NCA) Child Exploitation and Online Protection Centre (CEOP) receives reports related to online grooming and online distribution of indecent images. Further reports to CEOP relate to possession of indecent images (although it is not clear if all of these reports were online offences) and reports of contact abuse (both online and offline).

Surveys of young people suggest that meeting new people online is a common occurrence and very few offline meetings appear to lead to harm. In an EU study of over 25,000 children aged 9 to 16 years during 2011, 1 per cent reported expressing some concern about what happened at an offline meeting that followed online contact. Overall, less than 0.1 per cent reported some form of sexual contact (approximately 28 children). Whilst serious in nature, the number of police recorded grooming offences are low compared with other types of serious sexual offending. However, for grooming to be a recorded offence in accordance with the HOCR, there must also be an offline meeting. In a case where there was only an online meeting, this would not be recorded as 'grooming' and is likely to be recorded under another sexual offence category. Crime recording rules also set out that it is the most serious offence recorded by police, which may result in grooming cases being recorded under other serious sexual offence categories, such as rape of a child.

In recent surveys of UK children aged 11 to 16 years, 12 per cent reported receiving or seeing sexual messages online. However, by no means would all of these types of message constitute an offence and such studies do not specify if they were received from adults or peers. All in authority believe that there remains significant under-reporting of online crimes of child exploitation. The similarities between the online grooming process and the initial process of building online relationships can mean that some victimisation is going unnoticed. Some victims may perceive offenders as friends or romantic partners, rather than as abusers or offenders which may contribute to under-reporting. Offenders may also create fake online personas to portray themselves as a similarly aged peer, often of the opposite sex. They can use these personas to trick victims into sending self-generated indecent imagery. Offenders may coerce children not to report and some children may be too embarrassed to report or unsure who to tell. On the other hand, some children may be able to deal with unwanted advances online. In an EU survey of 11 to 16-year-olds, only 7 per cent of those who had received or seen messages that upset them said that they had done nothing to tackle it. Others undertook activities such as blocking the sender or changing filter settings, although these messages did not all necessarily relate to sexual messages.

More than one-fifth of industry reports submitted to CEOP relate to self-generated indecent imagery (SGII), involving practices such as 'sexting'. The emergence of 'sexting'—the self-generation and exchange of indecent user imagery—indicates a shift in the nature of online risks. CEOP suggests that SGII represents one of the biggest risks to young people but cyber crime investigators must recognise that some online sexual offending may never progress to the 'offline' world. Offenders do not appear to be a homogeneous group and there is little consensus regarding the links between online and offline forms of sexual offending. Sex offenders who access, share and create indecent images of children, along with those who groom children online, have been subject to more research than other cyber offenders, however most evidence relates to small samples of imprisoned offenders in the US. Although some offenders who share and create indecent images use highly sophisticated, technical methods to conceal themselves online, these behaviours are by no means universal. CEOP estimates that almost half of 'hidden' internet use, for example through hidden forms of communication, is involved in the proliferation of indecent imagery of children. Other research has also found evidence of technical methods being used, such as multiple identities incorporating several IP addresses, proxy servers to give the appearance of being in another country and illicit images being accessed through 'disguised' websites. However, other studies of convicted offenders suggest that these measures are by no means universal and many offenders who create, store and share indecent imagery take few security measures.

1.5.5 Online harassment—online stalking and hate crime

A recent British Government survey found that 1 per cent of respondents aged 16 to 59 years reported experiencing one or more forms of online or 'cyber stalking'. In this survey, cyber stalking was defined as:

- having received unwanted emails that were threatening or obscene; or
- respondents having personal, obscene or threatening information posted about them on the internet.

To set this in context, 3.5 per cent of people surveyed had experienced a form of stalking. Both men and women reported experiencing cyber stalking although women experienced a higher proportion of incidents than men. This was similar to the findings for all forms of stalking (where 4.2 per cent of women and 2.7 per cent of men were victims on one or more occasions). Overall, there continues to be limited evidence available regarding the nature and extent of online stalking in the UK. Evidence relating to online hate crime is even sparser than information regarding online stalking. Attempts have been made to calculate the number of online hate websites, for example the Internet Watch Foundation reported 982 websites hosted by the UK inciting racial hatred.

KEY POINT—ECONOMIC COST OF CYBER CRIME

The economic impact of cyber attacks across both the public and private sectors continues to increase. It is estimated that cyber crime costs the UK economy £27 billion per year which is significant and is likely to be growing. The rapid digitalisation of consumers' lives will increase the cost of data breaches to an estimated $2.1 trillion globally by 2019, increasing to almost four times the estimated cost of breaches in 2016. The financial impact of cyber crime is therefore a national threat to economic stability, security and well-being.

1.6 Changing Threat Landscape

Cyber crime continues to develop at a phenomenal rate and a major challenge for all cyber crime investigators is to keep pace with the changing technologies and techniques of contemporary cybercriminals. Table 1.5 illustrates recent changes in the dynamic and ever-evolving threat from cyber crime identified by Symantec internet security threat reports, informed by the most comprehensive source of internet threat data in the world through their Symantec Global Intelligence Network.

KEY POINT—CYBER CRIME IS CONSTANTLY CHANGING

The cyber threat landscape is subject to constant change with far-reaching vulnerabilities, faster attacks, files held for ransom and the continued presence of data breaches. Cyber vulnerabilities remain a big part of the security picture and all the evidence from cyber crime-related threat and risk assessments indicate that the attackers are moving faster than the practical and operational implementation of effective cyber defences and countermeasures. This position is unlikely to change and the cyber attackers will continue to have the upper hand unless more can be done to anticipate future threats and risks, which requires the ability to horizon-scan for the weak signals indicating the early signs of new trends.

Table 1.5 Changing threat landscape of cyber crime

Identified threat	Threat description
Cybercriminals are streamlining and upgrading their techniques, while companies struggle to fight old tactics	• Cyber attackers continue to breach networks with highly targeted spear-phishing attacks which are increasing in volume. • Cybercriminals have perfected watering-hole attacks, making each attack more selective by infecting legitimate websites, monitoring site visitors and targeting only the companies they wanted to attack. Further complicating companies' ability to defend themselves is the appearance of 'Trepanised' software updates. • Attackers identified common software programs used by target organisations and hid their malware inside software updates for those programs, and then waited patiently for their targets to download and install that software—in effect, leading companies to infect themselves. • More than half of all targeted attacks are striking small and medium-sized organisations. These organisations often have fewer resources to invest in security, and many are still not adopting basic best practices like blocking executable files and screensaver email attachments. This puts not only the businesses, but also their business partners, at higher risk.
Cybercriminals are leapfrogging defences in ways companies lack insight to anticipate	As organisations look to discover attackers using stolen employee credentials and identify signs of suspicious behaviour throughout their networks, savvy attackers are using increased levels of deception and, in some cases, hijacking a company's own infrastructure and turning it against them. Advanced cybercriminals are now: • deploying legitimate software onto compromised computers to continue their attacks without risking discovery by anti-malware tools; • leveraging a company's management tools to move stolen IP around the corporate network; • using commonly available crimeware tools to disguise themselves and their true intention if discovered; • building custom attack software inside their victim's network, on the victim's own servers; • using stolen email accounts from one corporate victim to spear-phish their next corporate victim; • hiding inside software vendors' updates, in essence 'Trojanising' updates, to trick targeted companies into infecting themselves.

(continued)

Table 1.5 Continued

Identified threat	Threat description
Malware used in mass attacks increases and adapts	Non-targeted attacks still make up the majority of malware, with millions of new pieces of malware being created every year. Some of this malware may not be a direct risk to organisations and is instead designed to extort end-users. Beyond the annoyance factor to IT, however, it impacts employee productivity and diverts IT resources that could be better spent on high-level security issues. Malware authors have various tricks to avoid detection; one is to spot security researchers by testing for virtual machines before executing their code. Certain malware like 'W32.Crisis', upon detecting a virtual machine, will search for other virtual machine images and infect them.
Digital extortion on the rise	Cybercriminals have used ransomware to turn extortion into a profitable enterprise, attacking big and small targets alike.
	Ransomware attacks are growing, driven by a huge rise in crypto-ransomware attacks. Instead of pretending to be law enforcement seeking a fine for stolen content, as has occurred with traditional ransomware, crypto-ransomware holds a victim's files, photos and other digital media hostage without masking the attacker's intention. The victim will be offered a key to decrypt their files, but only after paying a ransom that can range from £250–£500—and this is no guarantee that their files will be freed.
Cybercriminals are leveraging social networks and apps to do their dirty work	Email remains a significant attack vector for cybercriminals but there is a clear movement towards attacking social media platforms. 70 per cent of social media scams are manually shared. These scams spread rapidly and are lucrative for cybercriminals because people are more likely to click something posted by a friend. Mobile communication devices are also ripe for attack, as many people only associate cyber threats with their PCs and neglect even basic security precautions on their smartphones. 17 per cent of all Android apps (nearly one million in total) are actually malware in disguise.

Table 1.5 Continued

Identified threat	Threat description
Point of sale systems, ATMs and home routers are all network-connected devices	Cyber attacks against point of sale (POS) systems, ATMs and home routers continue. These are all network-connected devices with an embedded operating system, though they are not often considered part of the internet. Whether officially part of the internet or not, attacks on these devices further demonstrate that it is no longer only PCs at risk and the potential for cyber attacks against cars and medical equipment should be a concern to all of us. Risks to many home router devices are exacerbated by the use of smartphones as a point of control.

1.7 Cyber Crime Trends

The cyber crime landscape continues to evolve as criminals look to adopt more efficient and profitable attack tactics. At the same time, the market for cyber crime-as-a-service is advancing rapidly, with competition among malware vendors leading to increased innovation. And as smartphone penetration reaches record levels globally, cybercriminals are starting to switch their focus to stand-alone attacks on mobile devices. Table 1.6 illustrates a number of cyber crime trends identified by the RSA Research team of the EMC Corporation, who are at the forefront of threat detection and cyber crime intelligence, protecting global organisations with the shutdown of over a million cyber crime attacks.

KEY POINT—CYBER CRIME CHALLENGE

The population of cyberspace is estimated by the British Government to be in excess of 2 billion. While we do not accurately know the frequency or longevity, this means that one-third of Earth's population visit cyberspace and billions more are anticipated to join them over the next decade, putting more of their private lives online and exchanging over $8 trillion in commerce. For the UK, the threat from cyber crime is very real with over 90 per cent of small and medium-sized businesses reporting 'cyber breaches'.

Table 1.6 Contemporary cyber crime trends

Trend	Description
Cyber crime as a service marketplace continues to mature	The cyber crime marketplace has evolved tremendously and that evolution looks set to continue. Innovation among cyber crime-as-a-service provider will continue to be driven by a competitive marketplace, leading to a generalised increase in the quality of malware produced, and enabling a much larger pool of bad actors with no technical knowledge to profit from cyber crime.
Mobility provides a larger attack surface	The volume of mobile malware and rogue mobile apps is increasing as half the world's adult population owns a smartphone. The smartphone has become the go-to device over the computer, and the one to which people are always connected. Cybercriminals will increasingly look to exploit this change in user device preference by switching an expanding proportion of their attacks to mobiles. As a result, more stand-alone attacks on mobile devices are expected in the future. In addition, future attacks on payment systems are also expected to rise as their popularity and use grows.
Cybercriminals seek more bang for their buck and increase large-scale retail and financial attacks	The hacking of POS devices has shifted rapidly from being a premium attack to a commodity. Some vendors in the criminal marketplace even offer POS malware for free when they are starting out and want to build their reputation. The barriers to entry are low and some old code is even free, so almost anyone who can code can produce this malware. An increase in large-scale retail and banking breaches is anticipated, as cybercriminals seek more efficient and profitable types of attack.
Threats continue to grow more targeted and more advanced	Advanced persistent threats (APTs) and similar attacks by nation states are expected to grow with regional conflicts driving the perpetrators and their victim selection. Criminal groups are also expected to adopt nation-state tactics. Large enterprises and other organisations will be vulnerable through their use of commodity equipment, which attackers quickly learn how to bypass, so defending against these attacks will still be challenging.

Having separated cyber crime into cyber-dependent and cyber-enabled crime, in the same way that we might separate crime within a transport network from crime where a transport network is merely an enabler, cyber investigators now need to treat cyberspace for what it is; a separate socio-spatial dimension in which people choose not only to communicate, but also to dwell, trade, socialise and cultivate; to create intellectual property, generate economic wealth, to begin and end relationships; to forage, feud and thrive, to heal, harm and steal. Viewed in this way, cyberspace is another continent, vast, viable and virtual, a distinct jurisdiction requiring its own constitution and legal system with its own law enforcement agencies and agents. To police this new cyber continent effectively and protect all online citizens and communities requires a dedicated, determined and strategic response.

Chapter 2

Understanding Cyber Crime

2.1 **Introduction**

Law enforcement agencies are challenged on many fronts in their efforts to protect the public, themselves and their partners from all manner of cyber-related threats. Through constant innovation, cybercriminals are developing increasingly sophisticated malware and rogue mobile apps and more resilient botnets. And with the rapidly expanding cyber crime-as-a-service marketplace, all these products are becoming much more widely available—and more exploitable by criminals with little or no technical knowledge.

Advanced threats continue to evolve too, with watering-hole attacks helping to make them more efficient and successful; and criminal gangs increasingly adopting APT-type techniques that were previously the preserve of nation states. To combat these trends, organisations and law enforcement agencies are tending to favour intelligence-driven security approaches which can operate in mobile and cloud environments, making greater use of behavioural analytics and taking advantage of smart device capabilities to protect users and data. Even if attacks cannot be blocked completely, having access to the right intelligence makes it possible to detect an attack more quickly, significantly reducing the attacker's window of opportunity and minimising the potential for loss or damage.

While significant state and private sector resources have been invested in the detection and investigation of cyber crime, an increasing preventative approach with a focus on raising awareness and education of online security will best serve to minimise, mitigate and better manage the current level of threat from cyber crime. The aim of this chapter, therefore, is to provide the cyber crime investigator with an insight into the full range of criminality and crime types committed by cybercriminals, as well as exploring the psychology of the cybercriminal and offering practical online guidance and advice to prevent cyber crime, all of which is essential for today's cyber crime investigator.

2.2 **Diversity of Cyber Crime**

A key challenge for law enforcement in tackling cyber crime effectively is categorising and prioritising reports and investigations. Cyber crime cuts across traditional tiers of police prioritisation frameworks from lower level crimes of anti-social behaviour, harassment and bullying, to the more serious and organised crimes of sexual exploitation of children and human trafficking. Table 2.1 provides a series of case studies to highlight the diverse range of crime types that are committed within the domain of cyber-enabled and cyber-dependent crime, all of which have varying degrees of impact but which all serve to damage the safety and security of citizens, their communities and commercial industry.

KEY POINT—DIVERSITY OF CYBER-RELATED OFFENCES

The case studies provide an insight into the vast scale, reach and diversity of cyber crime. From online bullying to human trafficking, the use of cyberspace to plan, conduct and commit crime spans the traditional physical, legal and structural boundaries of policing. The totality of cyber crime to be tackled effectively requires a new approach and while the police have just begun to better understand the extent of online crime, and are gaining a better understanding of the challenges they face in keeping communities safe online, they have taken positive strides to disprove the incorrect perception that real-world laws do not apply online. The police are now showing that online harassment, intimidation and threatening behaviour will not go unpunished.

2.3 **Cyber Hate Crimes**

Cyber hate is currently understood as being the use of ICT to promote hate and to target individuals, groups and impressionable audiences that increasingly rely on these technologies for social

2 Understanding Cyber Crime

Table 2.1 Diversity of cyber crime

Online bullying—teenage harassment

During 2008, a 16-year-old male from Brighton, East Sussex, was driven to attempt suicide following a period of online bullying. The victim had swallowed 60 painkillers whilst alone in his bedroom. His parents had become concerned when he did not wake for breakfast and they found him unconscious. Their prompt actions saved his life; the suicide attempt being described by psychologists as 'serious and genuine'. The 16-year-old victim who was gay, had been the subject of bullying at the hands of a former friend who was later convicted of harassment in what was described as a landmark case within the UK. Following a disagreement between the two friends, the 17-year-old defendant created a fake online profile and lured the victim into an internet relationship on the popular site 'Bebo'. As this fake relationship developed, explicit messages were exchanged. The details of these conversations were then shared by the defendant with friends and teachers of the victim. The fake profile was only uncovered when the victim received an email, purporting to be from the fake person but accidentally sent from the defendant's personal email address. Suzanne Sooros, prosecuting said: 'The victim was then told by the defendant that not only had he made up the identity but he had been talking to friends and teachers, he was told all these people were colluding against him and laughing at him.' Sentencing the defendant to a 12-month referral order, confiscating the defendant's laptop and ordering the defendant to pay the victim £250, the chair of the bench, Tim Chittleburgh, said he hoped the case: 'Would send a message to other youngsters that this was a piece of planned and sustained harassment in public.'

Online hate crime—inciting racial hatred

During July 2009, two British citizens, Simon Sheppard aged 52, a former British National Party (BNP) organiser, and Stephen Whittle, aged 42, were convicted at Leeds Crown Court for a number of race hate crimes. Whilst this case was not unique in its nature, the conviction was the first conviction for inciting racial hatred via a foreign website. Sheppard had previous convictions for his extreme right-wing views but took to the internet to commit further offences with Whittle. Sheppard created a website and employed Whittle as a columnist under a pseudonym Luke O'Farrell.

The police investigation began when a complaint was made about a leaflet posted through the door of an address titled 'The tales of the Hollahoax'. Police investigators traced the address to a post office box registered to Sheppard in Hull, Yorkshire. This led officers to discover the web page where the pair posted grotesque images of murdered Jews alongside cartoons and articles ridiculing other ethnic groups. During the initial trial, the defendants failed to answer bail and fled to California where they sought asylum, claiming they were being persecuted for their right-wing views. They were arrested in the US and deported to the UK.

Table 2.1 Continued

During the trial, the court heard the constant theme of postings and publications which suggested the Holocaust was falsified by Jews as a slur on the German people. The defence argued that the online material did not fall under the jurisdiction of UK law as it was hosted on servers in California but the judge rejected this in a landmark ruling.

Sentencing the pair to 4 years 10 months and 2 years 4 months respectively, Judge Rodney Grant said: 'These are serious offences, I can say without any hesitation that I have rarely seen, or had to read or consider, material which is so abusive and insulting towards racial groups within our own society.'

Online organised crime—importation of illegal drugs

During 2013, Paul Lesley Howard, an Australian resident, became the first person in the world to be convicted of a 'Silk-Road-related crime'. Howard had been using the underground website to purchase and supply drugs as part of his organised criminal enterprise. Launched during 2011 as an online market, being operated as a Tor-hidden service, Silk Road allowed online users to browse the site anonymously and securely without the dangers of police monitoring. While visiting the Silk Road site, Howard purchased illegal drugs on 11 separate occasions, including marijuana and cocaine which were later posted directly to his home address from various countries including the Netherlands and Germany. Howard was one of thousands of criminals using Silk Road which facilitated monthly trade of an estimated value of £1.22 million. When Australian Customs officials intercepted mail destined for Howard's home, they found 14.5g of cocaine. A search of his home address soon followed where Australian Federal Police (AFP) found further evidence of his criminal enterprise, recovering cash and weapons. Howard pleaded guilty to two charges of importing a marketable quantity of a border-controlled drug. AFP Senior Investigating Officer, Peter Sykora, said: 'Criminals are attempting to exploit the international mail system through online networks but the recent arrest demonstrates that we are one step ahead of them. The AFP will continue to identify, investigate and prosecute individuals or groups importing narcotics into Australia, including via illicit ecommerce platforms such as Silk Road.'

Online fraud—back office burglars

During April 2013, Darius Bolder, aged 34, entered the back office of Barclays Swiss Cottage branch in London where he installed a Keyboard Video Mouse (KVM) switch, allowing an organised crime group (OCG) to access the IT system of the bank's branch. The group used the KVM device remotely from a nearby hotel to make 128 transfers worth £1,252,490 to a network of mule accounts set up to launder the stolen cash. Barclays reported the cyber attack later that day and have to date only managed to recover £600,000 of the stolen funds.

(continued)

Table 2.1 Continued

Just three months later, during July 2013, Dean Outram, aged 32, entered a Lewisham branch of Barclays and was able to unlawfully gain access to the bank's computers where £90,000 was stolen. Two months later, during September 2013, the same OCG made another attempt to unlawfully gain access to banking systems, this time attacking the IT infrastructure of Santander by fitting another KVM device. On this occasion, the Metropolitan Police Service (MPS) were able to arrest members of the OCG as part of a large-scale operation. Nine members of the OCG were convicted at Southwark Crown Court and sentenced in April 2014 to a total of 24 years and nine months' imprisonment. Detective Chief Inspector Jason Tunn of the MPS Cyber Crime Unit, said: 'Today's convictions are the culmination of a long and highly complex investigation into an organised crime group whose aim was to steal millions of pounds from London banks and credit card companies. Through working with industry partners such as Santander and Barclays, whose efforts in assisting us were immense, we have been able to bring this group to justice.'

Online child exploitation—the US approach to tackling child prostitution

During June 2014, the FBI Atlanta Field Office led a multi-agency investigation in support of operation Cross Country VIII, designed to tackle child sex trafficking throughout the US. Operation Cross Country is part of the Innocence Lost National Initiative that was established in 2003 by the FBI's Criminal Investigative Division, in partnership with the Department of Justice and the National Center for Missing and Exploited Children, to address the growing problem of online sexual exploitation. The operation included enforcement actions in and around Atlanta, Macon, Augusta and Savannah, Georgia, and led to the safe return of 11 juveniles who were being victimised through prostitution and other computer-based exploitation. In addition, 71 individuals were arrested on various state charges including pimping, criminal attempt child molestation/ enticement of a minor, prostitution and solicitation. Special Agent Johnson of the FBI Atlanta Field Office stated: 'The FBI's commitment and dedication toward the protection of our nation's children is clearly demonstrated in this latest national initiative and its primary objective of recovering juveniles being exploited and arresting those exploiting them. This is not an easy endeavor and the extensive participation and support from our various law enforcement partners is not only appreciated but is very much needed for these initiatives to be successful.' To date, the FBI and its task force partners have recovered and returned to safety more than 3,400 children from sexual exploitation, much of which is planned and carried out online.

Table 2.1 Continued

**Trafficking of human beings—sexual exploitation
of young women**

During January 2014, four Hungarian men, Mate Puskas, Zoltan Mohacsi, Ivtvan
Toth and Peter Toth, together with Puskas's British former girlfriend, Victoria Brown,
were found guilty of conspiring to traffic women into the UK for sexual exploitation
contrary to s 1 of the Criminal Law Act 1977. The charges related to 60 separate
incidents over a two-year period where the gang had flown over 50 young women
into the UK from Hungary with the promise of paid employment as nannies and
clerical workers. Having arrived in the UK, the gang uploaded the profiles of the
women onto websites advertising sexual services for sale. While the gang had
deceptively paid for the women's travel to the UK as part of the agreement, upon
arrival they were informed that in order to pay the 'debt' of the travel costs they
would be working in brothels managed by the group. To assert control over the
women, members of the gang removed their passports and identity documents and
threatened to harm their families in Hungary if they did not comply with their orders.
The gang conducted its entire business from an internet café in Croydon, organising
criminal activities online. The gang were found guilty at Croydon Crown Court and
were given custodial sentences which included 12 years' imprisonment for Vishal
Chaudhary, described as the leader of the gang. During sentencing, Judge Gower
said of the gang: 'Over a period of six years it exploited hundreds of women and was
a sophisticated business, it must have generated hundreds of thousands of pounds.'

interaction. Those individuals and groups who push and promote
online hatred achieve their goals in four main ways:

- promoting ideology;
- promoting hatred of other racial and religious groups;
- exerting control over others; and
- targeting opponents.

Hate crime remains an elusive concept yet its harmful and corrosive consequences for individuals, groups and societies are
becoming increasingly clear. Emerging powerful technologies
have presented new opportunities for the perpetrators of hate who
engage in a spectrum of hate crime running from abuse and harassment through to violent extremism. Cyber hate perpetrators
exploit the well-documented appeal of the internet in much the
same way as other cybercriminals. Its attractions centre on the following features:

- anonymity;
- sophistication;

- opportunities for empowerment;
- virtually instantaneous information transmission;
- manipulability of electric information;
- affordability, popularity and accessibility;
- potential as a 'force-multiplier' capable of enhancing the power and reach of extremist messages or relatively powerless individuals/groups.

KEY POINT—SUPPORTING VICTIMS OF CYBER HATE

It is essential for police officers responding to and investigating issues and allegations relating to cyber hate crimes to understand that even the lowest level of incident which causes harm can quickly escalate to serious consequences for the victim. While police officers may very well be able to recognise more severe forms of victims' harm and distress, they should not underestimate the cumulative 'drip-drip' effect of the so-called 'low level' incident which is now embedded as a constant feature of everyday life for many citizens, especially the young and most vulnerable in our society. It is absolutely essential that police officers acknowledge that 'minor' cyber hate crimes can produce as much emotional harm for victims as so called 'serious offences'.

2.4 Cyber-Terrorism

Cyberspace has changed—and continues to change—the very nature of terrorism. The internet is well suited to the nature of terrorism and the psyche of the terrorist. In particular, the ability to remain anonymous makes the internet attractive to the terrorist plotter. Terrorists use the internet to propagate their ideologies, motives and grievances and to plan and carry out their attacks. A growing phenomenon, and of critical concern to the security of the UK, is the increasing rise of cyber attacks by terrorists and terrorist groups and organisations. Now a global terrorist threat, according to the US Federal Bureau of Investigation (FBI), cyberterrorism is defined as any 'premeditated, politically motivated attack against information, computer systems, computer programs, and data which results in violence against non-combatant targets by sub-national groups or clandestine agents'.

In defining cyber terrorist activity, it is necessary to segment action and motivation. Security professionals and policymakers have come to understand that acts of hacking can have the same consequences as acts of the physical and more traditional forms of terrorist activity, but in the legal sense the intentional abuse of the information of cyberspace must be an integral part of the terrorist campaign or action. Cyber terrorists conduct unlawful attacks and threaten attacks against computers, networks and the information stored therein, with the primary purpose of intimidating or coercing a government or its people in furtherance of a political, religious or other ideological cause. Examples of cyber terrorist activity may include the use of information technology (IT) to organise and carry out attacks, disrupt essential public services and support group activities and perception-management campaigns which have adopted new IT as a means to conduct operations without being detected by counter-terrorist officials. Thus, the use of information technology and means by which terrorist groups and agents also constitute cyber-terrorism, other activities, which may be richly glamorised by the media, should be defined as cyber crime. It is essential for all cyber crime investigators to recognise the clear but subtle differences between cyber-terrorism and cyber crime which can be distinguished by the perpetrators' core motivations.

2.4.1 Understanding terrorism

First and foremost terrorism is a crime, a crime which has serious consequences and one which requires to be distinguished from other types of crime, but a crime nonetheless. Individuals who commit terrorist-related offences contrary to UK law are subject to the processes of the criminal justice system and those who are otherwise believed to be involved in terrorism are subject to restrictive executive actions. However, the key features of terrorism that distinguish it from other forms of criminality are its core motivations. Terrorism may be driven, as the legal definition provided in s 1 of the Terrorism Act 2000 states, by:

- politics;
- religion;
- race;
- ideology.

These objectives are unlike other criminal motivations, such as personal gain or pursuit of revenge. Terrorists may be driven by any one or any combination of the four core motivations but the primary motivator is political as Figure 2.1 illustrates.

Individuals who are driven by religious, racial or ideological beliefs have to gain some political ground to compel others to conform to their point of view, especially if they are operating within or intending to influence a democratic society.

Acts of terrorism whether motivated by politics, religion, race or ideology convey a message. This message attempts to persuade its audience or force them to accept its views and beliefs. The victims of terrorism are often distinct from this audience: victims may be passers-by on a train or those travelling on a plane but a political audience would be a government or the electorate. Terrorism, therefore, has a three-way relationship between the terrorist, the victim and the audience as Figure 2.2 illustrates.

This three-way relationship is not usually found in other types of crime. This unique relationship between the terrorist, the victim and the audience requires a greater degree of control and oversight to counter terrorism so that innocent and non-combatant victims are protected.

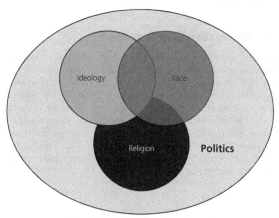

Figure 2.1 Core motivations of terrorism

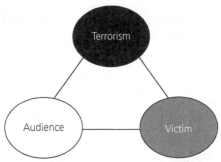

Figure 2.2 Terrorism, audience and victim relationship

KEY POINT—STATE LEGITIMACY

Terrorism is a very powerful way in which to promote beliefs and has potentially serious consequences for society. If allowed to grow and flourish, terrorism can undermine national security, it can cause instability to a country and in the most extreme of circumstances can lead to war. Terrorism seeks to undermine state legitimacy, freedom and democracy, the very fabric of our collective community values in Britain. These are a very different set of motivations and outcomes when compared against other types of crime. This is the reason why tackling terrorism is different to countering other types of criminality and why it requires a different and dedicated approach to prevent it.

2.4.2 Typology of terrorism

There are different types of terrorism and extremism and it is important to identify which type of terrorism an individual or group belongs to in order to counter it effectively. Terrorism and extremism can be classified into six broad categories which include:

- political;
- religious;
- ideological;
- nationalist;
- state sponsored;
- single issue.

2.4.2.1 Political and religious terrorism

Political and religious terrorism perceives itself as acting on the orders of a higher or divine authority. These terrorism organisations are often the most violent and robust as they believe that their actions are sanctioned by this higher authority. They believe that their actions are morally justified and that they will be vindicated of any wrongdoing when carrying out orders in pursuit of their objectives.

2.4.2.2 Ideological terrorism

Ideological terrorism and extremism seeks to change the social, economic and political systems of a country. Ideological terrorists and extremists are violent individuals and groups who can come from either the extreme left-wing or extreme right-wing of the political spectrum. Ideological terrorism objectives are set very high and attempt to achieve a great deal. In order to achieve these objectives, a full social revolution is often required to take place and the term 'social-revolutionary' is frequently used to describe this grouping.

2.4.2.3 Nationalist terrorism

Nationalist terrorism groups claim to be the authentic voice of a national culture. Through acts of violence, they attempt to restore their lands back to one single, larger country or seek complete independence from it by creating a new, separate state. Well-known nationalist terrorist organisations include the Irish Republican Army (IRA) and Euskadi Ta Askatasuna (ETA) of Spain.

2.4.2.4 State-sponsored terrorism

State-sponsored terrorism requires a state to support terrorism activities in pursuit of achieving its political objectives. These terrorist activities are sometimes carried out in the state's own territory or conducted in a third or neighbouring country. This tactic is often used to fulfil political agendas as any allegations of state involvement in terrorism can be easily denied or disassociated from political parties when such acts are conducted in other countries.

2.4.2.5 Single-issue terrorism and extremism

Single-issue terrorism and extremism focuses on a specific policy, practice or procedure. The key objective is to change, block or at the very least disrupt or deter one issue from continuing in its present form. Unlike purely ideological terrorism and extremism, single-issue groups do not seek a full-scale political revolution but they do want real action and changes to be made.

Cyber-terrorism has entered into the lexicon of IT security specialists and terrorist experts. A deeper understanding of cyber-terrorism by police officers and cyber investigators is required to better serve the early identification of potential terrorist threats. While the understanding of cyber-terrorism in the UK is generally associated with potential attacks on national critical infrastructures and the protection of essential public services, Table 2.2 provides a series of case studies highlighting the diverse range of large-scale cyber terrorist attacks which have not only served to affect and threaten issues of national security but have also substantially damaged and undermined the standing and reputation of government security measures. Such security embarrassments and failures which many cyber attacks have exposed, have led to negative impacts upon the public's confidence in their government to protect them, their essential services, businesses and economy from all manner of cyber terrorist threats.

2.4.3 Terrorist use of the internet

The internet enables terrorists and violent extremists to engage in sophisticated recruitment and radicalisation campaigns and to anonymously progress their attack-planning processes.

2.4.3.1 Attack planning

Early phases of terrorist attack planning include hostile reconnaissance which involves the gathering of information for use in a terrorist attack. It forms an integral part of the attack-planning process as terrorists seek to obtain a profile of a target. Hostile reconnaissance is a feasibility study to determine which method

Table 2.2 Cyber-terrorism case studies

Botnet 2009

During 2009, there were a series of coordinated attacks against major government and financial websites and news agencies of both the US and South Korea involving the activation of a botnet. This attack involved a number of hijacked computers that caused servers to overload due to the flooding of traffic from a DDoS attack. The numbers of hijacked computers varied depending on the source and included 50,000 from the Symantec's Security Technology Response Group, 20,000 from the National Intelligence Service of South Korea and more than 166,000 from Vietnamese computer security researchers as they analysed the two servers used by the invaders.

Cold War logic bomb

During the Cold War in 1982, the Central Intelligence Agency (CIA) in the US found a way to disrupt the operation of a Siberian gas pipeline in Russia without using traditional explosive devices such as missiles or bombs. Instead, they caused the pipeline to explode using a portion of a code in the computer system that controlled its operation in what they tagged as a 'logic bomb'. The chaos that ensued was so monumental that the resulting fire could be seen from space.

Estonia

The Government of Estonia was subjected to cyber terrorist attacks on 27 April 2007 by Nashi, a pro-Kremlin group from Russia. One of the largest cyber attacks following Titan Rain, Nashi employed a number of techniques such as ping floods and botnets to penetrate and take down key government websites rendering them useless. The attack method was so sophisticated that the Estonian Government believed that the attack had received state-sponsorship from the Russian Government. The trigger for the attacks appeared to arise from an important icon to the Russian people, the Bronze Soldier of Tallinn, an elaborate Soviet-era war grave marker that was relocated by the Estonian Government.

Flamer

Also known as Skywiper and Flame, Flamer is modular computer malware that was discovered in 2012 as a virus used to attack computer systems in Middle Eastern countries that run Microsoft Windows as their operating system. Used by hackers for espionage purposes, it infected other systems over a local network (LAN) or USB stick including over 1,000 machines from private individuals, educational institutions and government organisations. It also recorded audio, including Skype conversations, keyboard activity, screenshots and network traffic. It was discovered on 28 May 2012 by the MAHER Center of Iranian National Computer Emergency Response Team (CERT), the CrySys Lab and Kaspersky Lab.

Table 2.2 Continued

Government of Canada

The Canadian Government revealed in news sources that they became a victim of cyber attacks during February 2011 from foreign hackers with IP addresses in China. The hackers were able to infiltrate three departments in the Canadian Government and transmitted classified information back to themselves. Canadian security officials eventually cut off the internet access of the three departments in order to prevent the return transmission to China.

Government of India

Despite its international reputation for being an IT and software powerhouse, India reported 13,301 cyber security breaches in 2011 which has continued to grow year on year. The largest cyber attack that India faced occurred on 12 July 2012 where hackers penetrated the email accounts of 12,000 people, including high-level officials from the Defence Research and Development Organization (DRDO), the Indo-Tibetan Border Police (ITBP), the Ministry of Home Affairs and the Ministry of External Affairs.

Operation Shady Rat

An ongoing series of cyber attacks that started in mid-2006, Operation Shady Rat has hit at least 72 organisations worldwide including the International Olympic Committee, the United Nations and businesses and defence contractors. Discovered in 2011 by Dmitri Alperovitch, Vice President of Threat Research at McAfee, it was assumed that the People's Republic of China was behind the attacks. The operation was derived from the common security industry acronym for Remote Access Tool (RAT).

Opi Israel

A coordinated cyber attack by anti-Israel groups and individuals, #opiIsrael was a DDoS assault that was timed for 7 April 2012, the eve of Holocaust Remembrance Day, with the aim of erasing Israel from the internet. Websites targeted by these hacktivists included financial and business sectors, educational institutions, non-profit organisations, newspapers and privately owned businesses in Israel.

Jaschan

Sven Jaschan, a German college student who confessed to being the author of Netsky worms and Sasser computer worms, unleashed a virus in 2004 on his 18th birthday that had resounding impacts across the world. Although the estimated damage was believed to be $500 million, economic experts believe that it could have been more as it disabled Delta Air Lines' computer system and resulted in a number of cancellations of transatlantic flights. Microsoft placed a $250,000 bounty on his head and Sven was later captured after a three-month manhunt.

(continued)

Table 2.2 Continued

Moonlight Maze

One of the earliest forms of major infiltration where hackers penetrated US computer systems at will; Moonlight Maze was an accidental discovery made by US officials and was believed to be conceived by Russian security authorities, although they denied their involvement. In this cyber attack, hackers targeted military maps and schematics and other US troop configurations from the Pentagon, the Department of Energy, NASA and various universities and research labs in unremitting attacks that were discovered in March 1988 but which were believed to have been in place for several years.

PayPal

PayPal became a victim of a cyber attack in December 2010 after it permanently restricted the account used by WikiLeaks to raise funds, citing their violation of the Acceptable Use of Policy as their reason. The action by PayPal resulted in a backlash of multiple boycotts from individual users and invited hackers to attack PayPal systems.

Presidential election

During the 2008 US presidential election, suspected hackers from China or Russia attacked the computer systems used in the campaigns of both Barrack Obama and John McCain. The attack was successful in securing numerous emails and sensitive data used in the campaign. As a precautionary measure, and to aid the cyber investigation, the FBI confiscated all the computers and all the electronic devices connected with the attacks.

Stuxnet

Iran was subjected to cyber attacks during June 2010 when its nuclear facility in Natanz was infected by Stuxnet, a cyber worm that was believed to be a combined effort of Israel and the US, though no one claimed responsibility for its inception. The worm destroyed Tehran's 1,000 nuclear centrifuges and set back the country's atomic programme by at least two years, as it spread beyond the plant and infected over 60,000 computers.

Titan Rain

During 2004, Shawn Carpenter discovered a series of coordinated 'cyber raids', in what the FBI believed to have originated from government-supported cells in China. Dubbed 'Titan Rain,' hackers were able to infiltrate several computer networks including those at NASA and at Lockheed Martin, Redstone Arsenal and Sandia National Laboratories. Considered one of the biggest cyber attacks in history, these acts posed the dangers of not only procuring sensitive military intelligence and classified data but also paved the way for other hackers and espionage entities to infiltrate their systems as they purposefully left backdoor access.

Table 2.2 Continued

Yahoo

Yahoo fell victim to cyber attacks that originated from China in an action called 'Operation Aurora' which was intended to gain access to and modify their source code repositories. This operation was conducted by the Elderwood Group, which was based in Beijing and has ties with the People's Liberation Army, using advanced persistent threats that began in mid-2009 to December 2009.

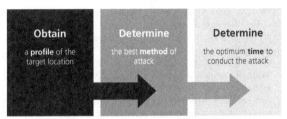

Figure 2.3 Primary role of hostile reconnaissance

of attack would be most appropriate, and when would be the preferred time of attack to ensure an operation is successfully completed. The three objectives of hostile reconnaissance are illustrated in Figure 2.3.

Identifying hostile reconnaissance is important as it very often provides the first indication that a terrorist cell or lone actor is planning an attack. A number of terrorist plots in the UK that have been disrupted by security forces have revealed evidence of hostile reconnaissance being conducted online; the first if its kind occurred more than a decade ago.

Case Study—Cyber Terrorist 007

When Metropolitan Police officers raided a flat in West London during October 2005, they arrested a young man, Younes Tsouli. The significance of this arrest was not immediately clear but investigations soon revealed that the Moroccan-born Tsouli was the world's most wanted 'cyber terrorist'. In his activities, Tsouli adopted the user name 'Irhabi 007' (Irhabi meaning 'terrorist' in Arabic), and his activities grew from posting advice on the internet on how to hack into mainframe computer systems to assisting in planning terrorist attacks. Tsouli trawled the internet searching

---

for home movies made by US soldiers in the theatres of conflict in Iraq and Afghanistan that would reveal the inside layout of US military bases. Over time, these small pieces of information were collated and passed on to those planning attacks against armed forces bases. This virtual hostile reconnaissance provided insider data illustrating how it was no longer necessary for terrorists to conduct physical reconnaissance if the relevant information could be captured and meticulously pieced together from the internet.

Police investigations subsequently revealed that Tsouli had €2.5 million worth of fraudulent transactions passing through his accounts which he used to support and finance terrorist activity. Pleading guilty to charges of incitement to commit acts of terrorism, Tsouli received a 16-year custodial sentence to be served at Belmarsh High Security Prison in London where, perhaps unsurprisingly, he has been denied access to the internet. The then National Coordinator of Terrorist Investigations, Deputy Assistant Commissioner Peter Clarke, said that Tsouli: 'provided a link to core al Qa'ida, to the heart of al Qa'ida and the wider network that he was linking into through the internet', going on to say: 'what it did show us was the extent to which they could conduct operational planning on the internet. It was the first virtual conspiracy to murder that we had seen.'

The case against Tsouli was the first in the UK which quickly brought about the realisation that cyber-terrorism presented a real and present danger to the national security of the UK. Law enforcement practitioners understood that the internet clearly provided positive opportunities for global information exchange, communication, networking, education and as a major tool in the fight against crime but that a new and emerging contemporary threat had appeared within the communities they sought to protect. The internet had been hijacked and exploited by terrorists not only to progress attack planning but to radicalise and recruit new operatives to their cause. It was also the core and affiliated networks of al Qa'ida which were quick to realise the full potential of the global platform provided by the internet.

2.4.3.2 Recruitment and radicalisation

The most powerful and alarming change for contemporary terrorism has been its effectiveness for attracting new terrorist recruits, very often the young and most vulnerable and impressionable in our societies. Modern terrorism has rapidly evolved, becoming increasingly non-physical, with vulnerable 'home grown' citizens being recruited, radicalised, trained and tasked online in the virtual and ungoverned domain of cyber space. With an increasing number of citizens putting more of their lives online, the interconnected and globalised world in which we now live provides an extremely large pool of potential candidates to draw into the clutches of disparate terrorist groups and networks.

The openness and freedom of the internet unfortunately supports 'self-radicalisation'—the radicalisation of individuals without direct input or encouragement from others. The role of the internet in both radicalisation and recruitment into terrorist organisations is a growing source of concern for security authorities. The internet allows individuals to find people with shared views and values and to access information to support their radical beliefs and ideas. The unregulated and ungoverned expanse of the internet knows no geographical boundaries, thus creating a space for radical activists to connect across the globe. This is especially problematic as easy access to like-minded people helps to normalise radical ideas such as the use of violence to solve grievances. Yet, solving the issue of radicalisation by simple processes, such as the suggestion to 'clean up' the internet, is impossible and well beyond the scope of any single government.

2.4.3.3 Tackling online radicalisation

The Home Office has published guidance for those citizens who are responsible for vulnerable individuals and work within communities to help to ensure that the internet is an environment where terrorist and violent extremist messages are challenged. As part of their wider efforts to counter the threat of radicalisation on the internet, a public-facing web page now encourages the public to take action against unacceptable violent extremist and hate websites and other online content. Where individuals believe that material they have located is potentially unlawful, they are provided with the opportunity to complete a form on the web page and refer it to the Counter Terrorism Internet Referral Unit (CTIRU).

Case Study—Role of the Counter Terrorism Internet Referral Unit

The CTIRU provides a national coordinated response to referrals from the public as well as from government and industry. It also acts as a central, dedicated source of advice for the police service.

The CTIRU provides the UK police service with a unit of experts who can carry out an initial assessment of material located on the internet. It is also responsible for alerting forces and the units of the UK Police Counter-Terrorism Network to online terrorist

---

offences that may fall within their jurisdiction. Powers under UK terrorism legislation provide for the CTIRU to take a national lead in serving notices on website administrators, web hosting companies, Internet Service providers (ISPs) and other relevant parties within the UK, to modify or remove any unlawful content.

The CTIRU also focuses on developing and maintaining relationships with the internet industry, an important part of ensuring the delivery of a safer and more secure online experience for citizens. A further challenge, given the global scope of cyberspace for UK law enforcement, was the majority of terrorist content online being hosted in other countries outside UK jurisdiction. To counter this challenge, the CTIRU continues to forge links with law enforcement counterparts abroad to help to target those websites hosted overseas. UK Counter Terrorism and Extremism Liaison Officers (CTELOs) based in countries around the world have a key role in supporting this work. The role of the CTIRU is to provide the opportunity to effectively enforce, and control, access to material believed to be extreme. In addition, the CTIRU helps to develop a culture of collaboration between police, partners and service providers dedicated to making the internet a safer place, particularly for young people.

KEY POINT—PREVENTING ONLINE RADICALISATION

The indoctrination of our citizens by online radicalisers and recruiters is a pressing concern for all in authority. The internet has become crucial in all phases of the radicalisation process, as it provides conflicted individuals with direct access to unfiltered radical and extremist ideology which drives the aspiring terrorist to view the world through this extremist lens. When combined with widely marketed images of the holy and heroic warrior, the internet becomes a platform of powerful material communicating terrorist visions of honour, bravery and sacrifice for what is perceived to be a noble cause.

The prevention of online radicalisation remains an ambitious undertaking, and we must still find new and innovative ways in which to expose and isolate the apologists for violence, and protect the people and places where they operate. Intelligence and law enforcement agencies across the world have come to learn more about how the processes of radicalisation develop, but their collective understanding remains far from perfect. If preventive measures are to have a chance in interdicting at least the most savage excesses of online extremism, countermeasures need to be informed by better definitions of online radicalisation and improved modelling of its causal mechanisms.

Case Study—School Boy Terrorist

In June of 2006, Hammad Munshi, a 16-year-old schoolboy from Leeds, was arrested and charged on suspicion of committing terrorism-related offences. He remains the youngest ever person in Europe to be formally charged and convicted of terrorist offences. Following his arrest, police searches were conducted at his family home where his wallet was recovered from his bedroom. It was found to contain handwritten dimensions of a submachine gun. At the time, Munshi had excellent IT skills; he had registered and ran his own website on which he sold knives and extremist material. He passed on, for example, information on how to make Napalm as well as how to make detonators for Improvised Explosive Devices (IEDs). At the time of his arrest, Munshi was still a schoolboy and had been directly influenced by being exposed to extremist rhetoric and propaganda on the internet from the comfort of his bedroom unbeknown to his family, friends and wider social network.

2.4.3.4 Foreign fighters

The new terrorist phenomenon is the sudden and dramatic increase of UK terrorist foreign fighters joining violent groups in Afghanistan, Iraq and Syria. Throughout the long and violent history of terrorism in the UK, young British men and women have left UK shores to join various causes and fight for their beliefs in foreign lands, but the sudden export of British-born violent jihadists this time has been amplified by a slick online cyber recruitment campaign, urging Muslims from across the world to join their fight and to post messages of support for Daesh.

Case Study—Daesh Call To Arms

Since the beginning of the Syrian uprising in March 2011, the International Centre for the Study of Radicalisation (ICSR) has compiled a database of foreign fighters travelling to the country. Based on an update of their earlier estimates, the ICSR now believes that over 500 British citizens have travelled to Syria with the intention of becoming foreign fighters. This figure includes deceased individuals and those who later left the conflict and have returned to their communities in the UK.

The ICSR continues to monitor the flow of foreign fighters from Western countries as part of a project exploring this aspect of the Syrian conflict. Though it may be too early to draw general conclusions, the ICSR project provides an insight into better understanding the threats and risks posed by foreign fighters. The ICSR data suggests that many of those British citizens travelling to Syria as foreign fighters are male, in their twenties, of Muslim faith and of South-Asian ethnic origin with recent connections to higher education and with links to individuals or groups who have international connections.

Spawned by the Syrian conflict, the violent progress of Daesh through towns and villages in Iraq has been swift—aided by foreign fighters from Britain. Daesh, the so-called Islamic State (IS), have now taken control of large swathes of Iraq leading the British Prime Minister to warn ministers that violent Daesh-inspired jihadists were planning attacks on British soil. The warning came amid growing concerns amongst senior security officials that the number of Britons leaving the UK to fight alongside extremist groups abroad was rising, which numerous government and research institute reports continue to confirm. The export of British-born violent jihadists is nothing new but the call to arms in Iraq this time has been amplified by a slick online recruitment campaign, urging Muslims from across the world to join their fight and to post messages of support for Daesh.

The reasons why some British Muslims would seek to engage in violent jihadist activity abroad remain varied. However, the ICSR suggests that some general observations about the key drivers which either serve to push or pull individuals towards fighting in Syria can be made. These include what has become known as the 'ummah consciousness', a viewpoint which informs Muslims that they belong to a global fraternity where issues such as loyalty and allegiance are defined through confessional identity. Some Muslims may, therefore, feel obligated to defend their 'brothers and sisters' in Syria.

The proximity of the Syrian conflict to Europe also makes it particularly attractive to potential fighters. Moreover, the main transit country, Turkey, does not require British citizens to have a visa and it is also relatively inexpensive to reach. While British involvement in previous conflicts over the last decade or more may have proved contentious, there was nonetheless an alternative narrative which counselled young Muslims against travelling abroad for jihad. With the present conflict in Syria, would-be jihadists find themselves adopting a not dissimilar view to Western governments—that Assad is guilty of committing atrocities against civilians, and that he should be removed.

Overseas conflicts, whether in Afghanistan, Iraq or in Syria, have served to raise a series of unintended consequences for UK national security which now have the potential to threaten the safety of British communities. These unintended consequences not only include the departure of British citizens as foreign fighters to conflict zones but the exportation of terrorism overseas by British citizens. The phenomenon of foreign fighters travelling to conflicts overseas raises two key issues for the British Government: first, the means used by these men to travel to conflicts and receive their training and, secondly, is the realisation that, while many of the volunteers may die in the theatre of conflict, some may well survive their experiences and return to the UK with military training and hardened combat experience. Such conflict-engaged citizens could put their skills and experiences to unlawful use when they return to their local communities in the UK continuing their violent jihadist crusade.

While the British Government remains committed to delivering security to the nation, and its primary responsibility is the safety of citizens at home, in the increasingly globalised and interdependent world in which we now live, it also has a responsibility to ensure that Britain does not become a staging post for terrorists and extremists to plan their next attacks overseas. As the intelligence machinery of the state continues to monitor the extent to which British nationals are joining violent jihadist groups in Syria, and analyses the potential threat to national security, it is the police service who have the potential to provide the richest intelligence picture of those members of our communities who hold a desire to fight in conflicts overseas.

The discovery of the British foreign fighter—embedded citizens living in local communities—has served to challenge the traditional pursuit of potential terrorists with a greater emphasis on local intelligence. Fuelled and facilitated by increased cyber connectivity on a global scale, all in authority have come to learn that national security increasingly depends on neighbourhood safety and good community-based intelligence to identify and prevent foreign fighters departing our shores has come to the fore. As a direct result, this renewed focus has now placed the diminishing resources of the police service centre stage of national counter-terrorism policy, and cyber investigators are increasingly becoming an essential part of UK defence against the threat from terrorism and violent extremism.

KEY POINT—IF YOU SUSPECT IT, REPORT IT

At all times members of the public should be encouraged by police to report any information which they believe to be unusual and out of place. By simply reporting suspicious activity to the police, terrorist attacks can be prevented. If something strikes you as being out of place, trust your instincts and report it. If cyber investigators suspect any terrorist activity then this must be reported immediately to their respective local or regional Counter Terrorism Branch, Counter Terrorism Intelligence Unit or Counter Terrorism Unit.

For reporting suspicious activity to the police that does not require an immediate response, members of the public should be encouraged to contact the confidential anti-terrorism hotline number, 0800 789321. For any incident that requires an immediate response, the emergency services number, 999, should be used.

2.5 **Psychology of Cybercriminals**

Over many years, understanding the psychology of criminals has proved an important part in designing effective measures to counter their activities. A richer understanding of criminal behaviours better serves the efficiency of police investigations. While significant research into the psychology of serial killers, paedophiles and terrorists has been conducted, all of which has helped to create an evidence-base of knowledge to inform the police investigator, there is little research with practical application on the psychology of the cybercriminal. One of the problems faced by those theorising the psychological aspects of perpetrators of cyber crime and cyber terror is that very few practitioners have been identified. Hence, psychologists have had to draw on what they know of cyber communications, the psychology of those who engage in crime and terror, to explain the phenomena. It is recognised by academics, professionals and practitioners working in the field of cyber crime that more research must be brought to operational reality to support the fight against cyber crime, because understanding the overall goals of the online criminal and asking how, who, when, what, why and where they conduct their cyber crime are essential questions to answer if strategies to defeat them are ever going to be effective. One type of cybercriminal, the 'hacker', has however been subject to the greatest amount of research in this field from which have arisen the beginnings of a better understanding of this phenomenon.

2.5.1 Profiling the hacker

During 2004, the United Nations Inter-regional Justice and Crime Research Institute (UNICRI) commenced the Hackers Profiling Project (HPP) to answer the many questions being raised by law enforcement agencies about the highest profile of cybercriminals, the 'hacker'. Over several years, the HPP has successfully identified the generations of the hacker subculture which are detailed in Table 2.3.

Table 2.3 Generations of hacker subculture

Generation	Timeline	Description
1st generation 'Academic'	1960–1980	The first generation of hacking was very much academic, with students at universities putting together various programs for the new mainframes being installed on campus, as well as early forays into the telephony system. The ethics of this era focused on shared ownership of data and information, as well as promoting the contribution of all those involved in the hacker culture.
2nd generation 'Curiosity'	1980–1985	The second 'hacker era' characterising the early 80s, was driven by curiosity, and the motivation to hack into external targets was often driven by the scarcity of technology: the mainframes and the unique operating systems running on them would cost vast sums of money and technology was not yet a common utility—even a Personal Computer was beyond reach for many, and dialling into modems half-way across the globe could result in exorbitant monthly phone bills.

(continued)

Table 2.3 Continued

Generation	Timeline	Description
3rd generation 'Crimeware'	1985–1999	The third wave of hacking covers a longer time frame and was a very active period, especially with the commoditisation of the internet in the latter half of that period. This was an extremely prolific time for the culture and many 'hacker periodicals', such as 2600 (1984) and Phrack (1985), began their publication in these years. The motives of hackers from this era were as eclectic as their geographical distribution and background but even in this period there were very few economically motivated Black Hat hackers. Interestingly, the diffusion of 'crimeware' and increases in frauds both rose as the 90s progressed, leading to the next and current era of hacking.
4th generation 'Monetisation'	2000–present	The current wave of hacking is just as convoluted as the previous but it is marked by a worrying trend, the monetisation of hacking. In the past couple of decades there has been a shift from hobbyist hacking primarily driven by ego and 'the thrill of the chase' to malicious and financially motivated crime conducted over the internet.

UNICRI reveal that the purpose of distinguishing between the modes and motives of hackers throughout the years is not to whitewash the second and third waves of hacking mentioned in the table as purely innocent or without consequence—crimes were in fact being committed—and even as early as 1991 there were cases of individuals peripherally related to the then-booming hacker scene being investigated and arrested for toll fraud or 'carding' (using stolen credit card information to purchase items or services). However, even a cursory glance at the literature and archived timelines of those days would show that the majority of the players involved tended to be uniform in their disdain of the outright criminal elements in their midst, such as virus writers and carders. Even today, the monetisation of hacking is being pursued by small, flexible and tight-knit criminal bands which, despite their size, have a considerable impact on the online ecosphere wherever the money is. It is no secret to police investigators that since the dawn of civilization criminals have sought out the 'low-hanging fruit', and the HPP have observed the cybercriminal shift away from targeted attacks on financial institutions or e-commerce with server-side attacks, to phishing scams and particularly virulent blended threats targeting end-users and consumers who do not have the luxury of an annual security budget ranging in the millions of dollars.

To profile the 'hacker' in more detail to support police investigators, the HPP has identified nine categories of attacker which are shown in Table 2.4. UNICRI used the word 'attacker' and not 'hacker' in the HPP simply because the evolution of the hacking world and of cyber crime itself has merged together different actors who do not always belong to the category of 'hackers'.

KEY POINT—HACKER PROFILES

While the list of hacker categories and profiles shown in Table 2.4 is not to be considered complete, it nevertheless provides a positive first step in developing a greater understanding of the hacker phenomenon to support cyber crime investigators.

An important element of the HPP was to gain a better understanding of hackers from the attackers themselves. The following provides an insightful interview with a Black Hat hacker from the current 'Monetisation' generation of the hacker evolution. Many police officers, investigators and prosecutors will no doubt observe some similarities from the psychology of the Black Hat hacker with the motivations of other, more traditional serious and organised criminals.

Interview with a Hacker—Chronicles of a Black Hat

Q: How would you define yourself with respect to the hacking activities you are conducting?

A: I'm a Black Hat. This means that hacking is my job and gives me a salary. I run black ops for those hiring me. I'm quite expensive.

Table 2.4 Hacker attacker categories

Wannabe (lamer)	The 'wannabe' often labelled a 'lamer', is the 'I would love to be a hacker' kind. They use hacker techniques without either knowing or having the curiosity to learn how they actually function. They use 'hacker toolkits', which can be downloaded free from the internet; these toolkits automate processes otherwise made manually and in a 'creative' way by more experienced hackers (and that often include mistakes and backdoors). They post a huge number of messages on forums and BBSs (Bulletin Board Systems), asking other hackers to teach them how to become a real hacker. They want to learn to be a hacker without really being one, and often their actions result in huge damage to some computer system or network.
Script kiddie	The 'script kid' term stands for 'the boy from the scripts', meaning those hackers relying on UNIX/Linux shell scripts written by others. They lack technical skills and sophistication, and the ones least capable are called 'point-and-clickers', since their attacks are called 'point-and-click attacks'. They are interested only in the result and not in learning how computer and hacking techniques work. They simply download from the internet (or from the 'crews' they belong to) software and hacker tools, and follow the related instructions.
Cracker	The term 'cracker' was created around the beginning of the 90s, when the hacker community wanted to somehow differentiate the malicious (or lame) actions highlighted by the media, from the serious hacker research done by many underground groups. Generally speaking, crackers have good technical skills, which allow them to pursue their purposes; in the latter years, due to the different players in the cyber crime arena (particularly when referring to skimming and phishing activities), crackers have been identified with poor or average technical background and field skills.

Table 2.4 Continued

Ethical hacker	'Ethical hacker' is not just a term but also designates an entire debate both in the underground community and in the information security market. An ethical hacker is somebody with excellent hacking skills, whose 'past life' may have been criminal, who decides to help the community, digging with software and discovering bugs and mistakes in widely (or poorly) used IT infrastructures (i.e. social networks), protocols or applications. They are creative hackers, since they try not to use software created by others and they prefer creating it themselves or improving it when there are no useful programs for their attacks. Ethical hackers prefer a manual attack rather than an automated one. They are also highly sophisticated and specialised in different operating systems, networks and attack techniques.
QPS (quiet, paranoid, skilled hacker)	If this type of attacker is on a system, and if they have even a remote feeling that they may be caught, they will disappear. This kind of hacker attacks IT systems not because they are looking for information but perhaps because they just love what they are doing. The QPS are creative hackers, using software made by others as little as possible, since they prefer creating their own. They share many similarities with ethical hackers.
Cyber-warrior/ mercenary	This type of hacker is a category that has appeared in the last few years because of the internet's globalisation and of the 'hacktivism' phenomenon. Cyber-warriors feel like heroes from their own environment (i.e. an extremist group with a political or religious background). Their skills may vary substantially, from the basic ones of a script kid to good or excellent ones, especially when specialised on focused particular areas (i.e. DDoS, or Web Defacing, or Wi-Fi). Not being 'exposed' in the business environment like the industrial spy profile, the mercenary hacker works on commission, getting money to attack specific targets.

(continued)

Table 2.4 Continued

Industrial spy hacker	The practice of industrial espionage has existed as long as business itself, infiltrating spies in companies throughout the years who walk out with information stored on paper files, microfilm, floppy disks, CD-ROMs and, today, USB keys or emails. Nevertheless, the scandals of industrial espionage that have emerged in recent years involve industrial spy hackers, who have modernised this practice by taking advantage of the new opportunities brought about by IT.
Government agent hacker	Current IT and the granularity itself of information allow external attackers from governments to run highly sophisticated attacks, specifically focused on nations' know-how in different business markets. Government agent hackers are state-sponsored and often conduct their activities under the guise of protecting and preserving a nation's security and economic well-being.

Q: How did you learn hacking techniques?

A: Mainly at school. At the university we also used to have a couple of cybercafés at the very beginning (around 1999–2000), which is basically where most of us started.

Q: What led you to become a hacker?

A: I'd say it was a mix of friends and free time. I was a teenager hanging out at that cybercafé and … everything began there, ya know. I was impressed by the things those guys were doing, I just fell in love with hacking … it was that much easier to accomplish goals, hacking into servers, stealing information, pictures … a lot of fun. Then I went into other things, meaning money.

Q: What were/are your aims?

A: Right now it's just money. People can hire me, I do the job, get the money, and disappear.

Q: Have your motivations for hacking ever changed over time?

A: I would say yes. At the very beginning it was all about curiosity and learning. Then I decided to step forward into the real world, where people pay you money because they don't know how to play as I do.

Q: Are you part of a group or do you act alone?

A: I was initially part of a group. Then some people left, others stayed, although they lacked real skills; in the meanwhile I grew up and updated myself. That's why right now I'm working mainly alone. I may work with some friends, but I prefer to run all jobs alone.

Q: What criminal offenses have you committed with a computer?

A: I guess they would include gaining unauthorised access to computer systems and networks; stealing accounts, personal information and selling them out. And I guess also industrial espionage and money laundering.

Q: Have you ever been arrested or convicted for computer crimes?

A: No.

Q: Have laws and penalties against cyber crimes had a deterrent effect on you?

A: Sort of … but I've decided to take the risk.

Q: Have technical difficulties encountered when penetrating a system represented a deterrent or a challenge?

A: They are basically a challenge. Whenever the target can't be hacked well … ya know, there's plenty of other targets out there.

Q: What is your main aspiration?

A: Stop working in two or three years, retiring, giving money to my family, buy my own house.

Q: Have you ever considered the negative effects of your hacking activities on people?

A: Are you talking about identity theft and this kind of things? Yes I did consider the effects, but … it's not my fault if the victim is an idiot, I'm sorry.

KEY POINT—UNDERSTANDING CYBER CRIME AND CYBERCRIMINALS

There is no technological or legislative 'silver-bullet' solution to tackling the increase in cyber crime: the criminals conducting online abuses, thefts, frauds and terrorism have already shown their capacity to defeat IT security measures, as well as an indifference to national or international laws focusing on them. As long as their activities remain profitable, the miscreants will continue; and as long as technology advances, they will keep on adapting. It is therefore important to learn and understand more about the psychology, motivations and operations of the cybercriminal to better inform strategies and tactics to prevent the harm they continue to cause.

2.6 **Public Attitudes to Cyber Crime and Cyber Security**

To help to understand the levels of awareness of cyber crime and cyber security amongst the public, the Home Office commissioned a survey which has served to highlight more about the behaviours people undertake to protect themselves online and their willingness to undertake additional security measures. The results of the 2012 survey continue to resonate today and provide evidence to support the ease with which cybercriminals go about their business and why more effort must be focused on the prevention of cyber crime at the most local level. As a summary, the key headlines from the survey were as follows.

In relation to internet users' online behaviours, internet security software is commonly used, but other 'good practices' are less well adopted:

- four-fifths (78 per cent) of internet users always used security software when connecting to the internet;
- one in ten never used security software (11 per cent) and a further one in ten did not use it on all devices (9 per cent);
- those who used the internet more often were more likely to use security software on all devices (82 per cent of those who used it every day/almost every day, compared with 63 per cent of less frequent users);
- wider internet security good practices were less well used—even amongst those who were frequent users. For example, just 43 per cent of internet users said they would check that a site was secure and 34 per cent said they did not use public Wi-Fi.

Amongst younger users, those in Black and Minority Ethnic (BME) groups or less affluent social groups and mobile phone users appear less likely to take up security features:

- users aged 15 to 24 years were less likely to use internet security software on all devices (70 per cent), compared to

users aged 65 and over (92 per cent). Whilst those aged 65
and over were less likely to have accessed the internet at all
in the last year compared to younger users (e.g. 44 per cent
of those aged 65 and over, compared to 93 per cent of 15
to 24-year-olds), they were still more likely to add security
software to their devices when they did access the
internet;

- BME users were less likely to use security software on all their
  devices (55 per cent) compared to users who defined themselves
  as white (81 per cent);

- less affluent users were less likely to use internet security on all
  their devices compared with more affluent users.

In relation to seeking security advice, many users do not seek
online security advice, but friends and family are key sources of
information for those that do:

- less than half (43 per cent) of internet security software
  users sought advice about different products. Where advice
  was sought, 59 per cent (n = 543) went to family, friends or
  someone else. Others went to their ISP (16 per cent) or to sales
  staff in a store (16 per cent). Three per cent went to government
  websites (e.g. http://www.gov.uk);

- most of those who did not seek advice (n = 545) either thought
  that it was not necessary (33 per cent) or they knew enough
  already (31 per cent); while a smaller proportion stated they
  had no interest in it (9 per cent). Around one in ten did not
  know where to look (7 per cent), whilst a small minority felt
  that it was the responsibility of their internet provider or
  security companies (4 per cent);

- for those who undertook various internet 'good practices', the
  largest proportion (39 per cent) said they did so because friends,
  family or someone else advised them to. Just 11 per cent did so
  because of government advertising/advice;

- just over two in five of those who used security software bought
  it separately from a specialist company such as Norton or
  McAfee (43 per cent). A quarter used free third party software
  (26 per cent), one in five used software provided with their
  computer or device (19 per cent) and one in seven had been
  provided with it as part of their current internet package (14
  per cent).

In relation to taking additional security measures, most internet
users were unwilling to pay more or undertake training courses
for additional online security. They were more in favour of

restricting access for users who had undertaken malicious or illegal activity:

- when given three options for increasing online security (internet users paying more for increased security, internet users receiving ongoing training on computer security and best practice and restricting access to those found to be engaged in malicious or criminal computer activity), most respondents were opposed to making additional payments to ISPs (47 per cent opposed, 27 per cent supported) and undertaking training on security (53 per cent opposed, 24 per cent supported);

- 66 per cent of respondents supported ISPs restricting access for people who showed signs of malicious online activity, such as sending viruses or malware from their computer. This compared with 13 per cent who opposed this measure;

- when internet users were asked to consider how much extra they would be willing to pay for improved security, the majority (62 per cent) said nothing, whilst 15 per cent stated £1–2 a month and 6 per cent stated less than £1 per month;

- those who support adding a monthly payment to their bill, and those who support having to undergo online training, are less likely to have engaged with the security practices. They are also more likely to have experienced one or more type of security breach than those who oppose either proposition (42 per cent compared with 33 per cent who oppose the payment proposition, and 46 per cent compared with 30 per cent who oppose the training proposition).

KEY POINT—UNDER-REPORTING OF CYBER CRIME

One of the most significant findings for law enforcement agencies arising from the survey was that just 2 per cent of online crime incidents were reported to the police.

Under-reporting occurred because incidents were perceived as too trivial and/or were dealt with internally. Other research corroborates these findings, also suggesting that concern over reputational damage further contributes to under-reporting for personal, professional and business reasons. Earlier findings from several surveys reveal a similar picture for members of the public with just 1 per cent of adult internet users who experienced hacking or unauthorised access to their data in the 12 months prior to

---

the surveys being conducted reporting the matter to the police. Evidence also suggests that under-reporting of cyber crime occurs for several reasons including:

- not perceiving that what had taken place was a crime (or worth reporting);
- not knowing where to report the matter;
- believing that the police cannot do anything; and
- individuals not realising that they are actually a victim of crime.

Whether or not an increase in the proportion of victims reporting negative online incidents will result in a subsequent increase in police recorded crime, depends on the nature of the crime reported and whether it meets criteria under the HOCR but a growing body of evidence now confirms policymakers' and practitioners' suspicions that cyber crime remains substantially under-reported and the full extent of its impact upon victims, business and the wider economy has yet to be accurately determined.

Part II

Responding to Cyber Crime

Chapter 3
Cyber Strategy

3.1 Introduction

To effectively tackle all manner of cyber threats requires a coherent strategic approach. An important part of this chapter is the explanation of the development, structure, strategic aim and objectives of the UK's cyber strategies which provide a framework for all cyber crime investigative activity. Contemporary cyber crime machinery now cuts across government departments, law enforcement agencies and intelligence agencies, all of which have an important role to play. The national cyber crime architecture has quickly developed over recent years in response to cyber threats and remains in its infancy. For police officers of all ranks and responsibilities, a better understanding of the role of the police in cyber security, cyber-terrorism and cyber crime will serve to contextualise their contribution to national strategies and reinforce the collaborative approach required to tackle cyber crime today. The primary UK strategies which provide the national frameworks to tackle cyber threats include;

- National Security Strategy;
- Cyber Security Strategy;
- Organised Crime Strategy;
- Cyber Crime Strategy;
- Counter-Terrorism Strategy.

3.2 National Security Strategy

To coordinate the UK's security response, the British Government has published a National Security Strategy which provides a cohesive, pan-government response to the variety of threats we face.

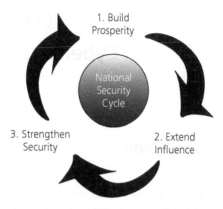

Figure 3.1 The national security cycle

The National Security Strategy sets out three key steps for a secure Britain. These steps include using all our national capabilities to build Britain's prosperity, to extend our nation's influence in the world and to strengthen our security, illustrated in Figure 3.1.

3.2.1 **National Security Council**

The British Government has given national security the highest priority creating the National Security Council (NSC). The NSC ensures a strategic and tightly coordinated approach across the whole of government to the risks and opportunities the country faces. The NSC is an essential part of the national security cycle ensuring that key decisions from across the full landscape of government are made to strengthen the UK.

3.2.2 **National risks**

The National Security Strategy requires all agencies of government engaged in law enforcement, security, intelligence collection and civil protection to identify the most pressing risks to our security, and to put in place the ways and means to address them. The national interest of the UK can also be threatened by natural disasters, man-made accidents as well as malicious attacks. These risks have different impacts if they occur and some are more likely to occur than others.

3.2.2.1 **National Security Risk Assessment**

A truly strategic approach to national security requires governments to go further than just simply assessing domestic civil emergencies. The National Security Strategy, as well as looking at short-term domestic risks, also considers aspects of national security. It is an 'all hazards' strategy which is underpinned by the first ever National Security Risk Assessment (NSRA) which assesses and prioritises all major areas of national security risk—domestic and overseas.

To develop the NSRA, subject-matter experts, analysts and intelligence specialists were asked to identify the full range of existing and potential risks to our national security which might materialise over a 5- and 20-year horizon. All potential risks of sufficient scale or impact so as to require action from government and/or which had an ideological, international or political dimension were assessed based on their relative likelihood and relative impact. The impact was assessed based on the potential direct harm a risk would cause to the UK's people, territories, economy, key institutions and infrastructure.

From the rigorous risk analysis process, the current NSRA suggest that, over the next 20 years, the UK could face risks from an increasing range of sources, and that the means available to our adversaries are increasing in number, variety and reach. Our increasingly networked world, which creates great opportunities but also new vulnerabilities, means that we must, in particular, protect the virtual assets and networks on which our economy and way of life now depend. This has quickly become just as important as directly protecting physical assets which presents a seismic shift in national security planning.

The NSRA serves to inform strategic judgements—it is not a forecast. The British Government cannot predict with total accuracy the nature or source of the next major national security incident we will face but it helps to make informed choices. In particular, it assists the British Government to prioritise the risks which represent the most pressing security concerns in order to identify the actions and resources needed to deliver our responses to those risks.

The NSRA is regularly updated and presented to the NSC which has currently identified 15 generic priority risk types and allocated them into three tiers in which cyber crime and cyber-terrorism were highlighted as being primary Tier One threats shown in Figure 3.2.

National Security Strategy: Priority Risks

Tier One

The National Security Council considered the following groups of risks to be those of highest priority for UK national security looking ahead, taking account of both likelihood and impact.

- **International terrorism** affecting the UK or its interests, including a chemical, biological, radiological or nuclear attack by terrorists; and/or a significant increase in the levels of terrorism relating to Northern Ireland.
- **Hostile attacks upon UK cyberspace** by other states and large-scale cyber crime.
- **A major accident or natural hazard** which requires a national response, such as severe coastal flooding affecting three or more regions of the UK, or an influenza pandemic.
- **An international military crisis** between states, drawing in the UK, and its allies as well as other states and non-state actors.

Tier Two

The National Security Council considered the following groups of risks to be those of highest priority for UK national security looking ahead, taking account of both likelihood and impact.

- **An attack on the UK or its Overseas Territories** by another state or proxy using chemical, biological, radiological or nuclear (CBRN) weapons.
- **Risk of major instability**, insurgency or civil war overseas which creates an environment that terrorists can exploit to threaten the UK.
- A significant increase in the level of **organised crime** affecting the UK.
- **Severe disruption to information received,** transmitted or collected by satellites, possibly as the result of a deliberate attack by another state.

Tier Three

The National Security Council considered the following groups of risks to be those of highest priority for UK national security looking ahead, taking account of both likelihood and impact.

- **A large-scale conventional military attack** on the UK by another state (not involving the use of CBRN weapons) resulting in fatalities and damage to infrastructure within the UK.
- A significant increase in the **level of terrorists, organised criminals, illegal immigrants and illicit goods trying to cross the UK border** to enter the UK.
- **Disruption to oil or gas supplies to the UK,** or price instability, as a result of war, accident, major political upheaval or deliberate manipulation of supply by producers.
- **A major release of radioactive material** from a civil nuclear site within the UK which affects one or more regions.

Figure 3.2 National Security Strategy: priority risks

3.2.2.2 National Security Tasks

The process of assessing national risks to the security of the UK identified, for the first time, eight cross-cutting National Security Tasks, shown in Table 3.1. These tasks, which are supported by more detailed planning guidelines, provide the ways in which the objective of the National Security Strategy will be achieved.

Table 3.1 National security tasks

1 Identify and monitor national security risks and opportunities.

2 Tackle at root the causes of instability.

3 Exert influence to exploit opportunities and manage risks.

4 Enforce domestic law and strengthen international norms to help to tackle those who threaten the UK and our interests.

5 Protect the UK and our interests at home, at our border and internationally, in order to address physical and electronic threats from state and non-state sources.

6 Help to resolve conflicts and contribute to stability. Where necessary, intervene overseas, including the legal use of coercive force in support of the UK's vital interests, and to protect our overseas territories and people.

7 Provide resilience for the UK by being prepared for all kinds of emergencies, able to recover from shocks and maintain essential services.

8 Work in alliances and partnerships wherever possible to generate stronger responses.

KEY POINT—CYBER CRIME AND NATIONAL SECURITY

Risk assessment involves making judgements about the relative impact and likelihood of each risk in comparison with others. In order to undertake the NSRA, an adapted methodology was used which involved consideration of the impact of an event (based on economic consequences, casualties and social/structural factors) and the likelihood of that event occurring over a determined time frame. The NSRA process compared, assessed and prioritised all major disruptive risks to our national interest which were of sufficient scale or impact to require action from government and/or which had an ideological, international or political dimension. The highest priority Tier One risks to national security are assessed to be of a higher relative likelihood and higher relative impact. Investigators of cyber crime must recognise that the UK Government has assessed hostile attacks on UK cyberspace by other states and large-scale cyber crime as a high risk to national security.

3.3 **Cyber Security Strategy**

Every day, millions of people across the UK rely on the services and information that make up cyberspace: that is, all forms of networked, digital activities. They may be aware of this if surfing the web, shopping or social networking online, or they may be unaware of the networked activity underpinning the services they rely on, and of just how critically dependent the work of government, business and national infrastructure is on this new domain of human activity. Either way, the effective functioning of cyberspace is of vital importance.

As the UK's dependence on cyberspace grows, so the security of cyberspace becomes ever more critical to the health of the nation. Cyberspace cuts across almost all of the threats and drives in the National Security Strategy: it affects us all, it reaches across international boundaries, it is largely anonymous and the technology that underpins it continues to develop at a rapid pace.

The threats to those who use cyberspace range from phishing to enable credit card fraud through to corporate espionage. These activities can affect organisations, individuals, critical infrastructure and the business of government.

To address the threats from cyberspace, the British Government has transformed its approach to cyber security over recent years, developing a Cyber Security Strategy. The strategy stresses that the UK needs a coherent approach to cyber security, and one in which the government, organisations across all sectors, the public and international partners all have a part to play. Figure 3.3 illustrates the high-level objectives of the Cyber Security Strategy designed to secure the UK's advantage in cyberspace.

The strategic vision for the UK Cyber Security Strategy is for the UK to derive huge economic and social value from a vibrant, resilient and secure cyberspace, where its actions, guided by its core values of liberty, fairness, transparency and the rule of law, enhance prosperity, national security and a strong society. To counter all cyber challenges, the strategy is divided into four strategic objectives shown in Figure 3.4.

KEY POINT—CYBER SECURITY RESPONSIBILITIES

The British Government understands that achieving its vision for cyber security in the framework of its guiding principles will require every organisation from the private sector, and individuals

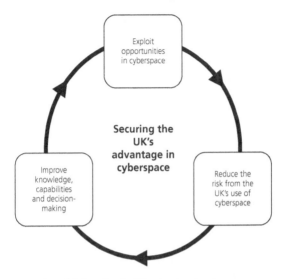

Figure 3.3 Securing the UK's advantage in cyberspace

Figure 3.4 The UK Cyber Security Strategy

and all government departments, to work closely together. Just as all citizens from all countries benefit from the use of cyberspace, all have a responsibility to help to protect it. The new approach by the British Government seeks to ensure that its citizens know how to provide themselves with a basic level of protection against online threats and that they have ready access to accurate and up-to-date information on the cyber-related threats that they face, together with the techniques and practices they can employ to guard against them. If citizens are careful about putting personal or sensitive information on the internet, are wary of email attachments or links from unrecognised senders and are cautious about downloading files from websites they know little about, then they can significantly assist in countering the cyber security challenge thereby making cyberspace increasingly resilient to all manner of cyber threats. It is, therefore, essential that everyone—in their homes, at their place of work and on the move—helps to identify threats in cyberspace and reports possible offences, thus making cyberspace a hostile environment for those seeking to unlawfully exploit its potential.

Cyber crime investigators must remember that cyber security is not an end in itself, but that it enables and protects economic and social activity, and should not discourage the use of new technologies. The government's goal is to enable the full benefits of cyberspace to be available for the UK, while protecting our society and allowing the UK digital economy to grow. All cyber crime investigators have an important role to play in keeping cyberspace safe and secure for all citizens.

3.4 Organised Crime Strategy

The complexity and volume of modern-day criminality is stretching the capacity and capability of law enforcement agencies (LEAs) across the world to near breaking point. The increasingly networked and sophisticated approach of organised crime groups (OCGs) is a major contributory factor. Driven by globalisation and the technological advancements of the internet and smart mobile communications, OCGs are no longer defined by nationality or ethnicity, and act undeterred by geographic boundaries. The British Government estimates that the overall costs to the UK from organised crime are between £20 and £40 billion a year. It involves around 38,000 individuals, operating as part of around 6,000 criminal gangs. These criminals have a global reach and a local presence. About half of all organised criminals are involved in the illegal drugs trade; others are involved in human trafficking, fraud and money laundering and organised acquisitive crime, ranging from armed robbery to organised vehicle theft. Many are involved in more than one crime type. As new opportunities arise, such as computer-enabled crime, organised criminals will be quick to take advantage and unless we have a flexible and effective response it will be the ordinary people of Britain who pay the price.

Recognising the need to develop a strategic approach to tackle organised crime, the British Government developed an Organised Crime Strategy which sets out the context and the nature of the risk from organised crime. The aim of the strategy is to:

> reduce the risk to the UK and its interests from organized crime by reducing the threat from organized criminals and reducing vulnerabilities and criminal opportunities.

The strategy offers a fresh tactical approach to reducing organised crime with the following key themes.

- **STEM** the opportunities for organised crime to take root. We will seek to stop individuals in the UK becoming involved in organised crime and tackle the causes of organised crime through overseas development and stabilisation work.

- **STRENGTHEN** enforcement against organised criminals. We will use the full range of lawful interventions against organised crime, with hard-edged enforcement through prosecutions where practicable; but also by using a wider range of innovative disruptions. We will particularly strengthen our focus on tackling criminal finances.

- **SAFEGUARD** communities, businesses and the state. We will help to reduce their vulnerability to becoming victims of organised crime. We will raise awareness of the threat and methods used by organised criminals; provide the public and businesses with information to enable them to protect themselves; and ensure closer working with partners.

When combined, the three key themes reduce the threat and vulnerability from organised crime, serving to diminish the overall risk to the UK and its interests from organised crime as Figure 3.5 shows.

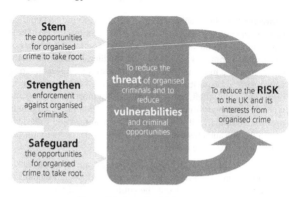

Stem
the opportunities
for organised
crime to take root.

Strengthen
enforcement
against organised
criminals.

Safeguard
the opportunities
for organised
crime to take root.

To reduce the
threat of organised
criminals and to
reduce
vulnerabilities
and criminal
opportunities

To reduce the **RISK**
to the UK and its
interests from
organised crime

Figure 3.5 Organised Crime Strategy

The government intends to deliver its response to organised crime through implementing a programme of activity which includes:

- enhancing intelligence—which drives the operational response;
- improving the law enforcement response to organised crime, particularly through establishment of the National Crime Agency (NCA);
- developing our international cooperation;
- improving our approach to research and communications.

3.5 Cyber Crime Strategy

The Home Office is the lead government department for developing policies to counter cyber crime and its impact on UK interests and specifically the citizen. It has developed a Cyber Crime Strategy which sets out the department's plan for coordinating and delivering cyber crime policies. The Cyber Crime Strategy recognises that the means of delivery will in some cases lie beyond the Home Office (e.g. the Department for Business, Innovation & Skills; as from July 2016, the Department for Business, Energy & Industrial Strategy) and that it will be necessary to work collaboratively with other departments and agencies to ensure a coherent approach.

The UK's Cyber Security Strategy identifies criminal use of cyberspace as one of the three principal threats to cyber security, alongside state and terrorist use. The Cyber Crime Strategy sets out the Home

Office's approach to tackling cyber crime, showing how it will tackle such crimes directly through the provision of a law enforcement response, and indirectly through cross-government working and through the development of relationships with industry, charities and other groups, and internationally. The Home Office ensures that this work to tackle cyber crime is coordinated with work to protect national security and the national infrastructure. This includes the development of overall strategies to prevent harm to the UK, to provide an effective government response and to ensure that all sectors of society work together to tackle the threats. To support and contribute to the vision of the Cyber Security Strategy, the strategy has five tactical tasks for the Home Office which include the following.

1. **Coordinate activity** across government to tackle crime and address security on the internet in line with the strategic objectives laid out in the UK Cyber Security Strategy.
2. **Reduce the direct harms** by making the internet a hostile environment for financial criminals and child sexual predators, and ensure that they are unable to operate effectively through work to disrupt crime and prosecute offenders.
3. **Raise public confidence** in the safety and security of the internet, not only through tackling crime and abuse, but through the provision of accurate and easy-to-understand information to the public on the threats.
4. **Support industry leadership** to tackle cyber crime, and work with industry to consider how products and online services can be made safer and security products easy to use.
5. **Work with international partners** to tackle the problem collectively.

The five priority tasks are underpinned by a series of objectives to ensure all tasks are delivered. Figure 3.6 shows the Cyber Crime Strategy strategic tasks and objectives.

KEY POINT—COMMITTED TO TACKLING CYBER CRIME

The development of the Home Office Cyber Crime Strategy provides evidence of the British Government's strong commitment to ensuring that cyber crime is tackled. The Home Office believes everyone in the UK must have safe and secure access to the benefits of the internet. The measures included in the Cyber Crime Strategy will allow the Home Office to take action against cybercriminals from the organised groups at the top end right through to the long tail of organised criminality that exists underneath. The Cyber Crime Strategy recognises that cyber crime threatens our safety and undermines our economy, and that the scope and sophistication of cyber crime in the 21st century demands an equally sophisticated and ambitious strategy with which to tackle it.

Home Office Cyber Crime Strategy: Strategic Tasks and Objectives

Task 1

To coordinate across Government the Home Office will:

- Provide clear ownership within Government, at ministerial level, for cyber crime and criminal conduct in the UK.
- Review all legislation affecting or relevant to cyber crime, to ensure that it is adequate to address our needs.
- With the Cabinet Office, Ministry of Justice and the Information Commissioner's office, establish standards of data handling and promote the requirement for a duty of care from all individuals and bodies that hold individuals [sic] personal data.

Task 2

To create a hostile environment for cyber criminals the Home Office will:

- Provide an effective law enforcement and criminal justice response, through specialist units, and ensure that intelligence is shared where appropriate.
- Develop, over time, a clear understanding of the scale and scope of cyber crime, including robust and easily accessible reporting systems for both the public and business, which we will monitor for trends.
- Develop tools, tactics and technology, working with the internet industry, to ensure that law enforcement are able to detect, investigate and pursue online criminals even when the technology changes.
- Produce a regular strategic overview of the threat to children and young people from those who use technology to harm and abuse them.

Task 3

To raise public confidence in the internet the Home Office will:

- Ensure the provision of safety information to the public on all types of cyber crime and internet harm, signposting to specialist units as appropriate.
- Continue to mount and support campaigns to raise awareness of internet safety issues.

Task 4

To support industry leadership the Home Office will:

- Work with the internet industry and commercial business to ensure that safety and security are factors in designing services and that criminals are deterred from exploiting the online environment.
- Ensure that there is successful liaison between all groups working to protect the public.

Task 5

To tackle cyber crime internationally the Home Office will:

- Work internationally to tackle cyber crime, including through effective collaboration with countries that have a well-developed understanding and capacity.

Figure 3.6 Cyber Crime Strategy strategic tasks and objectives

3.6 **Counter-Terrorism Strategy**

Cyberspace has changed—and continues to change—the very nature of terrorism. Cyberspace is well suited to the nature of terrorism and the psyche of the terrorist. In particular, the ability to remain anonymous makes cyberspace and the internet attractive to the terrorist plotter. Terrorists use the internet to conduct cyber attacks and propagate their ideologies, motives and grievances. The most powerful and alarming change for modern terrorism, however, has been its effectiveness for attracting new terrorist recruits, very often the young and most vulnerable and impressionable in our societies. Modern terrorism has rapidly evolved, becoming increasingly non-physical, with vulnerable 'home grown' citizens being recruited, radicalised, trained and tasked online in the virtual and ungoverned domain of cyberspace. With an increasing number of citizens putting more of their lives online, the interconnected and globalised world in which we now live provides an extremely large pool of potential candidates to draw into the clutches of disparate terrorist groups and networks.

The prevention of terrorist attacks remains the primary objective of counter-terrorism strategies operating throughout the world today, but they must also prepare emergency services to respond to the consequences of terrorism. In addition, counter-terrorism strategies need to be able to protect the public, having robust criminal justice systems in place to arrest and prosecute terrorists. Devising such a strategy is complex, as a free and democratic society offers terrorists the same freedoms in which to operate and a counter-terrorism strategy must preserve the very freedoms that the terrorists wish to exploit. This is a very difficult balance to achieve as human rights and civil liberties have to be maintained for all.

At the time of the catastrophic terrorist attack in the US on 11 September 2001, the British Government, like the US and many other countries in the developed world, had no sophisticated or coherent cross-departmental strategy to counter international terrorism. In short, the UK had no plan of any vigour to institute that would have been able to effectively respond to an indiscriminate attack. Of course, the UK security apparatus had memories of the long counter-terrorist campaign in Northern Ireland to draw on, and had the foundations that had been laid in terms of a corpus of emergency terrorism legislation on the statute book. Throughout the history of counter-terrorism practice in the UK, collaboration between government departments had been key to the success of many operations and the intelligence community had learned the value of close cooperation with the police service. Nevertheless, the characteristics of violent jihadist terrorism with its vaulting ambitions, strident ideology and disregard for civilian casualties—indeed for all human life, with adherents prepared to give their lives in their attacks—represented very new challenges for Parliament and public, government and law enforcement alike.

In the immediate aftermath of 9/11, the Cabinet Office in London initiated work on developing a comprehensive national counter-terrorism strategy. The strategy that emerged from this work was called CONTEST: COuNter-TErrorism STrategy. The strategic aim of CONTEST is: to reduce the risk to the UK and its interests overseas from terrorism, so that people can go about their lives freely and with confidence.

3.6.1 **CONTEST strategy structure**

The CONTEST strategy continues to be divided into four key pillars which provide the scope to counter terrorism effectively. The four pillars are commonly known as the four Ps, which are:

> **Prevent:** to stop people becoming terrorists or supporting violent extremism.
> **Pursue:** to stop terrorists.
> **Protect:** to strengthen our protection against terrorist attack.
> **Prepare:** where an attack cannot be stopped, to mitigate its impact.

The four-pillar structure of CONTEST is easily understood as a logical narrative, being translated into specific programmes of action across government, the private sector and the voluntary sector and is capable of being updated and extended in response to developments in the threat and in our technologies for countering it. It was important that the complexities of such a wide-ranging strategy were simplified and focused, as successful delivery would depend upon a joined-approach and the strength of partnerships. The creation of CONTEST as an overarching public strategy has given clarity and direction to all agencies and provided a framework to which separate organisations can allocate resources and assets for a combined effect.

The structure of CONTEST enables Prevent and Pursue to focus on the actual human threat from terrorists which is designed to reduce the risk by stopping them, while Protect and Prepare focus on the capacity and capability of the UK to reduce vulnerability to attacks when they occur. Simultaneously tackling areas to reduce

Figure 3.7 Mechanics of the CONTEST strategy

the risk and to minimise vulnerability, collectively serves to reduce the threat illustrated in Figure 3.7.

3.6.1.1 Prevent

The Prevent strand of CONTEST is concerned with tackling the radicalisation of individuals. It aims to do this by addressing structural problems in the UK and overseas that may contribute to radicalisation, such as inequality and discrimination. To prevent terrorism and its underlying causes requires a long-term approach. The strategy intends to deter those who facilitate terrorism and deter those who encourage others to become terrorists. This requires a change in the environment where extremists and those radicalising others operate. The Prevent strand also aims to engage in the battle of ideas, to win hearts and minds by challenging the ideologies that extremists believe can justify the use of violence.

3.6.1.2 Pursue

The Pursue strand of CONTEST is concerned with reducing the terrorist threat to the UK and to UK interests overseas by disrupting terrorists and their operations. To achieve this, the Pursue strand focuses on gathering intelligence and improving the ability to identify and understand the terrorist threat. It also aims to take action to frustrate terrorist attacks and to bring terrorists to justice by developing a legal framework. New legislation greatly assists in the pursuit of terrorists, but bringing them to justice also involves international cooperation and joint working with partners and allies overseas. This is an important element of the Pursue strand which also aims to reduce the global threat by strengthening the intelligence effort to achieve disruption of terrorists and their operations outside the UK.

3.6.1.3 Protect

The Protect strand of CONTEST is concerned with reducing the vulnerability of the UK and UK interests overseas. It aims to strengthen border security and to protect key utilities, transport infrastructures and crowded places. Protecting the UK is a vital component of the CONTEST strategy as target-hardening key and vulnerable sites will deter terrorist attacks from taking place. It also helps to reduce risks to the public in the event of an attack. An important part of Protect is informing the public and private sector industry about the level of threat the UK faces from international terrorism.

3.6.1.4 Prepare

The Prepare strand of CONTEST is concerned with ensuring that the UK is as ready as it can be to manage the consequences of a terrorist attack. It aims to identify the potential risks that the UK faces from terrorism and assesses their impact. It also aims to build the necessary capabilities to respond to any attacks, and will continually evaluate and test preparedness. Achieving the aims of the Prepare strand involves developing the resilience of the UK to withstand such attacks. This requires improving the ability of the UK to respond effectively to the direct harm caused by a terrorist attack, and in particular those individuals affected by it. It must also develop the UK's ability to quickly recover those essential services that are disrupted by an attack, and be able to absorb and minimise wider indirect disruption. The key elements of the strand are:

- identifying potential risk;
- evaluating and testing preparedness;
- assessing the impact of the risk;
- building capabilities to respond to the impact.

KEY POINT—SOPHISTICATED STRATEGY

The CONTEST strategy provides a framework to coordinate, direct and shape the government's response to the threat from terrorism, which includes cyber-terrorism and terrorist use of the internet

---

for attack planning, recruitment and radicalisation. The four-pillar structure of CONTEST provides a strategy that is easily understood as a logical narrative, and one that can be translated into specific programmes of action across government, the police, the private sector and the voluntary sector and, as has been shown, is capable of being updated and extended in response to developments in the threat and in our technologies for countering it. The creators of CONTEST understood that it was important that the complexities of such a wide-ranging strategy were simplified and focused, as successful delivery would depend on a joined-approach and the strength of partnerships. Developing and delivering CONTEST requires support from a plethora of Whitehall departments, intelligence and law enforcement agencies, local government and the voluntary sector. Ensuring that everyone agrees on the approach, is prepared to invest resources and sustain the project and programme, requires a great deal of time and effort. Often individual government departments will have other priorities and will experience tension between investing in short-term initiatives—often based on intelligence needs—and long-term policy—that will show no immediate results but have been identified as key to the strategy—which is a significant issue for civil servants to address. Despite a series of challenges for developing CONTEST, it has nevertheless produced successful results, providing policymakers with encouraging signs that their efforts across government are achieving the overarching aim of the strategy. More than a decade on from its first iteration, CONTEST is the most sophisticated counter-terrorism strategy currently in operation across the world and its structure provides a platform upon which to develop the next generation of cyber crime strategies to tackle contemporary cyber threats.

KEY POINT—STRATEGIC APPROACH TO TACKLING CYBER CRIME

The UK has rapidly established a plethora of strategies, directives, communications and guidance about how cyber crime, cyber-terrorism and cyber security should be addressed. Certain key themes consistently and continually emerge from these strategies: the need for an international perspective, the need for a partnership approach between private and public sectors and the importance of ensuring that the weakest element in the chain is strengthened in the interests of all. It is important for all in authority, and especially cyber crime investigators, to understand their role, responsibility and contribution to tackling cyber hazards in this complex tapestry of cyber-related strategies. For many police officers, the strategic picture to tackle cyber threats appears confused, especially by the multiplicity of bodies at both a domestic and international level that have identified a role for themselves around the determination of cyber security, cyber-terrorism and cyber crime policy.

The challenge for cyber policymakers is that while everyone is convinced that the solution to the problems of cyber security are global, nobody seems entirely clear how this might be achieved. There is, however, agreement amongst cyber security policymakers that there remains no one single way to protect the internet from criminal activities; many organisations have a role to play in this and national and international bodies have a role in protecting certain networks, but collaboration is essential to combat cyber crime.

The strategies outlined in this chapter provide a framework for all UK authorities which have a role in tackling cyber threats. Most importantly, the strategies have determined that tackling cyber threats is a priority for both national security and neighbourhood safety and, through these strategies, domestic agencies have been mobilised in response to the threat. The overarching National Security Strategy and NSRA process has given clarity and direction to all agencies, providing the framework for sub-strategies of cyber-related threats to which separate organisations can allocate resources and assets for combined effect.

The UK government response to tackle cyber security and cyber crime continues to develop in line with new and emerging threats, risks and challenges. To keep pace with new cyber strategy developments please refer to the following websites:

https://www.itgovernance.co.uk/what-is-cybersecurity;
https://www.gov.uk/government/policies/cyber-security.

Chapter 4

Policing Cyber Crime

4.1 Introduction

This chapter seeks to explain the role and responsibility of those agencies and organisations which have a primary role in keeping communities safe from the global phenomenon of cyber crime. A key message woven through the very fabric of this chapter is that law enforcement agencies must invest in the skills and resources necessary to police the ever changing digital environment. If the law enforcement community is to continue to prevent and reduce crime, improve the quality of cyber-related investigations as well as the administration of justice, it is absolutely vital that all in authority understand and address the contemporary challenges of tackling cyber crime at a local, regional, national and international level.

4.2 International Response to Cyber Crime

The borderless nature of cyber crime requires a coordinated approach across law enforcement not just in the UK but throughout EU member states and the wider international police community.

4.2.1 INTERPOL

INTERPOL is the world's largest international police organisation with 190 member countries. It works to ensure that police around the world have access to the tools and services necessary to carry out their roles effectively. INTERPOL provides targeted training, expert investigative support, relevant data and secure communications channels. The mission of INTERPOL is to prevent and fight crime through enhanced cooperation and innovation on police and security matters. It facilitates the widest possible mutual assistance between all criminal law enforcement authorities and ensures that police services can communicate securely with each other around the world. The INTERPOL vision is to enable police forces across the world to work together to make the world a safer place.

KEY POINT—INTERPOL AND CYBER CRIME

The day-to-day objectives and activities of INTERPOL focus on improving the quality and quantity of information in their databases, providing operational and specialised investigative support to member countries, developing a global approach to integrated border management and, most importantly for cyber crime investigators, providing a platform of technologically enabled threats, including cyber crime.

4.2.1.1 Tackling cyber crime

INTERPOL carries out a variety of activities to support member countries in the fight against cyber crime. It offers support to cyber crime investigations by:

- working to develop innovative new technologies;
- assisting countries to exploit digital evidence;
- conducting training sessions; and
- assisting countries in reviewing their cyber-fighting capacities.

INTERPOL is committed to the global fight against cyber crime and is the natural partner for law enforcement agencies looking to collaboratively investigate cyber crime. By working with private industry, INTERPOL is able to provide local law enforcement with focused cyber intelligence derived from combining inputs on a global scale. Its main initiatives in cyber crime focus on:

- operational and investigative support;
- cyber intelligence and analysis;
- digital forensics;
- innovation and research;
- capacity building;
- provision of National Cyber Reviews (NCRs).

INTERPOL is uniquely positioned to advance the fight against cyber crime on a global scale through proactive research into emerging crimes, the latest training techniques and the development of innovative new policing tools. Regional working groups bring together senior experts from national cyber crime units to assess the latest regional trends and current threats, and formulate action plans and transnational operations. An important element in the fight against cyber crime is the INTERPOL Global Cybercrime Expert Group (IGCEG). This cross-sector group brings together experts from different cyber-related fields to provide advice on several key areas of policing cyber crime including cyber strategy, research, training, forensics and operations.

INTERPOL coordinates transnational cyber crime investigations and operations, either on-site or remotely from the INTERPOL Global Complex for Innovation (IGCI) in Singapore. This can involve intelligence sharing and providing guidance on best practices in conducting cyber crime investigations. Located in the IGCI, the Cyber Fusion Centre (CFC) brings together cyber experts from law enforcement and industry to gather and analyse all available information on criminal activities in cyberspace to provide countries with coherent, usable intelligence.

Case Study—Global Operation Against Dorkbot Botnet

A coordinated global operation to disrupt the Dorkbot botnet, believed to have infected more than one million computers worldwide in 2015 alone, was supported by INTERPOL. A series of simultaneous actions involving law enforcement in North and Central America, Europe and Asia, with close collaboration from private industry, resulted in the takedown of the botnet's main servers and data channels.

Since its discovery in 2011, Microsoft has closely monitored Dorkbot via the Microsoft Malware Protection Center and the Microsoft Digital Crimes Unit. Analysis provided by Microsoft, Computer Emergency Response Team (CERT) Polska and technology security company ESET was provided to the private companies and law enforcement agencies involved in the action against the Dorkbot infrastructure.

The INTERPOL Digital Crime Centre (IDCC) supported the operation from the IGCI in Singapore through active coordination with law enforcement in its participating member countries to take down servers and domains.

This successful operation shows the value and need for close collaboration between law enforcement and the private sector to

---

detect, prevent and mitigate all manner of cyber threats', said Sanjay Virmani, Director of the IDCC. 'We encourage private sector companies with expertise in the cyber realm to work with INTERPOL to combat these very real security risks', he concluded.

The operation involved support from law enforcement agencies and industry partners including CERT Polska, ESET, Canadian Radio-television and Telecommunications Commission, US Department of Homeland Security's United States Computer Emergency Readiness Team, the FBI, Europol, the Royal Canadian Mounted Police, the Russian Ministry of Interior Department K, the INTERPOL National Central Bureau in Russia, the Indian Central Bureau of Investigation and the Turkish National Police.

KEY POINT—IMPORTANT ROLE OF INTERPOL

The operation to detect and disrupt the Dorkbot botnet provides a practical example of the important role of INTERPOL in coordinating multinational, large-scale cyber crime investigations.

Investigators from the affected countries and companies continue to identify the criminals behind the Dorkbot malware. The Dorkbot botnet is used for a variety of illegal activities, most commonly:

- stealing account credentials for online payment and other websites;
- DDoS attacks;
- providing a mechanism through which other types of dangerous malware can be downloaded to and installed onto the victim's computer.

Dorkbot spreads through USB flash drives, instant messaging programs and social networks. The malware can easily be removed with the appropriate anti-virus tools, therefore computer users are advised to scan their machines regularly.

For more information about INTERPOL and its role and responsibility for tackling cyber crime, visit the INTERPOL website at: http://www.interpol.int/Crime-areas/Cybercrime/Cybercrime.

4.2.2 Europol

Europol is the EU's law enforcement agency whose main goal is to help to achieve a safer Europe for the benefit of all EU citizens.

Europol delivers its mission by assisting the EU's member states in their fight against serious international crime and terrorism. Europol understands that large-scale criminal and terrorist networks pose a significant threat to the internal security of the EU and to the safety and livelihood of its people. It is positioned at the heart of the European security architecture and provides support for law enforcement operations.

Analysis is at the core of Europol activities, employing around 100 criminal analysts to provide Europol with one of the largest concentrations of analytical capability in the EU and who support the production of the European Organised Crime Threat Assessment (OCTA). The OCTA identifies and assesses emerging threats including cyber crime, and is an excellent source of information for all cyber crime investigators.

4.2.2.1 Europol Cybercrime Centre

A key element in Europol's fight against cyber crime is the development of the European Cybercrime Centre (EC3). EC3 is the focal point in the EU's fight against cyber crime: pooling expertise and intelligence; supporting and mobilising law enforcement resources for investigations; building operational and analytical capacity; and promoting EU-wide solutions. The EC3 team delivers high-level expertise through three specialist teams that focus on combating child sexual exploitation, payment card fraud and cyber crime, bringing cutting-edge support to EU law enforcement cyber crime investigations.

EC3 commenced its activities in January 2013 to strengthen the law enforcement response to cyber crime in the EU and to help to protect EU citizens, businesses and governments. Its establishment was a priority under the EU Internal Security Strategy. By situating the EC3 within Europol, EC3 was able to not only draw on Europol's existing law enforcement capacity but also to expand significantly on other capabilities, in particular the operational and analytical support to member states' investigations. EC3 is focused on delivering in the following three areas:

- cyber crimes committed by organised groups, particularly those generating large criminal profits, such as online fraud;
- cyber crimes which cause serious harm to the victim, such as online child sexual exploitation;
- cyber crimes (including cyber attacks) affecting critical infrastructure and information systems in the EU.

With regard to these three areas, Europol's EC3:

- serves as the central hub for criminal information and intelligence;
- supports member states' operations and investigations by means of operational analysis, coordination and expertise;
- provides a variety of strategic analysis products enabling informed decision-making at tactical and strategic levels concerning the combating and prevention of cyber crime;
- establishes a comprehensive outreach function connecting cyber crime-related law enforcement authorities with the private sector, academia and other non-law enforcement partners;
- supports training and capacity building, in particular for the competent authorities in the member states;
- provides highly specialised technical and digital forensic support capabilities to investigations and operations;
- represents the EU law enforcement community in areas of common interest (research and development requirements, internet governance and policy development).

Europol works within a framework of subject-focused analysis groups called Focal Points (FP). Three of these are under the EC3 scope, and, as a complementary element, the Europol Cyber Intelligence Team (CIT) enhances their work, bringing together relevant data from various sources, in order to enrich the information and intelligence available to law enforcement.

4.2.2.2 Joint Cybercrime Action Taskforce

To provide a dynamic response to cyber crime, Europol established the Joint Cybercrime Action Taskforce (J-CAT) on 1 September 2014. Hosted at EC3, J-CAT will further strengthen the fight against cyber crime in the EU and beyond. Commencing as a project with a six month pilot, J-CAT participating countries and agencies agreed on the benefit of the operational taskforce.

J-CAT is composed of cyber liaison officers from committed and closely involved EU member states (Austria, France, Germany, Italy, Spain, the Netherlands and the UK), non-EU law enforcement partners (Colombia, Australia, Canada and the US—represented by two agencies: the FBI and the Secret Service) and EC3. All J-CAT partners are located in a single office to ensure closer collaboration, increased information-sharing and interoperability.

The mission of J-CAT is to proactively drive intelligence-led, coordinated action against key cyber crime threats and top targets. It aims to achieve this objective by stimulating and facilitating the joint identification, prioritisation, preparation and initiation of cross-border investigations and operation by its partners. J-CAT is involved with high-tech crimes (e.g. malware, botnets and intrusion), crime facilitation (bulletproof hosting, counter-anti-virus services, infrastructure leasing and rental, money laundering, including virtual currencies, etc), online fraud (online payment systems, carding, social engineering) and various aspects of child sexual exploitation online.

In order to actively fight cyber crime, J-CAT chooses and prioritises which cases to pursue. For that purpose, country liaison officers submit proposals on what could be investigated. The taskforce members then select the most relevant ones and proceed to share, collect and enrich data. They then develop an action plan, which is led by the country which submitted the chosen proposal. Finally, J-CAT goes through all the necessary steps to make the case ready for action, which includes involving judicial actors, identifying the required resources and allocating responsibilities.

KEY POINT—STRATEGIC ROLE OF EUROPOL

Europol plays an important role in tackling cyber crime on an EU level, and the introduction of EC3 has served to galvanise member state support and focus in the fight against cybercriminals. The increasingly valuable role of EC3 within Europol is evident through the EC3 Cyber Strategy which combines expertise in strategic analysis, outreach, training, forensics and prevention, with the aim of gaining insight and understanding as to how high-tech criminals, child sex offenders and fraudsters think and operate in cyberspace. This knowledge is then shared to allow the more effective targeting of operations by law enforcement, to influence and inform changes on policy and legislation, to invite public–private partnerships for cooperation and, most importantly, advise citizens and businesses on how better to protect themselves in the digital world.

For more information about EC3, visit the Europol website at: www.europol.europa.eu/ec3.

4.3 **National Cyber Security Structure**

To ensure an effective response to cyber crime, the British Government has established an architecture which includes organisations with responsibility for cyber crime at a national, regional and local level. The apparatus includes:

- Office of Cyber Security & Information Assurance (OCSIA);
- Cyber Security Operations Centre (CSOC);
- Centre for the Protection of National Infrastructure (CPNI);
- Computer Emergency Response Teams (CERTs);
- National Technical Authority for Information Assurance (NTAIA).

4.3.1 **Office of Cyber Security and Information Assurance**

The OCSIA was formed in 2009 and is located in the Cabinet Office, coordinating cyber security programmes run by the British Government, including allocation of the National Cyber Security Programme funding. OCSIA supports the minister for the Cabinet Office and the National Security Council in determining priorities in relation to securing cyberspace. The unit provides strategic direction and coordinates the cyber security programme for the government, enhancing cyber security and information assurance in the UK.

The OCSIA works with other lead government departments and agencies including:

- Home Office (HO);
- Ministry of Defence (MOD);
- Government Communications Headquarters (GCHQ);
- Communications-Electronics Security Department (CESG);
- Centre for the Protection of National Infrastructure (CPNI);
- Foreign and Commonwealth Office (FCO);
- Department for Business, Innovation & Skills (BIS, now the Department for Business, Energy & Industrial Strategy).

The OCSIA is responsible for implementing a number of cross-cutting agendas including:

- providing a strategic direction for cyber security and information assurance for the UK including e-crime;
- supporting education, awareness, training and education (e.g. Get Safe Online and the Cyber Security Challenge);
- working with private sector partners on exchanging information and promoting best practice;
- ensuring that the UK's information and cyber security technical capability and operational architecture are improved and maintained;
- working with the Office of the Government Senior Information Risk Owner (OGSIRO) to ensure the resilience and security of government ICT infrastructures such as the Public Sector Network (PSN) and G-cloud;
- engaging with international partners in improving the security of cyberspace and information security.

4.3.2 Cyber Security Operations Centre

The CSOC was formed in 2009. CSOC is housed within GCHQ and is responsible for providing analysis and overarching situational awareness of cyber threats.

4.3.3 Centre for the Protection of National Infrastructure

The CPNI provides guidance to national infrastructure organisations and businesses on protective security measures, including cyber.

4.3.4 National Technical Authority for Information Assurance

The NTAIA is situated within GCHQ providing information security advice and a variety of information assurance services to government, defence and key infrastructure clients.

4.3.5 Computer Emergency Response Teams

CERTs exist in a number of public and private sector organisations. GovCERTUK is responsible for all government networks, while

CSIRTUK, CPNI's CERT, responds to reported incidents concerning private sector networks in the critical national infrastructure.

4.4 **National Response to Policing Cyber Crime**

To ensure an effective response to cyber crime, the British Government has established an architecture which includes organisations with responsibility for cyber crime at a national, regional and local level. The apparatus includes:

- National Crime Agency (NCA);
- Action Fraud;
- National Fraud Intelligence Bureau (NFIB);
- Regional Organised Crime Units (ROCUs);
- local police Cyber Crime Units (CCUs).

4.4.1 **National Crime Agency**

The NCA was established in 2013 and serves to strengthen the operational response to organised crime and cyber crime and provides a secure border through more effective national tasking and enforcement action. The creation of the NCA marked a significant shift in the UK's approach to tackling serious, organised and complex crime, with an emphasis on greater collaboration across the whole law enforcement landscape. The NCA continues to build effective two-way relationships with police forces, law enforcement agencies and other partners, and is made up of four separate commands.

- **Organised Crime Command (OCC)** targets organised crime groups operating across local, national and international borders. The command works with police forces and other agencies to ensure that prioritised and appropriate action is taken against every OCG identified.
- **Border Policing Command (BPC)** ensures that all law enforcement agencies operating in and around the border work to clear, mutually agreed priorities, ensuring illegal goods are seized, illegal immigrants are dealt with and networks of organised criminals are targeted and disrupted, both overseas and at ports up and down the UK.

- **Economic Crime Command (ECC)** provides an innovative and improved capability to deal with fraud and economic crimes, including those carried out by organised criminals.
- **Child Exploitation and Online Protection Centre (CEOP)** works with industry, government, children's charities and law enforcement to protect children from sexual abuse and to bring offenders to account.

The NCA has national and international reach and the mandate and powers to work in partnership with other law enforcement organisations to bring the full weight of the law to bear in cutting serious and organised crime. The NCA recognises that serious and organised crime is a global phenomenon which cannot be tackled in isolation. It continues to build multi-agency partnerships across police, law enforcement, the public sector, private industry and internationally to lead, support and coordinate the UK's response to a wide range of threats.

As well as leading its own operations, NCA officers support and coordinate operational activity, providing a range of specialist capabilities to partners who help to deliver criminal justice outcomes, recover assets and prevent and disrupt criminal activity. The NCA also has the power to direct chief officers of police forces and law enforcement agencies in England and Wales to undertake specific operational tasks to assist the NCA or other partners. The NCA operates across the UK, respecting the devolution of policing in Scotland and Northern Ireland. It works closely with partners to deliver operational results and has an international role to cut serious and organised crime impacting on the UK through a network of international liaison officers.

4.4.1.1 Child Exploitation and Online Protection Centre

The NCA's CEOP works with child protection partners across the UK and overseas to identify the main threats to children and to coordinate activity against these threats to bring offenders to account. CEOP protects children from harm online and offline, directly through NCA-led operations and in partnership with local and international agencies. Officers in CEOP and across the NCA, who specialise in this area of criminality, work side by side with professionals from the wider child protection community and industry. Intelligence developed in the NCA intelligence hub informs NCA-CEOP operational deployments, steers development of new capabilities and underpins a dedicated 'ThinkUKnow' education programme for children of all ages and for parents and carers.

CEOP pursues those who sexually exploit and abuse children, prevents people becoming involved in child sexual exploitation, protects children from becoming victims of sexual exploitation and sexual abuse and prepares interventions to reduce the impact of child sexual exploitation and abuse through safeguarding and child protection work. Activity in each of these areas is underpinned by specialist teams in CEOP command, and across the whole agency.

CEOP works to track registered offenders who have a sexual interest in children and who have failed to comply with their notification requirements under the Sexual Offences Act 2003. This includes disrupting or preventing travel by offenders and disseminating intelligence to international forces and specifically targeting offenders while they remain overseas. This includes non-UK nationals who travel to the UK. CEOP also focuses on organised criminal groups profiteering from the publication or distribution of child abuse images, supports local police forces with computer forensics and covert investigations and provides authoritative investigative advice and support to maximise UK law enforcement's response to crimes of child sexual abuse and exploitation. CEOP liaises with the online and technological industries, finetuning guidelines to minimise the possibility of present and future technology increasing the risk of sexual exploitation and sexual abuse to children. CEOP training and education specialists work together to raise the knowledge, skills and understanding of parents, carers, children and young people.

CEOP command receives invaluable assistance from its partners and supporters in the UK and internationally, allowing it to undertake more groundbreaking child protection work and support for victims of online child exploitation.

KEY POINT—FOLLOWING THE VICTIMS' CODE

Cyber crime investigators must follow the guidance contained in the Codes of Practice for Victims of Crime (Victims' Code). Introduced in 2006, it sets out the minimum levels of service which victims can expect from agencies that are signatories to it. In conjunction with existing legislation and regulations, the Victims' Code is the main mechanism used to transpose the EU Victims' Directive 2012/29/EU (the Victims' Directive) into domestic legislation. The Victims' Code has also been used to transpose into law parts of the Human Trafficking and Child Sexual Exploitation EU Directives.

The Victims' Code was revised in 2013 to reflect the commitments in the EU Victims' Directive. In addition, it introduced an enhanced level of service for victims of the most serious crime, vulnerable and/or intimidated victims and persistently targeted victims; and also introduced the Victim Personal Statement scheme and CPS commitments under the Victims' Right to Review scheme. Following a public consultation in 2015, further updates were made to the Victims' Code to complete the formal transition of the Victims' Directive into UK national laws and systems. The updated (2015) version of the Victims' Code was formally published on 22 October 2015 and came into effect on 16 November 2015, to coincide with the introduction of the Victims' Directive.

All cyber crime investigators must apprise themselves of the Victims' Code general principles which include:

- victims are entitled to receive services under the Victims' Code if they have made an allegation that they have directly experienced criminal conduct to the police or had an allegation made on their behalf;
- if that person has died, close relatives of the deceased are entitled to receive services as 'victims of the most serious crime';
- victims who have a disability, or who have been so badly injured as a result of criminal conduct that they are unable to communicate, are entitled to nominate a family spokesperson to act as the single point of contact to receive services under the Victims' Code;
- if the victim is under 18, their parent or guardian is entitled to receive services as well as the young person, except when investigated or charged themselves with an offence arising out of the criminal conduct complained of, or when the service provider is of the opinion that the parent/guardian does not represent the best interests of the young person;
- all businesses that are victims of crime are entitled to receive services under the Victims' Code, provided they give a named point of contact for all communication between the business and the service provider. Businesses will also be entitled to make an Impact Statement outlining how a crime has affected the business;
- a victim may opt out of receiving services under the Victims' Code, or may choose to receive services tailored to their individual needs which fall below the minimum standard.

The revised Victims' Code provides for an enhanced service for victims of the most serious crime (including cyber crime), persistently targeted victims and vulnerable or intimidated victims. Enhanced service refers to the time within which an entitlement is provided to the victim—that is, within one working day rather than five working days.

Once a service provider has identified that a victim is eligible for enhanced services, that service provider must ensure that this information is passed on as necessary to other service providers with responsibilities under the Victims' Code and to victims' services where appropriate. Service providers must share information about the victim with each other effectively and in accordance with their obligations under the Data Protection Act 1998.

Failure to comply with the Victims' Code does not of itself give rise to any legal proceedings but can be taken into account in determining any question in any proceedings. Breaches of the Victims' Code will initially be referred to the service provider but, if the complainant remains dissatisfied, the complaint can be investigated and may be the subject of a report by the Parliamentary Ombudsman.

4.4.1.2 National Cyber Crime Unit

The NCA's National Cyber Crime Unit (NCCU) is the national hub for the policing of cyber crime. The NCCU's remit includes:

- leading the investigation of the most serious incidents of cyber-dependent crime;
- driving the up-skilling of cyber investigation in law enforcement;
- leading law enforcement's relationships with key partners to tackle cyber crime, including industry, the intelligence agencies and international partners.

KEY POINT—INDEPENDENT OVERSIGHT AND SCRUTINY

The NCA is subject to rigorous external and independent scrutiny including by:
- Her Majesty's Inspectorate of Constabulary on efficiency and effectiveness, working with other inspection bodies as appropriate;

- the Independent Police Complaints Commission (IPCC) for activity undertaken in England and Wales and the Police Investigations Review Commissioner for Scotland;
- the Office of Surveillance Commissioners (OSC), which provides oversight of the use of covert surveillance and covert human intelligence sources;
- the Interception of Communications Commissioner (ICC), who provides oversight of the use of interception powers and the acquisition of communications data;
- the Investigatory Powers Tribunal (IPT) which can investigate complaints from the public about the use of intrusive powers;
- the NCA is also subject to scrutiny by Parliament, primarily by the Home Affairs Committee, the Public Accounts Committee and by the Scottish Parliament.

4.4.2 **National Fraud Intelligence Bureau**

The NFIB reviews the information provided to it by Action Fraud and other sources. It assesses whether there is sufficient evidence for the police or the appropriate law enforcement organisation, such as Trading Standards, to investigate the reported fraud. To assess reports of online fraud, the NFIB uses a system called 'Know Fraud', a highly sophisticated police intelligence system with the ability to process vast amounts of data to pinpoint patterns and linkages in offending. Data matching allows reports from different parts of the country to be linked through analysis, identifying the criminals behind the scams. Where NFIB crime reviewers and analysts see opportunities for law enforcement or partner agencies to take action, crime packages are compiled and disseminated for further action to be taken. On receipt of the crime packages, law enforcement and partner agencies then decide on the next most appropriate action and take responsibility for any further investigation.

4.4.3 **Action Fraud**

Action Fraud is the UK's national reporting centre for fraud and internet crime where members of the public should report fraud if they have been scammed, defrauded or experienced cyber crime. Action Fraud provides a central point of contact for information about fraud and financially motivated internet crime. The service provided by Action Fraud is run by the City of London Police, the national policing lead for economic crime. As Action Fraud does not have investigative powers, the reports it records are sent to the NFIB which is responsible for assessment of the reports and ensuring that reports of fraud reach the right place.

KEY POINT—CREATING A HOSTILE ENVIRONMENT FOR CYBERCRIMINALS

It is important to note that not all fraud reports result in an investigation, so the NFIB seeks to disrupt the fraud enablers who are causing harm by working with service providers to take down services abused by fraudsters. The NFIB will also alert members of the public and counter fraud agencies of emerging crime types, new methodologies and specific cases.

Even though not every report results in an investigation, every report helps to build a clearer picture of fraud within the UK. This contributes to making the UK a more hostile environment for fraudsters to operate and helps to keep other potential victims safe.

4.5 Strategic Policing Requirements

From November 2012, the Strategic Policing Requirements (SPRs) set by the Home Secretary set out those national threats that require a coordinated response in which resources are brought together from a number of police forces. Enacted by the Police Reform and Social Responsibility Act 2011—the same legislation that created elected Police and Crime Commissioners (PCCs)—SPRs apply to all police forces in England and Wales and are referred to by other law enforcement agencies throughout the UK.

The SPRs identify how police forces and their governance bodies often need to work collaboratively, and with other partners, national agencies or through national arrangements, to ensure that such threats are tackled efficiently and effectively. The current SPRs published by the Home Secretary include:

- terrorism (including cyber terrorism);
- organised crime (including cyber crime);

- threats to public order or public safety that cannot be managed by a single police force acting alone;
- other civil emergencies requiring an aggregated response across police force boundaries;
- a large-scale cyber incident, including the risk of a hostile attack upon cyberspace by other states.

The SPRs recognise that there may be considerable overlap between these areas. All elected PCCs and their respective Chief Officers must have regard to the SPRs in their planning and operational arrangements. This is an important obligation and PCCs and Chief Constables are now expected to drive collaboration between police forces and to ensure that forces can work effectively together and with their partners to address elements of cyber crime which fall under the SPRs. The SPRs support Chief Constables and PCCs to ensure they fulfil police forces' national responsibilities. They:

- help PCCs, in consultation with their Chief Constables, to plan effectively for policing challenges that go beyond their force boundaries;
- guide Chief Constables in the exercise of these functions; and
- enable and empower PCCs to hold their Chief Constables to account for the delivery of these functions.

In doing so, Chief Constables and PCCs must demonstrate that they have taken into account the need for appropriate capacity to contribute to the wider response to cyber crime. A major contribution to the cyber crime effort over recent years by PCCs and Chief Constables with regional organised crime responsibilities, has been the investment in building capacity and capability of local and regional units dedicated to deter, detect and disrupt cybercriminal activity.

4.6 **Regional Response to Policing Cyber Crime**

The regional response to cyber crime is led by the current structure of nine ROCUs in England and Wales which work across local police force boundaries to target the threat posed by serious and organised crime. The aim of ROCUs is to work with partners in law enforcement to create an effective response to tackle serious and organised crime in their respective regions. The mission of ROCUs includes:

- the provision of a specialist law enforcement capability for their region to relentlessly pursue and disrupt those who break the law;
- to protect communities from crime;
- to prevent people engaging in crime; and
- to minimise the impact of crime on regional communities.

The ROCUs investigate serious and organised crime in a range of areas including drugs, firearms and Child Sexual Exploitation (CSE). ROCUs liaise closely with local police forces and partners in their region to support their needs where possible with specialist resources and a prompt and effective response to disrupt and dismantle organised criminal networks. This regional capacity and capability supports the national efforts of the NCA and each ROCU has a senior NCA Organised Crime Command officer embedded within its organisational and operating structures. ROCUs also work in close partnership with other government departments and agencies which include the CPS, UK Visas and Immigration, Her Majesty's Prison Service (HMP), Her Majesty's Revenue and Customs and Crime Stoppers, a national public crime reporting service. Bringing these agencies together, shown in Figure 4.1, ROCUs provide a collaborative and unified response to tackling serious and organised crime at a local, regional and national level.

4.6.1 Regional Cyber Crime Units

An essential part of the ROCUs has been the creation of Regional Cyber Crime Units (RCCUs) which work with the NCA's NCCU and other partners in the UK and abroad, to investigate and prevent the most serious cyber offences. The RCCUs deal predominantly with the most serious pure cyber-dependent offences relating to malware-based cyber crime, including botnets, DDoS attacks, phishing, network compromise and extortion. RCCUs work with the other ROCUs and RCCUs and partners across the UK supporting a greater regional effort than local police forces are able to do, to tackle serious and organised crime by providing investigative and technical support and a proactive cyber capability.

The aim of RCCUs is to deliver a regional cyber capability that is feared by cybercriminals, considered professional by the judiciary, respected by industry and trusted and relied upon by victims

Figure 4.1 Regional Organised Crime Units

of cyber crime at a regional and national level. The work of the RCCUs cannot be conducted alone and their partnerships in the private sector, especially small to medium-sized enterprises (SMEs) are an essential ingredient in the fight against cyber crime. RCCUs provide support, guidance and advice to industry and support the work of 'Get Safe Online', a jointly funded initiative between several government departments and a number of private sector businesses. Get Safe Online is a unique public resource providing practical advice on how citizens can protect themselves online, their computers and their mobiles devices and how SMEs can better safeguard businesses against fraud, identity theft, viruses and many other problems encountered online. The protective cyber network of partners provides a rich source of publicly available information and support and is an important part of the efforts of RCCUs to keep citizens, communities and businesses safe online.

ROCUs provide a regional network of CCUs to support local police efforts and bridge the gap between neighbourhood safety and national security by supporting and informing the national threat intelligence picture. ROCUs provide essential specialist capabilities to tackle all manner of cyber-related crime which is beyond the scale and scope that local police forces are able to manage effectively and without drawing on and redirecting finite police resources from other essential duties at a local level. Given the current and continued scale of government cuts to policing, alongside Home Office and National Police Chiefs' Council (NPCC) encouragement to increase the effectiveness and efficiency of all police forces, it is recognised by senior police leaders that greater collaboration and integration between police forces and partner agencies through programmes of cyber crime innovation and transformation, will make better use of regional cyber crime assets and specialist capabilities at a local level.

4.7 Local Response to Policing Cyber Crime

Local police forces must be able to action reports of cyber-dependent crime and cyber-enabled crime directly from the public and as requests from Action Fraud and the NFIB, including crimes in action. As an example, this may include incidents of:

- malicious communication;
- fraud;
- harassment;
- child exploitation;
- money laundering.

Local police forces may also be asked by a ROCU or the NCA to undertake activity, or to support national or regional investigations. A number of police forces over recent years have established their own dedicated teams of cyber crime police investigators within a local CCU. These local teams of cyber crime specialists, who are focused on the prevention and detection of cyber crimes at a force-level, support and complement regional and national efforts to tackle cyber crime. Many of these local CCUs remain in their infancy being supported by force-level Cybercrime Boards and Cybercrime Groups at a tactical and strategic level. These groups bring together officers and staff from varying internal policing disciplines to ensure effective coordination, and are complemented by Independent Cybercrime Advisory Boards at force-level to ensure all activities to tackle cyber crime are not only plugged into the command and control structures of local forces, but that all officers and staff have ready access to specialists from academia and the private sector whose support, guidance, advice and contributions are vital in tackling contemporary cyber crimes.

To ensure local cyber crime activities are purposeful and directed, each local police force will have a set of identified key priorities as part of a Cyber Crime Control Strategy to specifically tackle cyber crime. This Control Strategy will be owned by a strategic lead, most likely to be a Deputy Assistant Commissioner or Commander in the Metropolitan Police Service, an Assistant Chief Constable in the larger strategic police forces across the country or a Chief Superintendent in smaller police forces. Whatever their rank in their respective police force, the responsibility will be the same, which includes overseeing cyber crime matters in their jurisdiction and setting key priorities to tackle cyber crime as well as monitoring performance to support the wider policing mission of their police force to prevent and reduce crime. The purpose of the Control Strategy is to ensure that across the four pillars of the national Cyber Crime Strategy and Organised Crime Strategy, all officers and staff within the CCU have clear direction to Prevent cyber crime, Prepare for cyber attacks, Protect against cyber attacks and Pursue cybercriminals. This approach also ensures that there is a consistent and coherent thread woven through local, regional and national cyber crime policing activity.

Force-level CCUs continue to build local capacity and capability to ensure they are able to meet the expectations of the public they serve in keeping them safe online. The CCUs remain the key local drivers to enable Chief Constables to meet their commitments set out in their own police force strategies. Local CCUs also provide the local Chief Constable with the ability to report to their respective PCC that the cyber crime-related priorities and outcomes contained in the local Police and Crime Plan published by the PCC is being achieved.

4.8 Police and Crime Commissioners

The locally democratically elected PCC (or Mayor of London for the metropolis) is responsible for the totality of policing within the jurisdiction for which they have been duly elected. Their legal duty is to ensure that the communities they represent have an efficient and effective police force. Primarily, PCCs meet these responsibilities by:

- appointing the Chief Constable or Commissioner of the Metropolitan Police;

- holding the Chief Constable or Commissioner of the Metropolitan Police to account;
- setting and updating a Police and Crime Plan;
- setting the police force budget and police precept in the council tax;
- engaging meaningfully with the public and communities they serve.

The PCC is also responsible for ensuring so far as possible that the communities they represent have an effective and efficient criminal justice system, for providing certain services to victims of crime and for working with partners—such as local authorities, health and well-being bodies, businesses and third sector voluntary organisations. As an elected representative in all matters affecting policing at a local level, PCCs are the voice for local communities in the areas they represent. Elected by local communities and accountable to them at the ballot box every five years, the PCC is not only responsible for policing at a local level, but also for policing issues that span larger geographical areas which include cyber crime.

It is important to note that the Chief Constable of a local police force, and the Commissioner of the Metropolitan Police for London, have operational independence in deploying police officers and staff across their jurisdiction and have direction and control of policing operations. They also set their own internal performance ambitions for measuring and driving the performance of the police, while the PCC makes relevant resources available to the Chief Constable for this purpose and will hold them to account for the use of those resources and the performance of the police.

Following a process of public and partner agency consultation, the PCC sets a Police and Crime Plan, usually for a five-year period, which is publicly available and includes police priorities and outcomes. These priorities include how the PCC will support the prevention and detection of crime which includes cyber crime.

KEY POINT—PREVENTATIVE GUIDANCE AND ADVICE

At the most local level, all police officers and Police Community Support Officers (PCSOs), whether working in neighbourhood policing, criminal investigation or other public-facing roles of the police, continue to play a vital role in ensuring that all the public, private businesses and police partners remain alert to cyber crime.

All police officers and PCSOs, as well as cyber investigators themselves, must be able to confidently offer practical advice to help to prevent cyber crimes, as well as signposting them to partner agencies which can provide additional specialist support and guidance. Practical cyber crime prevention advice is available for all police officers to communicate to the public, private business and partners from their local CCUs and force-level Crime Prevention Officers and such advice is readily available on police force internet and intranet websites.

The UK policing response to tackle cyber crime continues to develop in line with new and emerging threats, risks and challenges. To keep pace with new cyber crime developments please refer to the following website: http://www.nationalcrimeagency. gov.uk/about-us/what-we-do/national-cyber-crime-unit.

Part III

Investigating Cyber Crime

Chapter 5

Preventing Cyber Crime

5.1 Introduction

This chapter seeks to provide all police practitioners with an introduction to preventing cyber crime. The prevention of cyber crime remains the highest priority for all cyber crime investigators. This chapter seeks to guide all police practitioners through the complexities and challenges of effectively providing practical cyber crime prevention advice. Most importantly, this chapter sets out how cyber crime investigators can better protect themselves and their operational activities from all manner of cyber-related threats. There now exists a plethora of free and accessible information designed to keep all online users safe and to provide confidence and reassurance to the public, police partners and private industry; it is absolutely essential that all police officers are able to provide practical cyber crime preventative guidance and advice. It is also important for police officers to be able to readily signpost the public, partners and private businesses to trusted sources of information which will help to keep them safe online, leading to greater online protection and increased awareness of cyber crime prevention methods.

5.2 Password Protection

Passwords are the most common way to prove online identity when using websites, email accounts and personal and work computers via user accounts. The use of strong passwords is therefore essential for cyber crime investigators in order to protect online security and identity, as well as the integrity of police IT. With a few simple precautions, a strong password can dramatically reduce the risk from online identity theft and cyber fraud. Passwords are commonly used in conjunction with a username. However, on secure sites they may also be used alongside other methods of identification such as a separate Personal Identification Number (PIN) and/or memorable information. In some cases, users are asked to enter only certain characters of their password, for additional security. The risk of using weak passwords increases vulnerability to cybercriminals who will impersonate the victim to commit fraud and other crimes, including:

- accessing bank accounts;
- purchasing items online using the victim's money;
- impersonating the victim on social networking and dating sites;
- sending emails in the victim's name;
- accessing private information held on the victim's computer.

All police officers and staff **must** not only follow their own police force operational information technology security password protocols but they **must** also be able to advise partners and the public on the importance of choosing strong passwords and which are the most secure passwords to use. The following checklist provides guidance and advice for police, partners and the public to substantially minimise the risk of being a victim of online identify theft and fraud.

Cyber crime investigator's password protection checklist

ALWAYS use a password. Cyber crime investigators **must** consider the following suggestions when choosing a password.

- Select a password with at least eight characters (more if you can, as longer passwords are harder for criminals to guess or break), a combination of upper and lower case letters, numbers and keyboard symbols. However, be aware that some punctuation marks may be difficult to enter on foreign keyboards. Also remember that changing letters to numbers (e.g. E to 3 and i to 1) are techniques well known to criminals.
- Use a line of a song or from a film that other people would not associate with you.
- Use someone else's mother's maiden name (not your own mother's maiden name) or another surname that other people would not associate you with.
- Pick a phrase known to you and take the first character from each word to create your password.

You must NEVER use the following as passwords.

- Your username, actual name or business name.
- Family members' or pets' names.
- Your or family's birthdays.
- Favourite football team, film, pop group or other words easy to work out with a little background knowledge.
- The word 'password'.
- Numerical sequences.
- A single commonplace dictionary word, which could be cracked by common hacking programs.
- When choosing numerical passcodes or PINs, do not use ascending or descending numbers (e.g. 4321 or 12345), duplicated numbers (e.g. 1111) or easily recognisable keypad patterns (e.g. 14789 or 2580).

Once a strong password has been selected, you **must** protect it.

- Do not disclose or share your password with anyone else. If you think that someone else knows your password, change it immediately.
- Do not enter your password when others can see what you are typing.
- Use a different password for every website. If you have only one password, a criminal simply has to break it to gain access to everything.
- Do not recycle passwords (e.g. password2, password3).
- If you must write passwords down in order to remember them, encrypt them in a way that is familiar to you but makes them indecipherable by others.
- Do not send your password by email. No reputable firm will ask you to do this.

KEY POINT—CYBER CRIME COMPLACENCY

It is understandable that although members of the public should use different passwords for each of their online accounts, it can make them very difficult to remember, but cyber crime investigators must reinforce that this is a minor inconvenience when compared with the reality of becoming a victim of cyber crime through identity theft and online fraud. Cyber crime investigators at every opportunity should inform members of the public that using a strong password is a fundamental building block of online security, and that not using a password or using a weak password, is the offline equivalent of leaving a front door unlocked or leaving a car key in the ignition. Personal data and banking details are insecure without the use of strong passwords and there are consequences for poor online security measures. Cybercriminals exploit citizen complacency to cyber security.

5.3 **Get Safe Online**

Get Safe Online is the UK's leading source of unbiased, factual and easy-to-understand information on online safety and is an excellent resource not only for cyber investigators to gain practical knowledge and expertise, but also to access cyber crime information to disseminate to the public, partners and private industry. The Get Safe Online website is a unique resource providing practical advice on how to protect members of the public, computers and mobile devices and business against fraud, identity theft, viruses and many other problems encountered online. It contains guidance on many other related subjects too—including performing backups and how to avoid theft or loss of computers, smartphones or tablets. Every conceivable topic is included on the site—including safe online shopping, gaming and dating.

Get Safe Online is a trusted resource for police officers and a welcome addition to their cyber crime investigation toolkit as the site keeps all visitors up to date with news, tips and stories from around the world. Get Safe Online is not only a website, as they also organise national events—such as Get Safe Online week to raise awareness of cyber crime issues—and they work closely with law enforcement agencies and other bodies in support of their outreach activity, internal awareness and customer online safety. Get Safe Online is a public and private sector partnership supported by HM Government and leading organisations in banking, retail, internet security and other sectors. The following practical advice and guidance, including how to use the internet safely, protecting yourself, your computer and safeguarding children online, is all offered by Get Safe Online thus providing an excellent cyber security resource.

5.3.1 **Using the internet safely**

The internet has revolutionised the way we live our lives—enabling us to read the news, enjoy entertainment, carry out research, book our holidays, buy and sell, shop, network, learn, bank and carry out many other everyday tasks. There are, however, a number of risks associated with going online. These result from either visiting malicious websites or inadvertent disclosure of personal information, and Get Safe Online has provided guidance and advice to support the use of the internet. The following checklist summarises their advice which provides cyber crime investigators with excellent guidance to follow and to communicate to members of the public, partners and private industry.

Using the internet safely checklist

- Always be vigilant when supplying personal or financial details.
- Ensure the browser is up to date.
- Maintain privacy and avoid identity theft or fraud.
- Personal identity is precious. Keep it that way with a few simple precautions.
- When using the internet, the websites visited are visible to the ISP and browser provider, and it is possible that records are kept.
- It is very easy to clone a real website and does not take a skilled developer long to produce a very professional-looking but malicious site.
- Be wary of malicious, criminal or inappropriate websites; use your instincts and common sense and:
  - check for presence of an address, phone number and/or email contact—these are often indications that the website is genuine; if in doubt, send an email or call to establish authenticity;
  - check if the website's address looks genuine by looking for misspellings, extra words, characters or numbers or a completely different name from that the business would be expected to have;
  - roll the cursor over a link to reveal its true destination; displayed in the bottom left corner of your browser; be wary if this is different from what is displayed in the text of the link from either another website or an email;
  - if there is **no** padlock in the browser window or 'https://' at the beginning of the web address to signify that it is using a secure link, do not enter personal information on the site;
  - websites which request more personal information than you would normally expect to give, such as user name, password or other security details **in full**, are probably malicious;
  - avoid 'pharming' by checking the address in your browser's address bar after you arrive at a website to make sure that

it matches the address you typed—this will avoid ending up at a fake site even though you entered the address for the authentic one—for example, 'eebay' instead of 'ebay'.

+ Always get professional advice before making investment decisions. Sites that hype investments for fast or high return—whether in shares or alleged rarities like old wine, whisky or property—are often fraudulent.

+ Be wary of websites which promote schemes that involve the recruitment of others, receiving money for other people or advance payments.

+ If you are suspicious of a website, carry out a web search to see if you can find out whether or not it is fraudulent.

+ Be wary of websites that are advertised in unsolicited emails from strangers.

+ If you come across content that you consider to be illegal, such as child abuse images or criminally obscene adult material, you should report this to the Internet Watch Foundation (a charitable organisation working with government and private industry to remove harmful content from the internet) at: www.iwf.org.uk. If you come across content that you consider illegal, such as racist or terrorist content, you should report this to the police.

5.3.2 Protecting computers online

It is essential to take sensible measures to protect computers from the numerous threats encountered online. This should be relatively simple for anyone who can use a computer and is therefore essential for cyber crime investigators to increase their knowledge and awareness. Effective protection will safeguard against computers being infected with viruses and spyware that could result from online activities that seem completely harmless—such as searching the internet, downloading, playing games and even using email. In turn, it will safeguard online users against potentially serious consequences such as fraud and identity theft. A comprehensive guide to protecting personal computers is available from Get Safe Online.

5.3.3 Safeguarding children online

Police officers must be able to protect the most vulnerable in our society and it is essential that they equip themselves with the skills necessary to identify the online risks to children and are able to provide guidance and reassurance to both children and their parents, guardians and carers on keeping children safe online. Get Safe Online offers excellent advice for the safeguarding of children online which follows that of experts the world over by taking a balanced approach to children's online safety. Cyber crime investigators must adopt a proactive approach to safeguarding children online as doing nothing is a sure-fire way to let children get into trouble, whilst a heavy-handed approach will make them all the more determined to do the opposite of what parents or carers tell them. Get Safe Online suggests that a degree of technological monitoring and control (parental software)—balanced with age-appropriate education and guidance throughout their childhood—will show children that parents and carers actually care about their online activity and will go a long way towards keeping their digital lives safe and happy. Get Safe Online has identified and published a best approach model for parents to safeguard children online, shown in the following checklist, which provides effective guidance and advice for cyber crime investigators to consider when preventing and investigating online offences against children.

Get Safe Online best parental approach for safeguarding children online checklist

1. Guide your family in the digital world in the same way you do in day-to-day life—including not being afraid to set boundaries and rules for your children from a young age. Here are some questions that you could ask them at the outset, then raise them again and again as they get older and develop new online interests and activities. Use them as a base for discussion:
   - What are your friends doing online?
   - What are the newest and best websites and apps?
   - Can you show me your favourites?
   - Do you know what cyber bullying is, and have you ever experienced it in any way? Or have any of your friends?
   - Has anything you've seen online ever made you feel weird, sad or uncomfortable?

2. Try out some of the technologies your child enjoys for yourself. You could ask them to help to set you up on Facebook (if you don't already have a page), or play on the games console together.

3. Discuss with your friends, family and other parents how they help their children to progress and keep safe in their digital world. You might be able to exchange some interesting tips and even help them out too.

---

4. Ensure that you know how to use parental controls on computers, mobiles and games consoles, privacy features on social networking sites and the safety options on Google and other search engines.
5. Find out about software you can buy or download to keep children safe online, for example Norton Family which helps you to monitor web activity and prevents kids from trying to delete visits from their history.
6. Having said that, try not to rely purely on technology to babysit your child online. Use it to help you to set limits.
7. As your kids grow up, make sure they are aware of the 'basics' of online safety, such as not clicking on links in emails or instant messages, good password practice and not turning off anti-virus programs and firewalls.
8. Talk regularly with your child about their and your online lives. Show them that you understand how important technology is to them and talk about all its benefits, but don't be nervous about things like responsible online behaviour, bullying and pornography.
9. Sometimes as parents we have to take a step back and remember just how young or old our children are and what is the 'right thing' for people of their age.

KEY POINT—CYBER CRIME TOOLKIT

To keep updated on the latest cyber crime preventative guidance and advice, visit the Get Safe Online website at www.getsafeonline.org; it will add great value to the cyber crime toolkit of any cyber investigator.

There can be no complacency in the fight against cyber crime, so all cyber investigators must employ robust personal and operational security measures at all times to protect themselves, police operating systems and the confidentiality of the information held by them on behalf of the public they serve. Cyber crime investigators **must** not only follow internal local police IT security policy, practice and procedures but—given their role, responsibility and expertise—should be setting the standard for online and IT security and be role models for all police practitioners and ambassadors for cyber crime prevention to the public they serve.

See Appendix 2, 'Public Guidance to Prevent Online Fraud for Police Officers' which provides practical guidance and advice to prevent individuals becoming victims of online fraud.

5.4 **Cyber Crime and Cyber Security Guidance for Business**

The CESG, Cabinet Office, CPNI and BIS (now the Department for Business, Energy & Industrial Strategy) joined forces to publish '10 Cyber Security Steps' explaining how organisations can protect themselves in cyberspace. This ten-step guide, shown in Table 5.1, is supported by GCHQ which continues to identify real threats to the UK on a daily basis. The ten-step guidance was originally published in 2012 and was updated during 2015 and is now used by around two-thirds of the FTSE350 companies. The guidance from joint government departments with responsibilities for cyber security, all advocate a better understanding of the cyber environment for business leaders, and by adopting the Ten Steps will provide a more effective means for protecting organisations from all manner of cyber-related attacks. The Ten Steps also provide cyber investigators with practical guidance and advice to offer to businesses during the course of their investigations.

5.5 **Data Volume Classification**

In today's interconnected and interdependent world, being amplified by the internet, online social networks and smarter mobile communications, enormous amounts of data are being captured every day at an ever-increasing speed. The volume of information now stored and passing through computers, servers and other mobile devices of individual members of the public, public authorities and private industry is vast—all of which can be accessed and stolen by cybercriminals. To provide an insight into the size and scale of the amount of data generated by the internet, Table 5.2 provides a list of activity which provides a snapshot of what happens in an internet minute.

Most members of the public who use computers understand the relative size of their digital files: the report you just saved is 318 kilobytes (kB); those holiday photos tally 750 megabytes (MB); your new iPod holds 20 gigabytes (GB) of music. When data sets start to grow, however, their size becomes more difficult to explain. The understanding of these data sizes are important for all cyber crime investigators to know, not only to assess the size and scale of the crimes that may have been committed, but the time it may take to investigate and sift through piles of potential evidence.

Table 5.1 Ten steps to cyber security

Step	Title	Advice
1	Information Risk Management Regime	Assess the risks to your organisation's information assets with the same vigour as you would for legal, regulatory, financial or operational risk. To achieve this, embed an Information Risk Management Regime across your organisation, supported by the board, senior managers and an empowered information assurance (IA) structure. Consider communicating your risk management policy across your organisation to ensure that employees, contractors and suppliers are aware of your organisation's risk management boundaries.
2	Network security	Connecting to untrusted networks (e.g. the internet) can expose your organisation to cyber attacks. Follow recognised network design principles when configuring perimeter and internal network segments, and ensure that all network devices are configured to the secure baseline build. Filter all traffic at the network perimeter so that only traffic required to support your business is allowed, and monitor traffic for unusual or malicious incoming and outgoing activity that could indicate an attack (or attempted attack).
3	Managing user privileges	All users of your ICT systems should only be provided with the user privileges that they need to do their job. Control the number of privileged accounts for roles such as system or database administrators, and ensure this type of account is not used for high-risk or day-to-day user activities. Monitor user activity, particularly all access to sensitive information and privileged account actions.
4	Secure configuration	Introduce corporate policies and processes to develop secure baseline builds, and manage the configuration and use of ICT systems. Remove or disable unnecessary functionality from ICT systems, and keep them patched against known vulnerabilities. Failing to do this will expose your business to threats and vulnerabilities, and increase risk to the confidentiality, integrity and availability of systems and information (e.g. creating new user accounts, changes to user passwords and deletion of accounts and audit logs).

Table 5.1 Continued

Step	Title	Advice
5	User education and awareness	Produce user security policies that describe acceptable and secure use of your organisation's ICT systems. These should be formally acknowledged in employment terms and conditions. All users should receive regular training on the cyber risks they face as employees and individuals. Security-related roles (e.g. system administrators, incident management team members and forensic investigators) will require specialist training.
6	Incident management	Establish an incident response and disaster recovery capability that addresses the full range of incidents that can occur. All incident management plans (including disaster recovery and business continuity) should be regularly tested. Your incident response team may need specialist training across a range of technical and non-technical areas. Report online crimes to the relevant law enforcement agency to help the UK build a clear view of the national threat and deliver an appropriate response.
7	Malware prevention	Produce policies that directly address the business processes (e.g. email, web browsing, removable media and personally owned devices) that are vulnerable to malware. Scan for malware across your organisation and protect all host and client machines with anti-virus solutions that will actively scan for malware. All information supplied to or from your organisation should be scanned for malicious content.
8	Monitoring	Establish a monitoring strategy and develop supporting policies, taking into account previous security incidents and attacks, and your organisation's incident management policies. Continuously monitor inbound and outbound network traffic to identify unusual activity or trends that could indicate attacks and the compromise of data. Monitor all ICT systems using Network and Host Intrusion Detection Systems (NIDS/HIDS) and Prevention Systems (NIPS/HIPS).

(continued)

Table 5.1 Continued

Step	Title	Advice
9	Removable media controls	Produce removable media policies that control the use of removable media for the import and export of information. Where the use of removable media is unavoidable, limit the types of media that can be used together with the users, systems and types of information that can be transferred. Scan all media for malware using a stand-alone media scanner before any data is imported into your organisation's system.
10	Home and mobile working	Assess the risks to all types of mobile working (including remote working where the device connects to the corporate network infrastructure) and develop appropriate security policies. Train mobile users on the secure use of their mobile devices for locations they will be working from. Apply the secure baseline build to all types of mobile device used. Protect data-at-rest using encryption (if the device supports it) and protect data-in-transit using an appropriately configured Virtual Private Network (VPN).

Table 5.2 What happens in an internet minute?

Service	Activity
Google	2.4 million search queries
Email	150 million emails sent
Apple App Store	51,000 applications downloaded
Facebook	701,389 logins
WhatsApp	20.8 million messages sent
YouTube	2.78 million videos viewed
Spotify	38,052 hours of music played
Instagram	38,194 posts
Amazon	$203,596 value of sales
Twitter	347,222 new tweets
LinkedIn	120 new accounts

Computer hard drive capacity has increased 50-million-fold since 1956. It took 26 years to create a 1 GB hard drive, but between 2007 and 2011, hard drives quadrupled in size from 1 TB to 4 TB. Within the next ten years, 20 TB hard drives may even become commonplace. The smallest unit of measurement used for measuring data is a bit. A single bit can have a value of either 0 or 1. It may contain a binary value (such as On/Off or True/False), but nothing more. Therefore, a byte, or eight bits, is used as the fundamental unit of measurement for data. A byte can store 28 or 256 different values, which is sufficient to represent standard characters, such as letters, numbers and symbols. Since most files contain thousands of bytes, file sizes are often measured in kilobytes. Larger files, such as images, videos and audio files, contain millions of bytes and therefore are measured in megabytes. Modern storage devices can store thousands of these files, which is why storage capacity is typically measured in gigabytes or even terabytes. Larger units of measurement are usually reserved for measuring the sum of multiple storage devices or the capacity of large data storage networks. The list below provides all the standard units of measurement used for data storage, from the smallest to the largest:

- bit (b) 0 or 1 1/8 of a byte;
- byte (B) 8 bits 1 byte;
- kilobyte (KB) 10001 bytes 1,000 bytes;
- megabyte (MB) 10002 bytes 1,000,000 bytes;
- gigabyte (GB) 10003 bytes 1,000,000,000 bytes;
- terabyte (TB) 10004 bytes 1,000,000,000,000 bytes;
- petabyte (PB) 10005 bytes 1,000,000,000,000,000 bytes;
- exabyte (EB) 10006 bytes 1,000,000,000,000,000,000 bytes;
- zettabyte (ZB) 10007 bytes 1,000,000,000,000,000,000,000 bytes;
- yottabyte (YB) 10008 bytes 1,000,000,000,000,000,000,000,000 bytes.

KEY POINT: DATA SIZE MATTERS

A lowercase 'b' is used as an abbreviation for bits, while an uppercase 'B' represents bytes. This is an important distinction, since a byte is eight times larger than a bit. For example, 100 KB (kilobytes) = 800 Kb (kilobits).

5.5.1 **Internet of things**

The phenomenon of cyber crime remains in its infancy resulting in threats and harm to citizens' safety and national security which is set to grow. Law enforcement agencies must therefore continue to prepare and equip themselves for the challenges ahead which are to become increasingly acute as the Internet of Things rapidly grows, providing further opportunities for cyber crimes to be committed.

The Internet of Things (IoT) or Internet of Everything (IoE) refers to devices or objects that are connected to the internet, like your smartwatch, Fitbit or even your refrigerator. These devices are able to collect and transmit data via the internet, contributing to our big data world. Smart, connected devices are already transforming our way of life as well as the competitive forces in business. To demonstrate how fast this sector is growing, and what impact it will have on our lives and businesses, the following statistics prove that the phenomenon is here and is here to stay:

- the majority of people (87 per cent) have not heard of the term 'Internet of Things';
- ATMs are considered some of the first IoT objects, and went online as far back as 1974;
- back in 2008, there were already more objects connected to the internet than people;
- during 2016, the internet was estimated to have 4.9 billion connected things;
- by 2020, the number of internet-connected things will reach or even exceed 50 billion;
- in 2016, over 1.4 billion smartphones were shipped and by 2020 we will have a staggering 6.1 billion smartphone users;
- the IoT will connect many of the devices we have in our homes, from smart thermostats to smart fridges. Companies like Google and Samsung understand the business opportunities this will bring. Google purchased smart thermostat maker, Nest Labs, for $3.2 billion, and Samsung purchased connected home company SmartThings for $200 million;
- during 2016, cars that can drive on their own became a reality—Google's self-driving cars currently average about 10,000 autonomous miles per week;
- by 2020, a quarter of a billion vehicles will be connected to the internet, providing completely new possibilities for in-vehicle services and automated driving;

- the global market for wearable devices grew 223 per cent in 2016, with Fitbit shipping 4.4 million devices and Apple selling 3.6 million Apple Watches;

- internet-connected clothing is coming—estimates predict that 10.2 million units of smart clothing will be shipped by 2020, compared to a meagre 140,000 units in 2013;

- today, the market for Radio Frequency Identification (RFID) tags, used for transmitting data to identify and track objects, is worth $11.1 billion—this is predicted to rise to $21.9 billion by 2020;

- machine-to-machine (M2M) connections will grow from 5 billion at the beginning of 2016 to 27 billion by 2025;

- having a connected kitchen could save the food and beverage industry as much as 15 per cent annually;

- the IoT could generate $4.6 trillion over the next ten years for the public sector, and $14.4 trillion for the private sector.

The IoT is only set to grow. Current estimates reveal that less than 0.1 per cent of all the devices that could be connected to the internet are connected to the World Wide Web. Just think of the tremendous potential and limitless opportunities this brings for business and society and, as a cyber crime investigator, the innovative ways in which these new opportunities will be exploited by cybercriminals and cyber terrorists—tackling cyber crime will remain a national priority for the foreseeable future and a continued dedicated, determined and collaborative approach is essential to protect citizens' and business users' online activities.

KEY POINT—PREVENTION VERSUS INVESTIGATION

The government's Minister for Policing has stated that 80 per cent of cyber crimes can be prevented by individuals taking responsibility for their online security. More must be done by citizens to support the police in reducing their vulnerability to becoming a victim of cyber crime. Preventing cyber crime remains preferable to investigating increasing numbers of cyber-related crimes. Commander Greany of the City of London Police has stated: 'Given the nature of the cybercrime threat, victims must do everything they can to protect themselves; always being wary about who they are interacting with online and taking time to think before making any online transactions.'

Police officers must also be able to provide practical cyber crime preventative guidance, advice and support to members of the communities they serve and Chief Constables and PCCs are required more than ever to invest in the latest training for officers and staff, as well as encouraging local cyber crime prevention awareness campaigns for all police, partners, members of the public and the private sector.

Chapter 6

Cyber Crime Investigation Skills

6.1 **Introduction**

The complexity of cyber crime continues to challenge the capacity and capability of UK policing. Over recent years, in direct response to the threats from cyber crime, the need for a professionally trained, highly skilled cyber investigative workforce has been recognised. This workforce must prepare and equip itself for the cyber challenges that lie ahead and at its heart is the cybercriminal investigator whose skills and abilities are absolutely essential for the effective fight against cyber crime.

While it is recognised that cyber crime investigators require specialist knowledge and expertise to investigate the technical aspects of cyber crime, of critical importance is the understanding and practical application of the core investigative skills and doctrine required to effectively conduct contemporary criminal investigations. The development of new CCUs has attracted police officers with a rich mix of skills and expertise from across the operating landscape of policing. Some police officers will be nationally qualified and accredited detectives, while others have attained specialist skills in other areas with relevance to cyber crime investigation processes. In addition, new police staff have been recruited to tackle cyber crime including indexers, researchers, analysts, technicians and investigators, many of whom have been recruited from outside the police family. For a variety of reasons, these new cyber investigation teams need to increase their collective operational capacity and capability, and the purpose of this chapter is to outline the foundation of knowledge and skills required to do so, which includes the ethical frameworks for policing alongside national models, the importance of operational security and the core investigative skills to conduct effective cyber crime investigations.

KEY POINT—BALANCING SECURITY WITH LIBERTY AND HUMAN RIGHTS

It is absolutely essential that **any** investigation involving ICT is conducted with an acceptable balance between intrusion and privacy. Cyber crime investigators **must** consider Articles 6 and 8 of the Human Rights Act 1998 and the Regulation of Investigatory Powers Act (RIPA) 2000 throughout their operational activities.

6.2 Criminal Investigation

Criminal investigations are becoming increasingly complex and the investigation of cyber crime has brought many new challenges to the investigative capacity and capability of policing in the UK. As a direct result of highly sophisticated online crimes, contemporary police detectives, and especially those working in the domain of cyber crime, are expected to possess a wide range of knowledge, not just legislative powers and statutory offences, but also scientific approaches, crime scene management, collection of physical evidence, investigative interviewing, case file preparation, disclosure and management of the administration and investigative process.

Despite many challenges arising from the cyber crime phenomenon, the general and accepted definition of a criminal investigation remains unchanged. Put simply, a criminal investigation is best described as the collection of information and evidence for identifying, apprehending and convicting suspected offenders. It is, of course, much more complicated and challenging in reality but in the midst of a complex cyber crime investigation, cyber crime investigators should not forget the simplicity of what their role and responsibilities entail.

While there remains no official or universally accepted definition of criminal investigation within UK policing, a description is provided by the Criminal Procedure and Investigations Act 1996 (CPIA) Code of Practice, Part II, which defines a criminal investigation as:

An investigation conducted by police officers with a view to it being ascertained whether a person should be charged with an offence, or whether a person charged with an offence is guilty of it. This will include:

- investigations into crimes that have been committed;
- investigations whose purpose is to ascertain whether a crime has been committed with a view to possible institution of criminal proceedings; and
- investigations which begin in the belief that a crime may be committed.

KEY POINT—A NEW APPROACH

For many years, the criminal investigative default position was to prove points of law which presupposed that a crime had been committed, that an offender would be arrested and interviewed and that a prosecution would follow. Over recent years, the ethos of criminal investigations has significantly changed for the better, based on miscarriages of justice and a series of public inquiries concerning police investigations. Contemporary criminal investigations now focus on simply searching for the truth which provides for a range of possible outcomes.

KEY POINT—ROLE OF A CYBER CRIME INVESTIGATOR

Cyber crime investigators are expected to possess a wide range of knowledge, not just the knowledge traditionally associated with legislative powers and statutory offences. The contemporary professional cyber detective is required to embody a whole range of positive attributes and all cyber crime investigators, as a minimum, **must**:

- place their emphasis on 'searching for the truth' rather than 'searching for the proof';
- apply the investigative mindset and sceptically question and scrutinise;
- be confident, positive and optimistic;
- plan and prepare investigative activities with due consideration;
- reach out to specialist support and experts where required;
- **not** step outside the boundaries of training, competence or expertise;
- avoid 'tunnel vision' or 'closed minds' which are unethical.

6.3 **Code of Ethics**

The policing profession has a duty to protect the public and prevent crime. The public expect every person within the profession to fulfil this duty by being fair and impartial and giving a selfless service. While the great majority of people in policing act with honesty and integrity, any unprofessional behaviour detracts from the service provided to the public and harms the profession's reputation. The Code of Ethics sets out the principles and standards of behaviour that will promote, reinforce and support the highest standards from everyone who works in policing in England and Wales. The Code also has a preventive role. It requires everyone in policing to prevent unprofessional conduct by questioning behaviour which falls below expected standards. Additionally, it supports reporting or taking action against such behaviour.

KEY POINT—PROFESSIONAL APPROACH TO CYBER CRIME INVESTIGATIONS

The aim of the Code of Ethics is to support each member of the policing profession in delivering the highest professional standards in their service to the public. Ethical behaviour comes from the values, beliefs, attitudes and knowledge that guide the judgements of each individual. Everyone in policing has to make difficult decisions and complex choices every day of the week. These range from how to talk to a distressed member of the public through to how to allocate scarce resources and how to progress the next phase of a complex cyber crime investigation. The College of Policing, as the professional body for all in policing, has a responsibility to support the way these choices are made. The College of Policing believes that all involved in policing activity must make clear the ethical principles that are in place to guide decisions, whatever the context, and that the police service must be clear about what happens if those expectations are not met. Alongside the Code of Ethics, the College of Policing's commitment to helping police professionals to make the right decisions includes enhancing the knowledge and evidence base as well as developing a framework for continuous professional development.

The Code of Ethics is a first for everyone who works in policing in England and Wales. It sets out the principles and standards of behaviour expected to be seen from police professionals.

It applies to every individual who works in policing, whether a warranted officer, member of police staff, cyber crime detective and analyst, volunteer or someone contracted to work in a police force.

Policing has not previously adopted all the hallmarks of a profession but the Code of Ethics is one step towards obtaining full professional status for policing, similar to that seen in medicine and law. To maintain operational relevance, the College of Policing may from time to time revise the whole or any part of the Code of Ethics to keep pace with changes in policing.

The Code of Ethics underpins all of a cyber crime investigator's activities and, whether you are a seasoned detective drafted into a newly established cyber crime unit or have been recently recruited with technical or analytical expertise to support cyber crime investigations, a thorough understanding of the Code of Ethics is absolutely essential to ensure that all of the Code's principles and behaviours are embedded into everyday working practices.

6.3.1 Policing principles

Every person working for the police service must work honestly and ethically. The public expect the police to do the right thing in the right way. Basing decisions and actions on a set of policing principles will help to achieve this. The principles set out in the Code of Ethics originate from the 'Principles of Public Life' published by the Committee on Standards in Public Life in 1995, as these continue to reflect public expectations. The Code includes the principles of 'fairness' and 'respect' as research has shown these to be crucial to maintaining and enhancing public confidence in policing. The policing principles reflect the personal beliefs and aspirations that in turn serve to guide behaviour and shape the policing culture. The combination of principles and standards of behaviour encourages consistency between what people believe in and aspire to, and what they do. Table 6.1 shows the Code of Ethics Principles of Policing.

KEY POINT—ETHICS OF CYBER INVESTIGATIONS

The College of Policing Code of Ethics provides a firm foundation for all cyber crime investigators upon which to build a cyber crime investigation. Following the Code of Ethics, the Policing Principles and Professional Standards of Behaviour, will ensure that all overt and covert policing aspects of cyber-related investigations are conducted professionally, thereby providing confidence to the public that a new generation of online police investigators are progressing their work within a legal and ethical framework. Any cyber investigator's action which falls outside this framework serves to seriously damage the reputation of the police to carry out its duty in preventing and detecting cyber crime.

Table 6.1 Code of Ethics Principles of Policing

Principle	Description
Accountability	You are answerable for your decisions, actions and omissions.
Fairness	You treat people fairly.
Honesty	You are truthful and trustworthy.
Integrity	You always do the right thing.
Leadership	You lead by good example.
Objectivity	You make choices on evidence and your best professional judgement.
Openness	You are open and transparent in your actions and decisions.
Respect	You treat everyone with respect.
Selflessness	You act in the public interest.

6.4 **National Decision Model**

Making sound judgements is a core role and important attribute of any successful cyber investigator, particularly those leaders who are charged with the responsibility of managing and directing large-scale investigations. Effective decision-making, particularly at the very outset of cyber investigations, will ensure that opportunities are not missed and potential lines of enquiry are identified and rigorously pursued. In reality, law enforcement officers who are engaged in the early developments of an investigation do have to cope with a lack of sufficient information to begin with, and some important decisions may need to be made quickly and intuitively.

To support decision-making processes in the police service, the College of Policing have developed the National Decision Model (NDM), which is suitable for all decisions and should be used by everyone in policing. The NDM is shown in Figure 6.1 which can be applied:

- to spontaneous incidents or planned operations;
- by an individual or team of people;
- to both operational and non-operational situations.

Decision-makers can use the NDM to structure a rationale of what they did during an incident and why. Managers and others can use it to review decisions and actions, and promote learning. In a fast-moving incident, the police service recognises that it may not always be possible to segregate thinking or response according to each phase of the model. In such cases, the main priority of decision-makers is to keep in mind their overarching

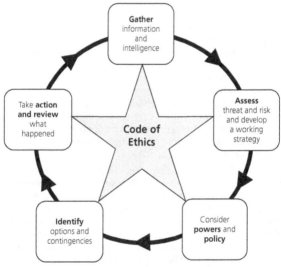

Figure 6.1 National Decision Model

mission to act with integrity to protect and serve the public. The mnemonic CIAPOAR can help users to remember the six key elements of the NDM. It also acts as an aide-memoire in aspects of decision-making.

- Code of Ethics—principles and standards of professional behaviour.
- Information—gather information and intelligence.
- Assessment—assess threat and risk and develop a working strategy.
- Powers and policy—consider powers and policy.
- Options—identify options and contingencies.
- Action and Review—take action and review what happened.

6.5 Developing an Investigative Hypothesis

Decisions to effectively progress cyber investigations may have to be based on or guided by a hypothesis. For cyber investigations, a hypothesis is a proposition made as a basis for reasoning without the assumption of its truth and supposition made as a starting point for further investigation of known facts. Developing and using a hypothesis is a widely recognised technique amongst criminal investigators which can be used to try to establish the most logical or likely explanation, theory or inference for why and how a cyber crime has been committed. Ideally, before cyber investigators develop a hypothesis there should be sufficient reliable material available on which to base the hypothesis, such as details of the victim, precise details of the incident or occurrence, national or international dimensions of the offence, motives of the crime and the precise modus operandi.

Of course, knowledge and experience of previous cases will also greatly assist in constructing a relevant hypothesis. Generating and building a hypothesis is an obvious and natural activity for cyber investigators, particularly during the early stages of an investigation. Clearly, if there is sufficient information or evidence already available then there will be no need to use the hypothesis method. However, cyber investigators are being increasingly called on to establish the most basic of facts at the commencement of an investigation, such as whether or not a crime has been committed.

Hypotheses are important to provide initial investigative direction where there is little information to work with. All cyber investigators must 'keep an open mind' and remember that it is better to gather as much information as possible before placing too much reliance on any speculative theory. It is a mistake for cyber investigators to theorise before sufficient data is collected, as it is easy to fall into the trap of manipulating and massaging facts to suit theories, instead of ensuring that theories suit the facts. The following provides a checklist for cyber crime investigators to consider when building a hypothesis.

Cyber crime investigator's hypothesis development checklist

When developing theoretical assumptions, cyber crime investigators would be well advised to give due consideration to the following.

- Beware of placing too much reliance on one or a limited number of hypotheses when there is insufficient information available.
- Remember the maxim 'keep an open mind'.
- Ensure a thorough understanding of the relevance and reliability of any material relied upon.
- Ensure that hypotheses are kept under constant review and remain dynamic, remembering that any hypothesis is only provisional at best.
- Define a clear objective for the hypothesis.
- Only develop a hypothesis that 'best fits' with the known information and material.
- Consult with colleagues and experts to discuss and formulate a hypothesis.
- Ensure sufficient resources are available to develop or test the hypothesis.

KEY POINT—COLLABORATION IN CYBER CRIME INVESTIGATION

Progressing cyber investigations is a collaborative effort and police officers must consult, listen and consider the advice and guidance provided by specialist hi-tech investigators. Any cyber crime investigator who fails to reach out to experts where appropriate to do so, or simply ignores specialist advice, does so at their peril.

6.6 **Evidence**

The primary role of the cyber crime investigator is to bring cyber-criminals to justice, which requires evidence to build a case for prosecution. Although cases against those suspected of cyber crime may still be regarded as specialist in nature, they are actually managed by the CPS in the same way as any other criminal case. It is important for the cyber crime investigator to clearly understand the role of the police and the prosecutor in the criminal justice system, and the sooner the CPS can be engaged in a cyber crime investigation the better.

All CPS decisions are made in accordance with the Code for Crown Prosecutors which states that a prosecutor needs to have sufficient evidence to afford a realistic prospect of a conviction before they can go on to consider the wider public interest. Commonly referred to as the 'Evidential Test', the CPS must be satisfied first of all that there is enough evidence to provide a realistic prospect of conviction against each defendant on each charge. This means that a jury or a bench of magistrates, properly directed in accordance with the law, is more likely than not to convict the defendant of the alleged charge. For there to be a conviction, the CPS have to prove the case so that the court is sure of the defendant's guilt. If the case does not pass the Evidential Test based on the strength of the evidence, it must not go ahead, no matter how important or serious it may be.

If the case does pass the 'Evidential Test', the CPS must then decide if a prosecution is needed in the public interest. A prosecution will usually take place unless there are public interest factors tending against prosecution which clearly outweigh those tending in favour. When considering the public interest test, one of the factors the CPS should always take into account is the consequences for the victim of the decision whether or not to prosecute, and any views expressed by the victim or the victim's family.

KEY POINT—CYBERCRIMINAL JUSTICE

Pursuing cybercriminals through the criminal justice system preserves and protects the democratic values of the prosecuting state while ensuring that the rights of all concerned are maintained. The role and responsibility of the CPS are essential for delivering justice to those who seek to use the internet and modern communications to steal, corrupt, harm and destroy our way of life.

The Code for Crown Prosecutors and the CPS Core Quality Standards can be found at http:www.cps.gov.uk and Her Majesty's CPS Inspectorate Report on the Counter-Terrorism Division at http://www.hmcpsi.gov.uk/index.php?id=116&inspection_id=0433.

The effective case management of cyber crime is an essential element in any cyber crime investigation and it is especially relevant to any lead cyber crime investigator. Mistakes and poor practice during the prosecution phase of a cyber crime investigative process can work against any chances of mounting a successful prosecution.

Cyber crime will continue to evolve at a rapid pace and all security practitioners must recognise that they are now operating in a world of low-impact, multiple victim crimes where bank robbers no longer have to plan meticulously for one theft of a million pounds; new technological capabilities mean that one person can now commit millions of robberies of one pound each. Paradoxically, effective contemporary cyber investigations rely upon a collaborative, multi-disciplinary and multi-agency approach where police detectives, hi-tech investigators, forensic analysts and experts from academia and the private sector work together to tackle cyber threats.

The complex nature and sophistication of cyber crime continues to demand a dedicated and determined response, especially from investigators who are critical to the success of tracking cybercriminals and bringing them to justice. Most importantly, however, no matter how complex and technical cyber investigations become in the future, all cyber crime investigators must develop their expertise founded on the core investigative skills and competencies outlined in this chapter.

6.7 **National Digital Evidence Guidance**

A national best practice guide for Digital Evidence has been produced by the Association of Chief Police Officers (ACPO) (now the National Police Chiefs' Council (NPCC)), Crime Business Area and was originally approved by ACPO Cabinet in December 2007. The purpose of the document is to provide guidance not only to assist law enforcement but for all partners and stakeholders who assist in investigating cyber security incidents and crime. The national guidance is regularly updated according to legislative and policy changes and republished as required, and all cyber investigators must keep themselves abreast of the latest version of the national guidance.

The *Good Practice Guide for Digital Evidence* has been created to ensure that the right information is available to practitioners and managers in the fight against cyber crime. A multi-disciplinary team consisting of practitioners, academics and individuals from the private sector contributed to its creation, drawing together their expert knowledge in tackling the criminal misuse of current and emerging technologies.

The most recent iteration of the *Good Practice Guide for Digital Evidence* reflects digital-based evidence and attempts to encompass the diversity of the digital world. As such, it is national guidance that will not only assist law enforcement but also the wider family that supports the investigation of cyber security incidents.

The national guidance recognises that the police service works in an area of constant change and that there is a continuing need to re-evaluate and revise police capacities to perform their duties. It also acknowledges that there is a need to recover and analyse digital data that can now be found in the many devices that are in day-to-day use, and can supply vital evidence in all our investigations.

KEY POINT—CYBER CRIME INVESTIGATIVE GOOD PRACTICE

It is important that people who work in the arena of digital forensics do not just concentrate on technology, as essential as that is, but that the investigative processes used are fit for the purpose, and that skills and capacities within the ever-increasing number of specialist CCUs reflect the demands that are made on them.

The *Good Practice Guide for Digital Evidence* is primarily written for the guidance of UK law enforcement personnel who may deal with digital evidence. This will include:

- persons who are involved in the securing, seizing and transporting of equipment from search scenes with a view to recovering digital evidence, as well as in the identification of the digital information needed to investigate crime;

- investigators who plan and manage the identification, presentation and storage of digital evidence, and the use of that evidence;
- persons who recover and reproduce seized digital evidence and are trained to carry out the function and have relevant training to give evidence in court of their actions. Persons who have not received appropriate training and are unable to comply with the principles should not carry out this category of activity;
- persons who are involved in the selection and management of persons who may be required to assist in the recovery, identification and interpretation of digital evidence.

6.8 Guiding Principles

To effectively establish national guidance and to build a firm foundation of cyber crime investigative doctrine, the authors of the *Good Practice Guide for Digital Evidence* have created four core principles to be followed by all cyber crime investigators. The four guiding principles are as follows.

- **Principle 1: (ACTION)**

  No action taken by law enforcement agencies or their agents should change data held on a computer or storage media which may subsequently be relied upon in court.

- **Principle 2: (COMPETENCY)**

  In exceptional circumstances, where a person finds it necessary to access original data held on a computer or on storage media, that person must be competent to do so and be able to give evidence explaining the relevance and the implications of their actions.

- **Principle 3: (ACCOUNTABILITY)**

  An audit trail or other record of all processes applied to computer-based electronic evidence should be created and preserved. An independent third party should be able to examine those processes and achieve the same result.

- **Principle 4: (RESPONSIBILITY)**

  The person in charge of the investigation (the case officer) has overall responsibility for ensuring that the law and these principles are adhered to.

KEY POINT—EXPLANATION OF THE PRINCIPLES

Computer-based electronic evidence is subject to the same rules and laws that apply to documentary evidence. The doctrine of documentary evidence may be explained thus: the onus is on the prosecution to show to the court that the evidence produced is no more and no less now than when it was first taken into the possession of the police.

Operating systems and other programs frequently alter and add to the contents of electronic storage. This may happen automatically without the user necessarily being aware that the data has been changed.

In order to comply with the principles of computer-based electronic evidence, wherever practicable an image should be made of the entire target device. Partial or selective file copying may be considered as an alternative in certain circumstances, for example when the amount of data to be imaged makes this impracticable. However, investigators should be careful to ensure that all relevant evidence is captured if this approach is adopted.

In a minority of cases, it may not be possible to obtain an image using a recognised imaging device. In these circumstances, it may become necessary for the original machine to be accessed to recover the evidence. With this in mind, it is essential that a witness, who is competent to give evidence to a court of law, makes any such access.

It is essential to display objectivity in a court, as well as the continuity and integrity of evidence. It is also necessary to demonstrate how evidence has been recovered, showing each process through which the evidence was obtained. Evidence should be preserved to such an extent that a third party is able to repeat the same process and arrive at the same result as that presented to a court.

It should be noted that the application of the principles does not preclude a proportionate approach to the examination of digital evidence. Those making decisions about the conduct of a digital investigation must often make judgements about the focus and scope of an investigation, taking into account available intelligence and investigative resources. This will often include a risk assessment based on technical and non-technical factors, for example the potential evidence which may be held by a particular type of device or the previous offending history of the suspect. Where this is done it should be transparent, decisions should be justifiable and the rationale recorded.

6.9 **Hi-Tech Investigations**

Despite major advancements in hi-tech investigation, it remains entirely possible for data to be beyond recovery by even the most eminent digital recovery expert. Understanding more about hi-tech investigations and their capabilities will provide the cyber crime investigator with realistic expectations of what can and cannot be achieved. Surprisingly, many cybercriminals and cyber crime investigators remain ignorant of the kind of data that can be scavenged from the various digital sources that will underpin an investigation. Digital devices are now part of any investigation in one way or another.

- **Used to conduct the activity under investigation:** the device is the main focus of the activity, such as the main storage and distribution device in a case of indecent images of children.
- **Target of the activity under investigation:** the device is the 'victim', such as in an incident of hacking.
- **Supports the activity under investigation:** the device is used to facilitate the activity, such as mobile phones used for communication.

Hi-tech investigations relate to the analysis and interpretation of data from digital devices, often called on when an incident has occurred. They are not purely about using the most advanced technology to perform the work. A good proportion of what is done is actually 'low-tech', in the sense that it is the investigator's mind doing the work and interpreting the data that is available. The primary objective of hi-tech investigations is to identify what happened and by whom it was carried out.

6.9.1 **Core concepts of hi-tech investigations**

Hi-tech investigations encompass four distinct components which represent the core concepts of all hi-tech investigations and include collection, examination, analysis and reporting, as shown in Figure 6.2.

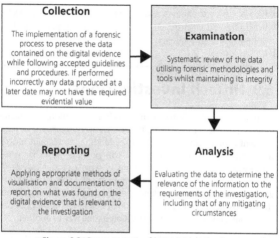

Figure 6.2 Core concepts of hi-tech investigations

KEY POINT—UNDERPINNING CORE CONCEPTS

The four core concepts of hi-tech investigation underpin the entire investigative process allowing hi-tech investigators and reviewers of the final product to have confidence that the captured evidence has authenticity, validity and, above all, accuracy.

6.10 Planning Cyber Crime Investigations

The proliferation of digital devices and advances in digital communications mean that digital evidence is now present or potentially present in almost every crime. Digital evidence can be found in a number of different locations:

- locally on an end-user device—typically a user's computer, mobile/smartphone, satellite navigation system, USB thumb drive or digital camera;

- on a remote resource that is public—for example, websites used for social networking, discussion forums and newsgroups;

- on a remote resource that is private—an ISP's logs of users' activity, a mobile phone company's records of customers' billing, a user's webmail account and, increasingly commonly, a user's remote file storage;

- in transit—for example, mobile phone text messages or voice calls, emails or internet chat.

KEY POINT—CONSIDERATIONS FOR PLANNING CYBER CRIME INVESTIGATIONS

It is quite common for evidence of a crime to be in more than one of the locations mentioned above. However, it might be much easier to obtain the evidence from one location rather than another; therefore, careful consideration should be given to the resources required to obtain the evidence.

For example, if evidence is required of contact between two mobile phone numbers, the best method would be to obtain call data from the Communication Service Providers via the force single point of contact (SPOC), rather than to request a forensic examination of the mobile phones. The call data is likely to be more comprehensive than call logs from a mobile phone and the times and dates can be relied on, which is not necessarily the case with logs from a mobile phone.

In addition, investigators seeking to capture 'in transit' evidence must be aware of the implications under the RIPA 2000 and the need to seek appropriate authorities for doing so. Further information to support cyber crime investigators will be available from local police force SPOCs.

With the above in mind, it is important that investigators develop appropriate strategies to identify the existence of digital evidence and to secure and interpret that evidence throughout their investigation. Due consideration should always be given by the investigators to the benefits to the overall investigation of conducting any digital forensic work. Proportionality should be assessed when a digital forensic strategy is being considered to ensure that limited resources for digital forensic investigation are directed appropriately.

6.11 **Capturing Digital Evidence**

There are many different types of digital media and end-user devices which may be encountered during the search of a crime scene, all of which have the potential to hold data which may be of value to the investigation. In order to preserve the data and achieve best evidence, these items must be handled and seized appropriately and should be treated with as much care as any other item that is to be forensically examined. This section is intended to assist police officers and cyber crime investigators to ensure that their actions in relation to the seizure of evidence at scenes of suspected cyber crime are correct. The section should be read in conjunction with Appendix 3, 'Cyber Crime Investigator's Guide to Network Forensics' and Appendix 4, 'Cyber Crime Investigator's Guide to Crimes Involving Websites, Forums and Blogs'.

The following guidance addresses the majority of scenarios that may be encountered by police officers. The general principles, if adhered to, will ensure the best chance of evidence being recovered in an uncontaminated and, therefore, acceptable manner. Items found during a search of a suspect's person, premises or property normally fall into the broad categories of:

- computer-based media items;
- CCTV systems; and
- mobile devices.

These will be considered separately.

KEY POINT—PROPORTIONALITY

Digital devices and media should **not** be seized just because they are present. Before seizing an item, police officers must consider whether their actions are proportionate and due regard **must** be taken concerning any possible contravention of the European Convention on Human Rights. The officer in charge of the search **must** have reasonable grounds to remove the property and there **must** be justifiable reasons for doing so. The search provisions of the Police and Criminal Evidence Act 1984 (PACE) legislation and its Codes of Practice equally apply to digital devices and media in England, Wales and Northern Ireland. In Scotland, officers should

---

ensure that they are acting within the terms of the search warrant. The proportionality checklist provided below provides guidance for all police officers to consider prior to seizing any item in pursuance of a cyber crime investigation.

6.11.1 **Proportionality checklist**

The following provides a checklist for cyber crime investigators to ensure their actions are proportionate to the crime being investigated.

Cyber crime investigator's proportionality checklist

Before seizing an item in pursuance of a cyber crime investigation, police officers must:

- consider whether an item is likely to hold evidence (i.e. is this a family computer or a computer belonging to a suspect?);
- ensure that details of where the item was found are recorded;
- consider when the alleged offence was committed;
- when seizing CCTV, consider narrowing down what is seized, by camera and/or time period and check whether another system may be better placed to record the evidence;
- differentiate between mobile phones found on a suspect and phones found in a drawer, as different levels of examination may be possible for these items;
- consider that evidence may be stored online, or on an ISP's systems, and end-user devices may only be needed to obtain the details necessary to request this evidence from the service provider. If so, it is best to seize items in current usage; that is, computers connected to the internet.

6.11.2 **What to take to cyber crime scenes**

All officers attending the scene of suspected cybercriminal activity should be prepared and appropriately equipped to seize items of evidence. The following checklist provides a suggested list of equipment that might be of value during planned searches. This basic toolkit should be considered for use in the proper dismantling of digital systems as well as for their packaging and removal.

Cyber crime scene equipment checklist

The following checklist provides a suggested list of equipment that might be of value during planned searches:

- property register;
- exhibit labels (tie-on and adhesive);
- labels and tape to mark and identify component parts of the computer system, including leads and sockets;
- tools such as screwdrivers (flathead and crosshead), small pliers and wire cutters for removal of cable ties;
- a range of packaging and evidential bags fit for the purpose of securing and sealing heavy items such as computers and smaller items such as personal digital assistants (PDAs) and mobile phone handsets;
- cable ties for securing cables;
- flat pack assembly boxes (consider using original packaging if available);
- coloured marker pens to code and identify removed items;
- camera and/or video to photograph the scene in situ and any on-screen displays;
- torch;
- forensically sterile storage material.

In addition, the following items may be useful when attending scenes to retrieve CCTV:

- laptop with USB and network connectivity. A selection of proprietary replay software could be installed, to enable the downloaded data to be checked;
- external CD/DVD writer;
- USB hard drives.

KEY POINT—RECORD-KEEPING

To comply with national digital evidence Principle 3, records **must** be kept in relation to digital evidence. For example:

- sketch map/photographs of scene and digital equipment;
- record location and contact details;
- of a business, record opening hours;
- details of all persons present where digital equipment is located;

- details of digital items—make, model, serial number;
- details of connected peripherals;
- remarks/comments/information offered by user(s) of equipment;
- actions taken at scene showing exact time;
- notes/photographs showing state of system when found.

6.11.3 **Computer-based devices and media**

Computer-based devices and media include desktop or laptop PCs and Apple Mac systems, digital cameras, memory cards, USB sticks, external hard drives and games consoles, amongst other items. Mobile devices which have wireless connectivity/communications capability (e.g. as tablet computers and satellite navigation systems) fall under the heading of 'mobile devices'. Systems which are powered on (running) need to be handled with care, as there is potential to make unwanted changes to the evidence if these are not dealt with correctly. Such systems should only be accessed by appropriately trained officers. In addition, volatile data of evidential value may be lost. Be aware of the potential to lose other valuable data, particularly when dealing with business systems, which could give rise to a claim for damages. In these cases, expert advice **must** be sought before seizing a business system which is powered on. A subsequent claim for damages against police due to the disproportionate, unjustifiable and incorrect seizure of business systems is both unnecessary and unwelcome—seek expert advice and guidance at **all** times.

6.11.4 **Desktop computers, laptop computers and games consoles**

Prior to seizing any desktop computers, laptop computers or games consoles, the cyber crime scene should be fully documented by written notes and/or a photographic record. If a device is powered on, it needs to be handled carefully to preserve any volatile data and to avoid unwanted changes to the stored data. Consideration should be given to removing the device from any network, as devices can be remotely accessed, causing alteration to the data—but balance this against the possibility of losing data of evidential value, such as the list of currently open connections. If unsure, officers **must** seek expert advice. Table 6.2 provides the sequential steps for investigating officers to follow while seizing desktop computers, laptop computers and games consoles.

Table 6.2 Sequential steps to seize desktop computers, laptop computers and games consoles

Steps	Action
1.	Secure and take control of the area containing the equipment.
2.	Move people away from any computers and power supplies and do not allow any interaction with digital devices by the suspect.
3.	Photograph or video the scene and all the components including the leads in situ. If no camera is available, draw a sketch of the plan of the system and label the ports and cables so that system(s) may be reconstructed at a later date.
4.	Allow any printers to finish printing.

If the desktop computers, laptop computers and games consoles are switched OFF:

5.	Do **not**, in any circumstances, switch the computer on.
6.	Be aware that some laptop computers may power on by opening the lid. Remove the battery from the laptop. Seize any power supply cables for future use.

If the desktop computers, laptop computers and games consoles are switched ON:

7.	Record what is on the screen by photographing it and by making a written note of the content of the screen.
8.	Do **not** touch the keyboard or click the mouse. If the screen is blank or a screensaver is present, the investigator should be asked to decide if they wish to restore the screen. If so, a short movement of the mouse should restore the screen or reveal that the screensaver is password-protected. If the screen restores, photograph or video it and note its content. If password protection is shown, continue as below, without any further touching of the mouse. Record the time and activity of the use of the mouse in these circumstances. (For games consoles, or tablet computers, the equivalent would be moving the controller joystick or touching the touchscreen.)
9.	If the system may contain valuable evidence in its current state (e.g. if it is currently displaying a relevant document or an instant message conversation), seizing officers should seek expert advice from their local DFU as this may be lost if the power is lost. This is especially important if the suspect is a technically knowledgeable user who may be using encryption, as there may be no way to retrieve evidence stored in encrypted volumes once the power is lost.

Table 6.2 Continued

Steps	Action
10.	Remove the main power source battery from laptop computers. However, prior to doing do, consider if the machine is in standby mode. In such circumstances, battery removal could result in avoidable data loss. This is normally evident by a small LED (light) lit on the casing. In this case, officers should seek advice from their local DFU.
11.	Unplug the power and other devices from sockets on the computer itself (i.e. not the wall socket). When removing the power supply cable, always remove the end connected to the computer, and not that attached to the socket. This will avoid any data being written to the hard drive if an uninterruptible power supply is fitted. If the equipment was switched on, do not close down any programs or shut down the computer, as this will cause changes to the stored data and may trigger wiping software to run, if this is installed.
12.	Ensure that all items have signed and completed exhibit labels attached to them. Failure to do so may create difficulties with continuity and cause the equipment to be rejected by the DFU.
13.	Search the areas for diaries, notebooks or pieces of paper with passwords on them, often attached to or close to the computer.
14.	Ask the user about the setup of the system, including any passwords, if circumstances dictate. If these are given, record them accurately.
15.	Allow the equipment to cool down before removal.
16.	Track any cables that can be seen as they may lead you to other devices in other rooms.

6.11.5 **Mobile devices**

Mobile devices include mobile phones, smartphones and other devices which may have wireless connectivity or communications capability such as tablet computers, PDAs, personal media players and satellite navigation systems. Table 6.3 provides the sequential steps for investigators to follow when seizing mobile devices.

Table 6.3 Sequential steps to seize mobile devices

Steps	Action
1.	Secure and take control of the area containing the equipment. Do **not** allow others to interact with the equipment.
2.	Photograph the device in situ, or note where it was found, and record the status of the device and any on-screen information.
3.	If the device is switched on, power it off. It is important to isolate the device from receiving signals from a network to avoid changes being made to the data it contains. For example, it is possible to wipe certain devices remotely and powering the device off will prevent this.

In exceptional circumstances, the decision may be made to keep the device on. Timely access to the handset data is critical for the decision.

Steps	Action
4.	Seize cables, chargers, packaging, manuals, phone bills etc as these may assist the enquiry and minimise the delays in any examination.
5.	Packaging materials and associated paperwork may be a good source of PIN/PUK details.
6.	Be aware that some mobile phone handsets may have automatic housekeeping functions, which clear data after a number of days. For example, some Symbian phones start clearing call/event logs after 30 days, or any other user-defined period. Submit items for examination as soon as possible.

6.11.6 Handling and transporting digital evidence

Following national guidance for capturing and seizing digital evidence is essential for the effective investigation of cyber crime but equally as important is the correct handling and transporting of digital evidence. Table 6.4 provides guidance and advice for cyber crime investigators when handling and transporting different types of digital evidence.

Table 6.4 National Guidance for handling and transporting digital evidence

Digital devices	Handle with care. If placing in a car, place upright where they will not receive serious physical shocks. Keep away from magnetic sources (loudspeakers, heated seats and windows and police radios).
Hard disks	As for all digital devices, protect from magnetic fields. Place in anti-static bags, tough paper bags or tamper-evident cardboard packaging or wrap in paper and place in aerated plastic bags.
Removable storage (floppy disks, memory sticks, memory cards, CDs/ DVDs)	Protect from magnetic fields. Do not fold or bend. Do not place labels directly onto floppy disks or CDs/DVDs. Package in tamper force-approved packaging to avoid interaction with the device whilst it is sealed.
Other items	Protect from magnetic fields. Package correctly and seal in plastic bags. Do not allow items to get wet.

Other handling and transporting considerations of digital evidence include the following:

- If fingerprints or DNA evidence are likely to be required, always consult with the investigator.
- Using aluminium powder on electronic devices can be dangerous and result in the loss of evidence. Before any examination using this substance, consider all options carefully.
- Any seized equipment should be stored at normal room temperature, without being subject to any extremes of humidity and free from magnetic influence such as radio receivers. Dust, smoke, sand, water and oil are also harmful to electronic equipment.
- Some devices are capable of storing internal data (e.g. the time and date set on the system) by use of batteries. If the battery is allowed to become flat, internal data will be lost. It is not possible to determine the life expectancy of any one battery. However, this is an important consideration when storing a device for long periods before forensic examination and should be addressed in local policy.

KEY POINT—PROPORTIONALITY ISSUES RELATING TO SEIZURE OF DIGITAL EVIDENCE

There are a number of key proportionality issues that cyber crime investigators must consider relating to the seizure of digital evidence.

- Before seizing an item, consider whether the item is likely to hold evidence. For example, is this a family computer or a computer belonging to a suspect?
- Ensure that details of where the item was found are recorded, which could assist in prioritising items for examination at a later stage.
- Consider when the offence was committed; when seizing CCTV, give consideration to narrowing down what is seized, by camera and/or time period. Check whether another system may be better placed to record the evidence.
- Differentiate between mobile phones found on a suspect (likely to be in current use) and phones found in a drawer (may not be in current use), as different levels of examination may be possible for these.
- Also consider that evidence may be stored online, or on an ISP's systems, and end-user devices may only be needed to obtain the details necessary to request this evidence from the service provider. If so, it is best to seize items in current usage; that is, computers connected to the internet.

All cyber crime investigators must remember that digital devices and media should **not** be seized just because they are there. The person in charge of the search **must** have reasonable grounds for removing property and there must be justifiable reasons for doing so. Remember that the search provisions of PACE legislation and its Codes of Practice equally apply to digital devices and media in England, Wales and Northern Ireland. In Scotland, officers should ensure that they are acting within the terms of the search warrant. Due regard **must** also be given to the application of the European Convention on Human Rights.

6.12 **Analysing Digital Evidence**

Devices that are lawfully seized as part of a search in pursuance of a cyber crime investigation will typically be submitted to the local police force Digital Forensic Unit (DFU) in accordance with the local police force policy in place. Due to the volume and complexity of data stored on digital devices, it is neither possible nor desirable to extract all data held on a device for review by investigators. Instead, a forensic strategy needs to be formulated to enable the examination to be focused on the relevant data.

KEY POINT—EXAMINATION PRIORITIES

When moving towards the forensic analysis phase of a cyber crime investigation, the investigator needs to properly consider the nature and purpose of the digital examination. The investigator **must** be clear on what priorities are placed on the examination as it may well be that key information needs to be found in order to preserve evidence that may exist elsewhere. This is particularly the case where it relates to the existence of additional evidence, offenders and victims.

When submitting evidence to DFUs, investigators must supply specific requirements. It is not practically possible to examine every item of digital data and clear tasking is needed to ensure that the digital forensic practitioner has the best chance of finding any evidence which is relevant to the investigation.

For more complex or lengthy investigations, an initial triage/review of the digital evidence (whether or not this is done using a specific triage tool) will give investigators and practitioners a better understanding of the nature of the digital evidence held. The forensic strategy should be regularly reviewed to take account of any changes in the direction of the investigation, which may occur as a result of digital forensic examination (e.g. finding emails identifying a co-conspirator) or investigations elsewhere (a witness identifying another person as being of interest to the investigation). For this reason, it is vital that the investigator and the digital forensic practitioner communicate regularly regarding the progress of the investigation.

If initial examination results in a large amount of data to be reviewed, consideration must be given to who is best placed to review that data. Often this will be the investigator, due to their greater knowledge of the case. Dependent on the source, this data may include:

- internet history records;
- emails;

- instant messaging logs;
- media files (images and videos);
- text documents;
- spreadsheets;
- CCTV;
- text messages.

Collaboration with the DFU will ensure that the significance of any reviewed data is not misunderstood. For example, when reviewing keyword hits which exist in deleted files, the significance of a hit's location may need explanation from a digital forensic practitioner. For mobile phone examinations, different levels of examination may be appropriate depending on the intelligence relating to the device and the requirements of the investigation. For example, a phone that has been found in a drawer may be examined only to retrieve the necessary information to request billing details and to establish whether it is owned by the suspect. A phone that is known to be in regular use by a suspect in a high-profile investigation may be subject to a much more in-depth examination involving the retrieval of deleted data and potentially the physical removal and examination of memory chips.

KEY POINT—INTERPRETATION OF DIGITAL DATA

As with other forensic evidence, interpretation is often required to ensure that the evidential weight of recovered digital evidence is clear. Practitioners who undertake the interpretation of digital data must be competent to do so and have had sufficient training to undertake the task assigned to them. As an example, the presence of indecent images of children on a computer would not in itself be sufficient evidence of possession, as the possessor must be aware of the existence of the images. A digital forensic practitioner may interpret the presence of other digital evidence (e.g. a list of recently opened files, recent search terms, the name and location of folders/files containing the material or whether or not the computer is password-protected) to establish the likelihood of the user being aware of the existence of those images.

Establishing the provenance of digital evidence is another key task of the forensic practitioner, who must use their knowledge and skills to identify not just that the evidence exists but also how it came to be there. This is common to all forensic disciplines; for example, the presence of a defendant's fingerprint on a bottle at the crime scene may not have any bearing on whether the defendant committed the crime if the bottle may have been carried there by someone else. It is the responsibility of the practitioner to carry out analysis to identify the provenance where necessary, to mitigate the risk of their findings being misinterpreted.

Often the role of the digital forensic practitioner will be to make investigators and prosecutors aware of the limitations of the digital evidence as well as its strengths. It must also be borne in mind that the development of digital technology is dynamic and practitioners may well face significant challenges to their knowledge. It is not possible to be an expert in all aspects of digital forensic examination, but a practitioner should be aware of the limits of their knowledge and where further research or additional specialist knowledge is required, especially given the increasingly sophisticated measures being put in place by cybercriminals to conceal their activities.

6.13 Anti-Forensics

Cybercriminals are becoming progressively more aware of forensic analysis methods. As a result they often implement countermeasures to prevent an investigator harvesting useful information. This practice is called anti-forensics, the purpose of which is to destroy or hide evidential data. There are a number of techniques that are used to apply anti-forensics and it is important for cyber crime investigators to develop awareness of the practices used by cybercriminals in an attempt to conceal their activities. Table 6.5 provides a list of anti-forensic approaches.

KEY POINT—AWARENESS OF ANTI-FORENSICS

Anti-forensics is a reality. Criminals conducting their activities online are just as devious as criminals operating offline, making every attempt to conceal their crimes. Every cyber crime investigation will include some element of anti-forensic tools or approach.

Of course, cybercriminals may adopt operational security protocols that are not necessarily designed with anti-forensics in mind. For instance, passwords, code words and file shielders may be used that are in place simply to provide an appropriate level of safety, security and privacy but they can be used as an anti-forensic tool since they can protect and conceal data. The work of the cyber crime forensic investigator is to be a 'safe hacker' and use the full range of legitimate and lawful investigative tools to retrieve vital intelligence and evidence to bring cybercriminals to justice. Cybercriminals continue to develop new and increasingly sophisticated anti-forensics tools and technologies to thwart law enforcement efforts. The identification of anti-forensics and the sharing of knowledge of new and emerging anti-forensics tools and approaches between cyber investigators is essential to maintain an effective cyber investigative capability.

Table 6.5 Digital anti-forensics tools and approaches

Anonymous actions	Includes any action that can be completed by a false or unknown identity.
Anti-forensics in flushable devices	Taking advantage of devices that can be 'flashed' to install malicious codes.
Digital media wiping	A thorough wiping of the media that contains digital evidence.
Digital memory anti-forensics	Programs that are able to hide processes or other evidence from memory.
Encryption	Used in any anti-forensic approach in order to obscure and render data unreadable.
File signature modification attacks	The alteration of a file signature to make it appear as something different.
Forensic detection	A mechanism installed and designed to be triggered after any computer forensic-related presence.
Homographic attacks	An attack designed to mislead the investigator by using one of two or more words, letters or symbols that have the same spelling but differ in origin, meaning and sometimes pronunciation.

Table 6.5 Continued

Metadata anti-forensics	Information about data itself can be altered in order to conceal actions such as time, day and dates the actions were taken.
Misleading evidence	The planting of evidence designed to mislead a forensic investigation.
Packers/binders	The use of a program to transform a file by changing its structure to bypass security mechanisms that search for malicious behaviour patterns inside files.
Privacy wipers	Tools aimed to delete any privacy traces from applications or operating systems.
Resource waste	Purposefully leaving false traces in a large network intended to waste valuable forensic investigator's time and resources.
Rootkits	Designed to subvert the operating system kernel and react to forensic acquisition processes by hijacking the way an operating system uses areas such as process management or memory management to extract evidence.
Secure digest function collision generation	The modification of a file to be able to bypass a forensic integrity check.
Slack space anti-forensics	Hiding malicious software in reserved, empty or spare capacity areas that are not being used by operating systems.
SMART anti-forensics	Technology used by a cybercriminal to identify whether a hard drive has been removed for a forensic duplication process.
Steganography	The art and science of hiding information by embedding messages within other, seemingly harmless messages. Steganography works by replacing bits of useless or unused data in regular computer files (e.g. graphics, sound, text) with bits of different, invisible information. This hidden information can be plain text or even images. Steganography is sometimes used when encryption is not permitted or, more commonly, steganography is used to supplement encryption. An encrypted file may still hide information using steganography, so even if the encrypted file is deciphered, the hidden message is not seen. Special software is used for steganography.

6.14 **Forensic Awareness**

Whilst it is not possible within the scope of this Handbook to write a simple and complete forensic manual for the cyber crime investigator, it is essential that all practitioners have a greater awareness of cyber crime investigative forensic issues and good practice. Table 6.6 provides a summary of issues regarded as national good practice.

KEY POINT—COMMERCIAL FORENSIC PROVIDERS

Where the services of commercial forensic service providers are required by law enforcement, it is important to select external consulting witnesses/forensic practitioners carefully. Any external practitioner should be familiar with, and agree to comply with, the national guiding principles of digital evidence referred to in this guide.

Selection of external providers, particularly in the more unusual or highly technical areas, can be a problem for the investigator. DFUs may be able to offer more advice on the criteria for selection. Issues regarding security clearance, physical security and procurement rules must be carefully considered when selecting an external forensic service provider. Investigators **must** also ensure that any forensic service provider engaged on law enforcement work is able to work in accordance with the Forensic Regulator's Codes of Practice and Conduct which requires ISO accreditation (ISO 17025 and ISO 17020).

When engaging the services of digital forensic contractors, processes and policies for the retention of case-related data should be considered, both on an ongoing basis and following the termination of the contract. Contractors and those engaging them must comply with the terms of the Data Protection Act 1998, and with any local policies of the engaging organisation.

6.15 **Disclosure Challenges for Cyber Crime Investigations**

The particular issues relating to disclosure of digital evidence are typically those of volume. A digital investigation may involve the

Table 6.6 Good practice guidance for cyber crime forensics

Good practice	Rationale
Peer review	There have been a number of cases where the processes followed during a forensic investigation have been questioned successfully by the defence. It is therefore important that the quality of forensic examinations is kept at a high level despite the pressure of work that units operate under. It is unfortunate that some personnel feel under pressure to produce quick results, sometimes at the expense of reliability, accuracy and even, it has been alleged, impartiality.
	In order to identify processes that are questionable or, for whatever reason the unreliability of evidence produced from a unit, it is strongly recommended that each unit subject itself periodically to a peer review. This can be carried out at one level locally and continuously by analysts checking their colleagues' work on a regular basis. The main recommendation in this area from the working party is that independent reviews are carried out. This can be achieved by either internal or external review.
	Internal review can be completed by forces combining with a reciprocal arrangement to review each other's work. External review is more difficult, due to the material examined, but could be carried out by other law enforcement organisations or trusted partners involved in the field.
Dual tool verification	It is accepted that many cases involve large amounts of evidence pointing to the guilt of the defendant. However, in some cases, the actual evidence recovered may be just a few files, a single file or a few bytes of data. In these cases, it is highly recommended that the examination is repeated with a totally different software process and tool. All software has 'bugs' (minor programming anomalies) which can cause the erroneous reports of what appears to be, for instance, a fact, a date and time. The repeat of the examination should conclude in the report of the same result, thus giving the one 'nugget of gold' more reliability and credibility.

(continued)

Table 6.6 Continued

Good practice	Rationale
Horizon scanning/ internet research	Computer and digital storage technology changes very quickly. In an effort to keep up to date as well as prepare for future developments, it is highly recommended that the following two steps are taken which can be done at little cost:

- A subscription to a monthly computer magazine such as *PC PRO* will bring with it a number of advantages. Changes in technology go to press early so the arrival of those changes can be planned for; this could also have an effect on the updating of hardware in particular, and good planning can save sizeable amounts of money by the avoidance of purchasing 'old' technology. Discussions in the press about the use of particular pieces of software, and the most popular software for particular tasks, provide useful reference when that software is encountered on suspect machines. The internet is also a useful source of information.
- The identification of hardware availability and its competitive price can assist in negotiations with retailers wishing to sell on at 'list' prices when purchasing upgrades or new kit.

The internet is a vital tool for any computer crime unit. Used for software upgrades, answers to technical questions, software downloads, open-source research, resolution of IP addresses and research into paedophile material, it offers a vast resource at little or no cost. Time should be built in to Unit task lists to carry out such research. Broadband connections are the minimum acceptable connection for this type of work.

If the staff of the Unit find it difficult to put aside time to conduct research, an approach could be made to the Computer Science Faculty of a local university to see if a student is willing to conduct research on behalf of the Unit for a small payment.

Asset and job database	If not already implemented, Units should equip themselves with an asset and job database. The asset part of which should record equipment kept within the Unit. The job part should contain details of each job, all exhibits and continuity trails for all items. A fully functional relational database system can be built from software already provided within Microsoft Office.

Table 6.6 Continued

Good practice	Rationale
Preview of machines and triage	Forensic software often provides a preview function which permits a 'safe' (with a proviso) look at a disk. Previous practice might have been to avoid previewing computers and mobile devices as a preview might miss some evidence that would otherwise be found on a full examination and risk the return of a computer in that state to a suspect.
	However, it is not uncommon now to witness seizures of multiple computers and mobile devices in domestic settings where there might be ten or more digital devices recovered. With many Units suffering large backlogs of forensic examinations, especially given that there is a consistently high proportion of work related to paedophilia, a triage solution would thus provide numerous benefits, especially when considering investigation priorities and resources. Where there are insufficient resources to cope with the volume of digital devices being presented for examination, a triage tool in combination with assessment of the intelligence available in the case could be used to reduce the number of digital devices being given a full examination. Triage could especially help to identify:
	• media likely to contain evidence; • those investigations that require a more detailed and technical examination; • the investigations that could be subject to limited examination by qualified practitioners; • material requiring urgent investigation; • examinations suitable for out sourcing; • the extent of the assistance the Unit will need to provide to an investigation.

examination of a vast amount of data and it is not always straightforward for investigators and prosecutors to discharge their disclosure obligations in respect of this. For example, the average hard disk is now larger than 200 gigabytes and this, if printed out on A4 paper, would be 10 million pages long. In addition, the nature of digital evidence means it is not always possible to create a static representation which preserves the nature of the original evidence (e.g. of a database) and in some cases data can only be disclosed electronically, such as CCTV.

The CPIA 1996 came into force on 1 April 1997. The Act, together with its Code of Practice, introduced a statutory framework for the recording, retention, revelation and disclosure of unused material obtained during criminal investigations commenced on or after that date. Additional guidance for investigators and prosecutors to assist them in complying with their statutory duties is set out in the Attorney General's Guidelines on Disclosure (revised April 2005).

The CPIA, as amended by the Criminal Justice Act 2003, requires a single objective test for the disclosure of prosecution material to the defence. This test requires the prosecutor to disclose 'any prosecution material which has not previously been disclosed to the accused and which might reasonably be considered capable of undermining the case for the prosecution against the accused, or of assisting the case for the accused'. Disclosure affects not only material seized by law enforcement, but may extend to other relevant material held by third parties.

Where there is a large volume of computer-held material, inspection and description of it may present difficulties. Due to this, the Attorney General has provided some helpful guidance:

> Generally material must be examined in detail by the disclosure officer or the deputy but, exceptionally, the extent and manner of inspecting, viewing or listening will depend on the nature of the material and its form. For example, it might be reasonable to examine digital material by using software search tools, or to establish the contents of large volumes of material by dip sampling. If such material is not examined in detail, it must nonetheless be described on the disclosure schedules accurately and as clearly as possible. The extent and manner of its examination must also be described together with justification for such action.

The CPIA Code of Practice also provides guidance concerning the duty to pursue all reasonable lines of enquiry in relation to computer material (CPIA Code of Practice, para 3.5). Where seized material is of a significant volume, and where it is not felt a reasonable or proportionate use of police resources to examine all or part of it and the data is retained, a statement—disclosed as part of the disclosure schedule—should be prepared by the Disclosure Officer detailing, in general terms, the material and justification for not examining it.

In a case where inextricably linked material or various categories exists on the same media and, due to the large volume or fragmentary nature of the data, viewing all of it may be impossible, or require a disproportionate use of resources, the defence should be advised in statement form, included in the disclosure schedule, of the existence and extent of the material, categories and examination made upon it including lists of keyword searches.

There may be instances where automatic disclosure cannot be permitted, for example:

- malicious code, the return of which to a suspect could result in further criminal acts;
- in cross-disclosure cases of multiple defendants, legally privileged material or personal data relating to persons not under suspicion or who may become at risk if disclosure is made to other suspects;
- commercially sensitive data contained within the material;
- CCTV images, where the collection of data is indiscriminate, consideration must be given to possible collateral intrusion into privacy;
- in the above cases, agreement should be sought with the defence to manage access, for example the listing of file structure or directories or inviting the provision of additional keyword searches.

In cases where the defence is not permitted full access to the seized material, it is the responsibility of the Senior Investigating Officer and the Disclosure Officer to ensure full account is taken of this. Where appropriate, a partial disclosure of a file set or subset could be made of files that do not fall within the areas outlined above. Such disclosure will considerably reduce the need for extensive examination of that area of data by the Disclosure Officer. Figure 6.3 provides guidance for the recommended disclosure procedure to be followed in such circumstances.

KEY POINT—PURSUING ALL LINES OF ENQUIRY

Even in relatively straightforward cyber crime cases, investigators may obtain, and even generate, substantial quantities of material. Some of this material may in due course be used as

---

evidence: for example, physical exhibits recovered from the scene of the crime or linked locations, CCTV material, forensic evidence, statements obtained from witnesses and tape recordings of defendants interviewed under caution before charge. The remaining material is the 'unused material', and it is this material that is the subject of the procedure for disclosure created under the CPIA.

Generally, material must be examined in detail by the Disclosure Officer or the deputy but, exceptionally, the extent and manner of inspecting, viewing or listening will depend on the nature of the material and its form. For example, it might be reasonable to examine digital material by using software search tools. If such material is not examined in detail, it must nonetheless be described on the disclosure schedules accurately and as clearly as possible. The extent and manner of its examination must also be described, together with justification for such action.

The CPIA Code of Practice also provides guidance concerning the duty to pursue all reasonable lines of enquiry, in relation to computer material. Examination of material held on a computer may require expert assistance and, in some cases, Digital Evidence Recovery Officers (DEROs) may be commissioned to help to extract evidence and assist with unused material. DEROs may be police officers, police staff or external service providers. The use of DEROs and related matters is discussed in detail in Annex H of the Disclosure Manual.

It is important that the material is inspected and described on the unused material schedule, in accordance with the above guidance, as the schedules (non-sensitive and sensitive) are in due course revealed to the prosecutor, in order that the latter can comply with the duty under s 3 of the CPIA to provide primary disclosure to the accused (or initial disclosure, where the criminal investigation in question has commenced on or after 4 April 2005).

Whether the material is disclosed under s 3 of the CPIA, following service of a statement, or after an application for specific disclosure under s 8 of the Act, disclosure may be in the form of providing a copy or copies of the material in question to the defence. It may also be by permitting the defence (or a suitable expert, instructed by the defence) access to the actual material.

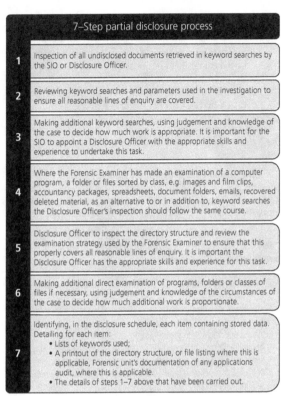

Figure 6.3 Seven-step partial disclosure process

6.16 **Presenting Digital Evidence**

Forensic computing and investigation requires a very high standard of documentation and exhibit handling. Each examiner is involved in a specialised and responsible field of endeavour which requires considerable knowledge, skill and impartiality. The following checklist provides general national recommended guidance for cyber crime investigators in progressing a case through to prosecution.

Cyber crime investigator's prosecution checklist
- Get a full understanding of the facts of the case and the chain of custody in relation to the storage media to be investigated.
- Know the crimes that are suspected or charged and the elements to prove in order to convict.
- Having found the key evidence, focus on the challenges the defence expert could raise in relation to it.
- When testifying, be prepared and consider any question carefully before answering.
- Draw on all the experience available to you.

How the examiner/investigator presents the evidence for consideration by the CPS and then by the court is an issue which is subject to considerable debate. What is clear is that evidential points **must** be properly put and supported by factual detail. Table 6.7

Table 6.7 Queen's Counsel advice for presenting cyber crime investigation digital evidence.

1. The main body of the evidence should be contained in the witness statement.
2. All witness statements/reports should list the relevant qualifications of the 'expert'.
3. Do not put diagrams in the body of the statement.
4. Append a glossary of the technical terms you have used in the statement.
5. Simply because you call something an exhibit does not mean that it is!
6. Placing a commentary on an exhibit may provide the defence with a legitimate objection to it going before the jury.
7. If a commentary is required in order to make an exhibit more jury friendly, the commentary should be as brief and uncontentious as possible.
8. Accurate diagrams may be attached as an exhibit.
9. Always put what exhibits/documents you have been provided with and what you have used to draw your opinions on.
10. Where in the course of examining an exhibit, that exhibit is altered/ destroyed, photographs should be taken at each stage. These may then form part of the record of work or be exhibited themselves.
11. Where pictures/diagrams etc are being used as exhibits, they should be as jury friendly as possible, for example:
    - exhibits should be of a size easy to read;
    - use of specialised terms should be kept to a minimum;
    - where there are a series of exhibits, if at all possible make all icons and colours consistent with the exhibit throughout.

provides national advice to practitioners from members of the Queen's Counsel, and specifically from those with direct experience of prosecuting and defending when digital and/or electronic evidence forms part of the case. Although these points may be considered 'basic', it could be argued that sometimes the 'basic' is very often forgotten.

6.17 Communicating Digital Evidence

The communication of the results of a digital forensic examination may be through a number of means including:

- verbally to an investigator/officer throughout a case;
- by a statement or report on conclusion of the case;
- in court if witness evidence is required.

In all cases, a digital forensic practitioner must be aware of their duty of impartiality and that they must communicate both the extent and the limitations of the digital forensic evidence. This is especially important as, due to the nature of digital forensic evidence, it is not always immediately understandable by the layperson.

6.17.1 Verbal feedback

Verbal feedback should be given regularly throughout the progress of an examination. In this way it will enable the cyber crime investigator to pursue relevant lines of enquiry as these become evident, and will ensure that the practitioner is up to date with any information required to better target their investigation. It is important that this communication is recorded for potential disclosure at a later date. Good practice would be for a verbal conversation to be followed up via email or to be recorded in contemporaneous notes.

6.17.2 Statements or reports

The statement or report is the ultimate product of the forensic examination. It should outline the examination process and the significant data recovered. Whilst an initial report may be relatively brief, the practitioner should be in a position to produce a full technical report should one be required later. The report should be written to be understandable to the reader; this may include the use of a glossary, diagrams/screenshots to illustrate points, the use of examples and avoidance of technical jargon.

When particular items are reproduced in a report, care should be taken to ensure that their presentation is accurate. For example, pictures should not be reproduced at a larger size without this being made clear in the report. If a report is produced digitally, items should be reproduced where possible in their original file formats, to ensure that those viewing them will see the item as close as possible to its original appearance. If this is not appropriate (e.g. if a file needs to be converted to a more common format for reviewing), then the fact that it has been converted must be stated in the report. Where it is not possible to reproduce the item as it would have originally been viewed, for example when a web page is retrieved some time after the original page was accessed, this must also be clearly stated in the report.

The report should make clear the strength of any conclusions reached and always identify where an opinion is being given, to distinguish this from fact. Where opinion evidence is provided, the practitioner must state the facts on which this is based, and how he or she came to this conclusion.

6.17.3 **Witness evidence**

A cyber crime practitioner may need to testify about not only the conduct of the examination, but also the validity of the procedure and their experience and qualifications to conduct the examination. Expert witness training should be considered for digital forensic practitioners so that they are familiar with the process of giving evidence and aware of their responsibilities as witnesses. A digital forensic practitioner will not always be giving expert evidence and should clearly understand the distinction between expert evidence and evidence of fact. When giving evidence, practitioners must make clear when they are expressing facts and when they are giving opinions, as above. Practitioners, when giving expert evidence, must take care to do so only where it relates to their own area of expertise and remember that their duty when giving evidence (whether it be in report form or as a witness) is to the court, regardless of which party has instructed them.

It is worth repeating at this point that full records should be made of all actions taken. These must be disclosed to the defence who may subsequently cause a further examination to be conducted. A significant part of such an examination will be to validate the actions and results of the original examination. Such records are also part of the unused material for the case under investigation.

KEY POINT—PRESENTATION OF EVIDENCE

To reinforce the importance of not only gathering, examining and presenting evidence, it is well worth repeating that forensic computing requires a high standard of documentation and exhibit handling. The examiner is involved in a specialised and responsible field which requires considerable knowledge and impartiality and the examiner is an essential and integral part of any cyber crime investigation. Additional guidelines are included in Appendix 6, 'Presentation of Evidence for Documents and Exhibits in Forensic Computing' which provides further recommended national guidance discussing the writing of notes, statements and reports together with the production of exhibits in forensic computing cases. This guidance provides evidence of the continued efforts by all in authority associated with the investigation of cyber crime to produce a national standard.

The rise of cyber criminality has increased the need for the police service to invest in cyber crime investigators. Great efforts have been made to develop cyber crime investigative doctrine underpinned by national and accredited levels of professional competence. While work continues to develop the UK cyber crime capacity and capability, it remains the professional responsibility of all cyber investigators to share knowledge, expertise and effective practices. Cyber crime tactics, modus operandi, technology and methodology continue to change at a rapid pace. In order to prevent, detect and bring cybercriminals to justice, police officers and the wider policing family and their partners have to raise their knowledge, awareness and operational competence to tackle contemporary cyber crime.

Part IV

Cyber Law

Chapter 7

Cyber-Dependent Crime

7.1 Cyber Crime Definitions and Computer Misuse Offences

There have been several attempts to define cyber crime but they are most commonly viewed as falling into one of two categories. Those offences which are used against new technologies—cyber-dependent and are catered for within the Computer Misuse Act 1990, and the older type of offence where the new technology is being used to facilitate it. This chapter will explore those offences created to address those cyber-dependent crimes which in essence 'attack the machine and networks'.

The cyber-enabled offences are explained in later chapters and will look at those including fraud, child online protection, terrorism and hate crimes. The two distinctions will ensure an ease of understanding and some separation of the offences that are commonly committed either with or by the use of computer, internet, social media and other applications.

Cyber-dependent crimes are those which are only able to be committed by using the computer, programs, data and its associated networks and other forms of ICT. Quite often there will be a secondary outcome; for example, personal details that have been obtained being used in a fraud.

One type of this crime would include the disruption or reduction of computer functionality and its network space by the spread of what are commonly known as viruses and other malicious software (**malware**).

Malware is often distributed by means of a **botnet** which is a network of private computers infected with the malicious software and controlled as a group without the owner's knowledge e.g. to send spam or distribute viruses (see below).

On a larger scale, this would most commonly occur by what are known as **DDoS**—distributed denial of services—attacks, which seek to take down a whole structure or service.

Hacking into systems or networks is an illegal invasion or intrusion of computer networks and in effect a person's space. It is the cyber form of trespass and is quite often perceived as such. It is unauthorised and most often is used to gather personal data, which can be used later for unlawful purposes. It can also be used to deface websites or even as a precursor to a DDoS attack, which will flood an internet server and sometimes cause it to crash.

There are a wide variety of types of malware, which it is worth noting.

- **Viruses** are damaging to the computer and network in that they can cause malfunction, delete files and damage hard and software. By the very nature of their name, they will replicate and spread quite easily between computers but they cannot affect a computer without human action. This is usually by opening the infected file which quite often will be sent by spam (unsolicited junk) email.

- **Worms** are similar but are more dangerous in that they can run without human instigation (e.g. opening an email).

- **Trojans** appear to be legitimate programs but facilitate illegal access to a computer (e.g. online games). They are able to steal data and hide behind routine tasks within the computer.

- **Spyware** is usually hidden within adware (software that requires you to watch adverts so that you can use it). One example is key logging which will capture and follow key strokes made on the keyboard which will allow the installer to acquire personal information even relating to the sites that are visited. This is the most extreme form of an invasion of privacy.

The offences, which have stood the test of time and are wholly appropriate to deal with these types of crime, were introduced by the Computer Misuse Act 1990. It was enacted at a time when computers were a relatively new concept and without having full vision of what was around the corner with the advent of the internet and social media.

However, there does appear to have been some foresight in that the Act does not provide a definition of a computer because it was feared that with the advance of technology any definition would be outdated the moment the Act was created! The Act also provides that there is jurisdiction to prosecute all Computer Misuse Act offences if there is at least one significant link with the domestic jurisdiction—which is England and Wales—in the circumstances of the case.

On 5 May 2015, the territorial scope of the Act's offences was changed by s 43 of the Serious Crime Act 2015 and now includes 'nationality'. This will provide the legal basis to prosecute a UK national who commits any of the offences within the Act while outside the UK, where the offence has no link to the UK other than that offender's nationality, provided that the offence was also an offence in the country where it took place. Obviously, an individual cannot be tried twice so double jeopardy rules will apply.

Interpretation and definition has been left to the courts and in the next chapter some of those decisions are explained.

Most recently, the Act has had one amendment inserted by the Serious Crime Act 2015. This created the offence of unauthorised acts causing or creating a risk of serious damage—where the damage affects the national infrastructure. The Act uses a new term of 'material kind' which is defined in the new section. The maximum sentence of 14 years is believed to be commensurate with the seriousness of the offence.

7.2 **Unauthorised Access to Computer Material**

This offence is created by s 1 of the Computer Misuse Act 1990 and is most often used when hacking takes place or viruses through malware are distributed.

Offence

(1) A person is guilty of an offence if—
    (a) he causes a computer to perform a function with intent to secure access to any program or data held in any computer or to enable any such access to be secured;
    (b) the access he intends to secure, or enable to be secured, is unauthorised; and
    (c) he knows at the time when he causes the computer to perform the function that that is the case.
(2) The intent a person has to have to commit an offence under this section need not be directed at—
    (a) a particular program or data;

(b) a program or data of a particular kind; or
(c) a program or data held in a particular computer.

Computer Misuse Act 1990, s 1

Points to prove

Section 1(1)

✓ caused a computer to perform a function

✓ with intent to secure unauthorised access

✓ to a program/data held in the computer or to enable any such access

✓ to be so secured

Meanings

Computer

No definition is provided by the Act but courts are expected to adopt the everyday meaning of the word, where it has previously been described as a device for storing, processing and retrieving information. This can therefore include smartphones, tablets and even online gaming machines.

The words 'any computer' do not restrict the offence to the circumstances where the offender uses one computer to secure unauthorised access to another. An offence will also be committed where the offender causes a computer to perform a function with intent to secure unauthorised access to any program or data held in the same computer—*Attorney General's Reference (No 1 of 1991)* [1993] QB 94.

Program

Is defined in the IT sector as a set of instructions which tell a computer what to do. In addition, s 17 of the Act includes program and data when held in a computer as well as references to a program or data held in a removable storage medium (memory stick, removable hard drive) which is for the time being in the computer, and a computer is to be regarded as containing a program or data held in such a medium.

Data

Is defined by the IT sector as the quantities, characters or symbols on which operations are performed by a computer, which may be stored and transmitted in the form of electrical signals and recorded on magnetic, optical or mechanical recording media.

Secured access

A person secures access to a program or data held in a computer if by causing a computer to perform a function he:

(a) alters or erases the program or data;
(b) copies or moves it to a storage medium other than that in which it is held or to a different location in the storage medium in which it is held;
(c) uses it; or
(d) has it output from the computer in which it is held (whether by having it displayed or in any other manner).

Unauthorised access

Access of any kind by a person to a program or data held in a computer is unauthorised if:

(a) he is not himself entitled to control access of the kind in question to the program or data; and
(b) he does not have consent to access by him of the kind in question to the program or data from a person who is so entitled.

There has to be knowledge on the part of the offender that the access is unauthorised. Recklessness is not sufficient. Hackers are therefore captured as well as employees who exceed their authority and access parts of a system which they know are officially denied to them.

Explanatory notes

- There is jurisdiction to prosecute all Computer Misuse Act offences if there is at least one significant link with domestic jurisdiction—which for these purposes is within England and Wales.
- A significant link is defined by s 4 of the Act and states that:

  It is immaterial for the purposes of an offence under section 1 whether an act or other event required to be proved for a conviction of the offence, occurred in the home country concerned; or whether the accused was in the home country concerned at the time of such act or event.

- Another way of expressing this would be:
  (a) that the accused was in the home country concerned at the time when he did the act which caused the computer to perform the function; or

(b) that any computer containing any program or data to which the accused by doing that act secured or intended to secure unauthorised access, or enabled or intended to enable unauthorised access to be secured, was in the home country concerned at that time.

- To support this, the Court of Appeal, 6 April 2000, in *R v Waddon* held that the content of US websites could come under British jurisdiction when downloaded in the UK.

- In proceedings brought in England and Wales in respect of a s 2 offence, it is immaterial whether or not the accused was a British citizen at the time of any act or omission.

Related cases

Attorney General's Reference (No 1 of 1991) [1993] QB 4 The computer, which a person uses to cause to perform a function with the required intent, does not have to be a different computer from the one to which he intends to secure unauthorised access. The offence would be committed where the person's intention is to enable someone else to secure unauthorised access to a computer or to enable the person himself to secure unauthorised access to a computer at some later time.

R v Bignall [1998] 1 Cr App R 1 Two police officers who were only authorised to request information from the Police National Computer (PNC) for policing purposes, made a request for their own use. The Divisional Court decided that they had not committed the s 1 offence as the actual operator had not exceeded his authority.

R v Bow Street Magistrates Court and Allison (AP), ex p Government of United States of America [2002] 2 AC 216 It was determined that s 1 can include individuals who have lawful access to specific files on a system, but then look at other material on the same system (e.g. an operator who is given a number of computer files to work on who then accesses other files which do not concern them).

Practical considerations

- No damage, loss or gain need be proven.

- Section 55 of the Data Protection Act 1998 which is only punishable with a fine, is in some circumstances an alternative charge to s 1 of the Computer Misuse Act 1990.

- Where any case involves an employer/employee relationship, then any contracts in existence should be examined carefully to see if they cover what exactly the employee's authority entails.
- Seize any computers or storage mechanisms as evidence under s 20 of PACE and bag and tag in accordance with local procedures.
- Leave the device as you find it—do not attempt to gain access. Leave it to the experts who have the remit to recover digital evidence.
- Ensure authority has been obtained for examination of the computer whether desktop, laptop, tablet or even smartphone.
- Only in extraordinary circumstances will devices be examined in situ.

 Either way offence

 Time limit for prosecution: none

 Summary: maximum 12 months' imprisonment and/ or fine
Indictment: maximum 2 years' imprisonment and/or fine

7.2.1 **Unauthorised access with intent to commit another offence**

This offence is created by s 2 of the Computer Misuse Act 1990 and, to be considered, the previously described offence under section 1 has to be proved. However, in addition there has to be shown an intent to either commit or facilitate the commission of a further offence which quite often will be fraud.

Offence

(1) A person is guilty of an offence under this section if he commits an offence under section 1 ('the unauthorised access offence') with intent—
  (a) to commit an offence to which this section applies; or
  (b) to facilitate the commission of such an offence (whether by himself or by another person);
and the offence he intends to commit or facilitate is referred to in this section as the further offence.

Computer Misuse Act 1990, s 2

Points to prove

✓ caused a computer to perform a function

✓ with intent to secure unauthorised access

✓ to a program/data held in a computer

✓ with intent to commit/facilitate the commission of a further offence

Meanings

Computer (see 7.2)

Program (see 7.2)

Data (see 7.2)

Unauthorised access (see 7.2)

Further offence

An offence for which the sentence is fixed by law; or for which a person of 21 years of age or over (not previously convicted) may be sentenced to imprisonment for a term of five years.

Explanatory notes

- There is no need for there to be a significant link with domestic jurisdiction in proving the unauthorised access relevant to the s 2 offence as you have to do with a straightforward s 1 offence.

- The commission of the further offence (the one intended to be committed or facilitated) outside the home country would apply as if it happened in the home country concerned. For example, if the offence intended to be committed in the US is one to which s 2 applies then it would be applied as if it took place in the home country concerned (England and Wales).

- It is immaterial for the purposes of this section whether the further offence is to be committed on the same occasion as the unauthorised access offence or on any future occasion.

- A person may be guilty of an offence under this section even though the commission of the further offence is impossible.

- In proceedings brought in England and Wales in respect of a s 2 offence, it is immaterial whether or not the accused was a British citizen at the time of any act or omission.

Practical considerations

- Unauthorised access to data will quite often reveal an offence contrary to s 55 of the Data Protection Act 1998. Where it is difficult to prove the necessary points for a s 2 offence, then this offence should be considered.

- If the access is authorised but there is still an intent to use the data/material to commit/facilitate the commission of another offence, then there will be no offence under s 2 (consider the full offence).

- Seize any computers or storage mechanisms as evidence under s 20 of PACE and bag and tag in accordance with local procedures.

- Leave the device as you find it—do not attempt to gain access. Leave it to the experts who have the remit to recover digital evidence.

- Ensure authority has been obtained for examination of the computer whether desktop, laptop, tablet or even smartphone.

- Only in extraordinary circumstances will devices be examined in situ.

 Either way offence

 Time limit for prosecution: none

 Summary: maximum 6 months' imprisonment and/ or fine
Indictment: maximum 5 years' imprisonment and/or fine

7.2.2 **Unauthorised acts with intent to impair**

This offence is created by s 3 of the Computer Misuse Act 1990 and is the offence which is usually considered for DDoS attacks.

Offence

(1) A person is guilty of an offence if—
  (a) he does any unauthorised act in relation to a computer
  (b) at the time when he does the act he knows that it is unauthorised; and
  (c) either subsection (2) or subsection (3) below applies.

(2) This subsection applies if the person intends by doing the act—

    (a) to impair the operation of any computer;

    (b) to prevent or hinder access to any program or data held in a computer; or

    (c) to impair the operation of any such program or the reliability of any such data.

(3) This subsection applies if the person is reckless as to whether the act will do any of the things mentioned in paragraphs (a) to (c) of subsection (2) above.

Computer Misuse Act 1990, s 3

Points to prove

✓ did an unauthorised act when it was known to be unauthorised

✓ intending by doing the act; or

✓ being reckless as whether the act would

✓ impair or enable the operation of a computer to be impaired; or

✓ prevent or hinder access to a program or data held in a computer; or

✓ enable access to a program or data held in a computer to be prevented or hindered

✓ enable the operation of a program or the reliability of data held in a computer to be impaired

Meanings

Unauthorised act

Different to unauthorised access as defined in s 1 of the Computer Misuse Act 1990, although it will be included within the meaning. However, s 17(8) of the Act states:

An act done in relation to a computer is unauthorised if the person doing the act (or causing it to be done)—

(a) is not himself a person who has responsibility for the computer and is entitled to determine whether the act may be done; and

(b) does not have the consent to the act from any such person.

In this subsection "act" includes a series of acts.

Intend or being reckless

This offence is different to s 1 and 2 offences as it allows reckless-ness to be included. This is the main reason behind the s 3 offence capturing the DDoS attacks where recklessness could have been a defence.

Impair or enable impairment

To weaken functionality, to reduce operational effectiveness, to impede or spoil an operation.

Prevent or hinder access

To shut out, impede, hamper or make things difficult to carry out.

Explanatory notes

- Every act relied upon for this offence to be proved must have taken place after it was updated by the changes made under s 36 of the Police and Justice Act 2006 on 1 October 2007.
- Any impairment can be temporary.
- There is no need for any modification to have occurred.
- When DDoS attacks take place they are aimed at specific websites and this offence should be considered as being the appropriate one to charge. The attacker floods the web server with messages endlessly repeated. This ties up the system and denies access to legitimate users as exampled by Kent Police and the Ministry of Justice in 2013.
- Section 127 of the Communications Act 2003 is a summary offence that may be considered if s 3 of the Computer Misuse Act 1990 is not appropriate (see **8.1.2**).

Related cases

R v Lennon [2006] EWHC 1201 (Admin) This was the mail-bombing case where the Divisional Court stated that although the owner of a computer which is able to receive emails would nor-mally be seen to consent to emails being received, such consent did not extend to emails that had been sent for the purpose of communicating with the owner purely for the purpose of inter-rupting the operation of the system.

R v Christopher Weatherhead, Ashley Rhodes, Peter Gibson and Jake Burchall, Southwark Crown Court, 24 January 2013 Charged with conspiracy to carry out an unauthorised act: DDoS attacks against PayPal, Visa and MasterCard between August 2010 and January 2011 after they had withdrawn their services to WikiLeaks. One of the online attacks was said to have cost PayPal over £3 million. Sentences of between 6 and 18 months administered.

R v Pavel Cyganok and Ilja Zakrevski, Southwark Crown Court, 2 July 2012 It was alleged that a SpyEye Trojan was used to steal login ID for online banking accounts and was uploaded to servers controlled by the defendants. As a result of information being provided by the Estonian authorities, both were arrested in London and it was estimated that over 1,000 computers were infected with victims located all over the world. Cyganok was sentenced to 5 years' imprisonment and Zakrevski to 4 years' imprisonment.

R v Zachary Woodham, Southwark Crown Court, 13 May 2011 The offender, who was a teenager, attacked a web hosting company and caused it to cease trading. Sentenced to 12 months' imprisonment suspended for two years and 240 hours' community service.

Practical considerations

- Seize any computers or storage mechanisms as evidence under s 20 of PACE and bag and tag in accordance with local procedures.
- Leave device as you find it—do not attempt to gain access. Leave it to the experts who have the remit to recover digital evidence.
- Ensure authority has been obtained for examination of the computer whether desktop, laptop, tablet or even smartphone.
- Only in extraordinary circumstances will devices be examined in situ.

 Either way offence

 Time limit for prosecution: none

 Summary: maximum 12 months' imprisonment and/or fine
Indictment: maximum 10 years' imprisonment and/or fine

7.2.3 Making, supplying or obtaining articles for use in a s 1 or 3 offence

Section 3A of the Computer Misuse Act 1990 was inserted by s 37 of the Police and Justice Act 2006 to close a loophole at the time and ensure that those who supply, make, offer to supply or obtain with a view to supply, articles that are going to be used in s 1 or 3 offences can be prosecuted. Section 42 of the Serious Crime Act 2015 inserted a new offence in s 3A(3)(a) which ensures that an individual is caught by the section regardless of an intention to supply to another—for example, the lone wolf operator.

Offences

(1) A person is guilty of an offence if he makes, adapts, supplies or offers to supply any article intending it to be used to commit, or assist in the commission of, an offence under section 1 or 3 or 3ZA.

(2) A person is guilty of an offence if he supplies or offers to supply any article believing that it is likely to be used to commit, or to assist in the commission of, an offence under section 1 or 3 or 3ZA.

(3) A person is guilty of an offence if he obtains any article—
   (a) intending to use it to commit, or to assist in the commission of, an offence under section 1, 3 or 3ZA, or
   (b) with a view to its being supplied for use to commit, or assist in the commission of, an offence under section 1, 3 or 3ZA.

Computer Misuse Act 1990, s 3A

Points to prove

Section 3A(1)
✓ made/adapted/supplied/offered to supply an article
✓ intending that it should be used to
✓ commit/assist in the commission of an offence
✓ under s 1, 3 or 3ZA of the Computer Misuse Act 1990

Section 3A(2)
✓ supplied/offered to supply an article
✓ believing that it was likely to be used to
✓ commit/assist in the commission of an offence
✓ under s 1, 3 or 3ZA of the Computer Misuse Act 1990

Section 3A(3)(a)
✓ obtains any article
✓ intending to use it to commit an offence
✓ or intending for it to assist in the commission of an offence
✓ under s 1, 3 or 3ZA of the Computer Misuse Act 1990

> **Section 3A(3)(b)**
> ✓ obtains any article
> ✓ with a view to its being supplied for use to commit
> ✓ for use to commit/assist in the commission of an offence
> ✓ under s 1, 3 or 3ZA of the Computer Misuse Act 1990

Meanings

Article

Includes any program or data held in electronic form and that could be a username and/or password.

Supplies

Furnishes or provides a person with an article, that a person wants, needs or requires for their purpose (commission of an offence under s 1, 3 or 3ZA).

Offer to supply

Can be related to a current or future use of the article.

Obtains

To get, acquire, come into possession of.

Explanatory notes

- If a person were charged with a s 3A(2) offence and it related to a quantity of articles, the prosecution would need to prove its case specifically around one or more of those articles; it would not be sufficient to prove that the person believed that a certain proportion of the articles were likely to be used in connection with an offence under s 1 or 3 or 3ZA.

- 'Likely' is not defined in the Computer Misuse Act but is used in s 3A(2). In deciding whether an article is 'likely' to be used to commit an offence, the functionality of the article should be looked at, at the same time as the intention of the 'user'.

- If the article was supplied in the course of or in connection with fraud, then always consider if there is also an offence of making or supplying articles for use in frauds contrary to s 7 or 6 of the Fraud Act 2006 (see **9.2.2**).

- Dual-use articles are those which can be used for lawful and unlawful purposes.

- Section 42 of the Serious Crime Act 2015 extends this offence (through s 3A(3)(a) so that it now covers obtaining an article for use to commit an offence under s 1, 3 or 3ZA regardless of an intention to supply that article and therefore ensures personal use is captured within the computer misuse offence as well as removing the requirement for the involvement or intended involvement of a third party.

Practical considerations

- Any prosecutions under this section should put some emphasis on ascertaining whether criminal intent is present as some articles are described as dual use. This is due to there being a legitimate industry concerned with the security of computer systems via penetration tests when testing hardware or software. This is likely to either generate or need 'articles' and includes programs or data held in electronic form.
- In determining the likelihood of an article being used or misused to commit a criminal offence, questions should be asked concerning:
  + the purpose of its primary development (does it have another use or was it deliberately created for the sole purpose of committing a Computer Misuse Act offence?);
  + whether the article sold is through normal commercial channels;
  + whether the article has a legitimate use.

 Either way offence

 Time limit for prosecution: none

 Summary: maximum 6 months' imprisonment and/or fine to statutory maximum
Indictment: maximum 2 years' imprisonment and/or fine to statutory maximum

7.2.4 **Unauthorised acts causing or creating risk of serious damage**

Offence

(1) A person is guilty of an offence if—
  (a) the person does any unauthorised act in relation to a computer;
  (b) at the time of doing the act the person knows that it is unauthorised;

(c) the act causes, or creates a significant risk of, serious damage of a material kind; and

(d) the person intends by doing the act to cause serious damage of a material kind or is reckless as to whether such damage is caused.

Computer Misuse Act 1990, s 3ZA

Points to prove

✓ did an unauthorised act in relation to a computer

✓ knew at the time of doing the act it was unauthorised

✓ caused/created a significant risk of serious damage of a material kind

✓ intended to cause serious damage/reckless as to whether such damage was caused

Meanings

Unauthorised act (see 7.2.2)

Material kind

Damage is of a material kind for the purposes of this section if it is:

(a) damage to human welfare in any place (includes outside the UK);

(b) damage to the environment in any place;

(c) damage to the economy of any country; or

(d) damage to the national security of any country.

And an act causes damage to human welfare only if it causes:

(a) loss to human life;

(b) human illness or injury;

(c) disruption of a supply of money, food, water, energy or fuel;

(d) disruption of a system of communication;

(e) disruption of facilities for transport;

(f) disruption of services relating to health.

Explanatory notes

- This offence creates a more serious offence which addresses those instances where the impact of the action is to cause serious damage or the risk of serious damage.

- It is designed to address the most serious cyber attacks; for example, when the systems controlling power supply, communication, food or fuel distribution are damaged or left unable to operate.

- The attacks this offence is meant to deal with are those which have a significant impact resulting in loss of life, serious illness or serious social disruption or even serious damage to the economy (of any country).

- The unauthorised act must result directly or indirectly in the damage of a material kind described above.

- The offender must know that the act he or she does is unauthorised.

- The offender must know that the act is going to cause the material harm or must have been reckless as to whether the harm would be caused. Reckless is previously defined in the chapter.

- The sentences available for this offence are commensurate with how seriously it is viewed by the legislators.

 Indictable only offence

 Time limit for prosecution: none

Sentence: maximum life imprisonment where the unauthorised act results in serious damage to human welfare or national security

Sentence: maximum 14 years' imprisonment where the act results in serious damage to the economy or environment

Chapter 8

Cyber-Enabled Hate Crime

8.1 Cyber-Enabled Crimes

'Cyber-enabled crimes' are traditional crimes, which can be increased in their scale or reach by the use of computers, computer networks or other forms of ICT. These crimes can also be committed without the use of ICT so they are not 'cyber-dependent'.

Social media now plays a large part in all cyber-enabled crime, more particularly those offences where the small minority are spoiling the outstanding pieces of work on this form of media which enhances social networking and enables worldwide connectivity leading to internet interaction. There are many ways where the potential for that positive and informative interaction is being spoiled by that minority and these include the following.

- **Cyber bullying** using social media or other ICT means.
- **Revenge porn** is typically sexually explicit media that is publically shared online without the consent of the pictured individual and is usually uploaded by ex-partners. The images are often accompanied by personal information including the pictured individual's full name, links to social media profiles and address, and are shared with the intent to cause distress or harm to the individual.
- **Trolling**, which has been shown on many recent occasions, is the intentional disruption (and quite often without evidence) of online conversations or blogs which start arguments and cause offence.
- **Virtual mobbing** is where online communities are used via social media and messaging systems to make vile and corrosive comments about another individual, usually because they have a difference of views or have fallen out with them in the past.

All these activities are catered for within current legislation under the following.

- **Section 1 of the Malicious Communication Act 1988** (see **8.1.1**) which deals with the sending of electronic communications which are indecent, grossly offensive, threatening or false, provided there is an intention to cause distress or anxiety to the recipient.

- **Section 127 of the Telecommunications Act 2003** (see **8.1.2**) which makes it an offence to send or cause to be sent through a public electronic communications network a message that is grossly offensive or of an indecent, obscene or menacing character.

- **Section 33 of the Criminal Justice and Courts Act 2015** (see **8.1.3**) is the most recent piece of legislation which addresses the so-called offence of revenge porn which is illustrated by an adult ex-partner uploading onto the internet intimate sexual images of the victim which cause them humiliation and embarrassment. There are various defences available and all are explained below under the relevant heading.

- **The Protection from Harassment Act 1997** (see **8.2**) addresses where there is more than one incident or the incident forms part of a course of conduct directed towards an individual.

The government launched its three-year action plan on hate crime in March 2012 when it explained that it wanted to:

- prevent hate crime by challenging the attitudes that underpin it and early intervention to prevent it escalating;

- increase reporting and access to support—by building victim confidence and supporting local partnerships;

- improve the operational response to hate crimes—by better identifying and managing cases, and dealing effectively with offenders.

This chapter will identify, define and explain those offences relating specifically to hate crime and which quite often begin online.

At present, the police and the CPS record 'hate crimes' as any crime that is perceived, by the victim or another person, to have been motivated by hostility or prejudice based on a person's race, religion, sexual orientation, disability or transgender identity. Although crimes are recorded for all these 'protected characteristics', the criminal offences that specifically deal with hate crime only cover some of them.

There are 'aggravated offences' contained in the Crime and Disorder Act 1998 where if an offender commits one of a list of offences and is shown to have been motivated by hostility or has demonstrated hostility whilst committing the basic offence only on the grounds of race or religion, it becomes a separate aggravated offence with the potential for a greater sentence. Currently, these aggravated offences do not address any hostility based on sexual orientation, transgender identity or disability.

The other types of hate crime created by legislation are called ones which are stirred up by hatred. These are contained in the Public Order Act 1986 and address the pure offences of stirring up hatred on the grounds of race, religion or sexual orientation. At present, these offences do not cover hatred on grounds of transgender identity or disability.

However, the courts are also enabled to enhance sentences under ss 145 and 146 of the Criminal Justice Act 2003 where the offence was motivated by hostility or involved a demonstration of hostility on the basis of any of the five protected characteristics (race, religion, sexual orientation, disability or transgender identity). A paper was submitted by the Law Commission in 2013 (Consultation Paper 213) to assess the need to widen the hate crime offences.

The internet has provided an avenue for prolonged and consistent activities which amount to 'hate crime' over an extended period of time. This could be conveyed by email, Twitter, Facebook or even a website dedicated to the spreading of evil and hateful messages.

There is a wide scope of offences covered by a variety of Acts of Parliament, which have changed over the years to address ongoing concerns of the public and the courts. This includes those referred to in the preceding paragraphs and those which relate to the specific method of communication of threats from which hate can be concluded.

8.1.1 **Offensive/false messages**

The Malicious Communications Act 1988 concerns the sending and delivery of letters, other articles or electronic communications to cause distress or anxiety; the Communications Act 2003 regulates all types of media, including the sending of grossly offensive material via the public electronic communications network.

Section 1 of the Malicious Communications Act 1988 creates offences relating to the sending of indecent, offensive or threatening letters, electronic communications or articles with intent to cause distress or anxiety to the recipient.

Offences

Any person who sends to another person—

(a) a letter, **electronic communication** or article of any description which conveys—
  (i) a message which is indecent or grossly offensive;
  (ii) a threat; or
  (iii) information which is false and known or believed to be false by the sender; or
(b) any article or electronic communication which is, in whole or part, of an indecent or **grossly offensive** nature,

is guilty of an offence if his purpose, or one of his purposes, in sending it is that it should, so far as falling within paragraph (a) or (b) above, cause distress or anxiety to the recipient or to any other person to whom he intends that it or its contents or nature should be communicated.

Malicious Communications Act 1988, s 1(1)

Points to prove

Section 1(1)(a) offence

✓ sent a letter/an electronic communication/an article
✓ which conveys an indecent/grossly offensive message/ threat/false information which you knew/believed to be false
✓ for the purpose of causing distress/anxiety
✓ to the recipient/any other person
✓ to whom its contents/nature were intended to be communicated

Section 1(1)(b) offence

✓ sent to another person
✓ an article/an electronic communication
✓ wholly/partly of an indecent/grossly offensive nature
✓ for the purpose of causing distress/anxiety
✓ to the recipient/any other person
✓ to whom its contents/nature were intended to be communicated

Meanings

Electronic communication

Includes any:

- oral or other communication by means of an electronic communications network; and
- communication (however sent) that is in electronic form.

Electronic communications network

Means:

- a transmission system for the conveyance, by the use of electrical, magnetic or electro-magnetic energy, of signals of any description; and
- such of the following as are used, by the person providing the system and in association with it, for the conveyance of the signals—
  + apparatus comprised in the system;
  + apparatus used for the switching or routing of the signals; and
  + software and stored data.

Grossly offensive

This has to be judged by the standards of an open and just multi-racial society. Whether a message falls into this category depends not only on its content but on the circumstances in which the message has been sent (*DPP v Collins* [2005] EWHC 1308 (Admin)).

Explanatory notes

- Sending includes delivering or transmitting and causing to be sent, delivered or transmitted; 'sender' will be construed accordingly.
- Offence only requires that the communication be sent—not that the intended victim actually received it.

Defences

A person is not guilty of an offence by virtue of subsection (1)(a)(ii) above [threat] if he shows—

(a) that the threat was used to reinforce a demand made by him on reasonable grounds; and

(b) that he believed, and had reasonable grounds for believing, that the use of the threat was a proper means of reinforcing the demand.

Malicious Communications Act 1988, s 1(2)

Practical considerations

- As well as letters and telephone systems, this offence would include emails, fax, text messages, Facebook, Twitter or other social media.
- What was the intended purpose of the defendant in sending the communication?
- If the intent is to cause the victim annoyance, inconvenience or needless anxiety, then consider the offence under s 127 of the Communications Act 2003 (see **8.1.2**).
- If there has been more than one incident, an offence under s 2 or 2A of the Protection from Harassment Act 1997 may be appropriate (see **8.2.1** or **8.2.3**).
- If any threat used includes an unwarranted demand, consider the more serious offence of blackmail.
- Preserve the means or item that was used to deliver the message to the victim.
- The original message can be retrieved from phones or computers; the original letter or envelope can be fingerprinted or examined for DNA.

 Either way offence

 Time limit for prosecution: none

 Summary: maximum 12 months' imprisonment and/or fine
Indictment: maximum 2 years' imprisonment and/or fine

8.1.2 **Improper use of electronic public communications network**

Section 127 of the Communications Act 2003 creates offences regarding improper use of a public electronic communications network.

Offences

(1) A person is guilty of an offence if he—
    (a) sends by means of a public electronic communications network a message or other matter that is grossly offensive or of an indecent, obscene or menacing character; or
    (b) causes any such message or matter to be so sent.

(2) A person is guilty of an offence if, for the purpose of causing annoyance, inconvenience or needless anxiety to another, he—

    (a) sends by means of a public electronic communications network, a message that he knows to be false,

    (b) causes such a message to be sent, or

    (c) persistently makes use of a public electronic communications network.

Communications Act 2003, s 127

Points to prove

Section 127(1) offence

✓ sent

✓ by means of a public electronic communications network

✓ a message/other matter

✓ being grossly offensive/indecent/obscene/menacing character

or

✓ caused such a message/matter to be so sent

Section 127(2) offence

✓ to cause annoyance/inconvenience/needless anxiety to another

✓ sent by means of a public electronic communications network

✓ a message known to be false

or

✓ caused such a message to be sent

or

✓ persistently made use

✓ of a public electronic communications network

Meanings

Public electronic communications network

Means an electronic communications network provided wholly or mainly for the purpose of making electronic communications services available for use by members of the public.

Electronic communications network (see **8.1.1**)

Grossly offensive (see **8.1.1**)

Menacing

Means a message which conveys a threat; which seeks to create fear in or through the recipient that something unpleasant is going to happen. Here the intended or likely effect on the recipient must ordinarily be a central factor (*DPP v Collins* [2005] EWHC 1308 (Admin)).

Persistently

Includes any case in which the misuse is repeated on a sufficient number of occasions for it to be clear that the misuse represents a pattern of behaviour, or practice, or recklessness as to whether people suffer annoyance, inconvenience or anxiety.

Explanatory notes

- 'Electronic communications network' includes current and future developments in communication technologies (e.g. telephone, computers (internet), satellites, mobile terrestrial networks, emails, text messages, fax, radio and television broadcasting including cable TV networks).

- These offences do not apply to anything done in the course of providing a broadcasting service, such as a television programme, public teletext, digital television, radio programme or sound provided by, for example, the BBC.

- Sections 128 to 130 empower OFCOM (Office of Communications) to enforce this Act to stop a person persistently misusing a public electronic communications network or service.

Practical considerations

- These offences do not apply to a private/internal network. In these instances consider s 1 of the Malicious Communications Act 1988 (see **8.1.1**).

- Under subsection (1) there is no requirement to show any specific purpose or intent by the defendant.

- Consider s 1 of the Malicious Communications Act 1988 (see **8.1.1**) if the offence involves intent to cause the victim distress or anxiety.

- Also consider an offence under the Protection from Harassment Act 1997 (see **8.2**).

- If threats or information relate to bombs, noxious substances or the placing of dangerous articles, consider offences under the Anti-terrorism, Crime and Security Act 2001 and the Criminal Law Act 1977.

- Possession or control of apparatus which may be used dishonestly to obtain an electronic communications service, or in connection with obtaining such a service is also an offence under s 126.

- A Penalty Notice for Disorder may be issued by a police officer, PCSO or other accredited person for an offence under s 127(2).

- Recent changes to time limits (s 127(5)) are that an information or complaint relating to an offence (which came to light after this subsection came into force: 12 March 2015) under this section may be tried at the magistrates' court in England, Wales and Northern Ireland if it is laid:
  + before the end of three years beginning with the day on which the offence was committed; and
  + before the end of the period of six months beginning with the day on which evidence comes to the knowledge of the prosecutor which the prosecutor considers sufficient to justify proceedings.

 Summary offence

 Time limit for prosecution: none

Sentence: maximum 6 months' imprisonment and/or level 5 fine

8.1.3 **Disclosure of private sexual photographs and films with intent to cause distress—revenge porn**

Section 33 of the Criminal Justice and Courts Act 2015 creates the new criminal offence of disclosing private sexual photographs or films with intent to cause distress commonly referred to as 'revenge porn'.

Offence

(1) It is an offence for a person to disclose a private sexual photograph or film if the disclosure is made—

(a) without the consent of an individual who appears in the photograph or film, and

(b) with the intention of causing that individual distress.

Criminal Justice and Courts Act 2015, s 33

Points to prove

✓ disclosed

✓ a private sexual photograph/film

✓ without consent of an individual who appeared in the photograph/film

✓ with the intention of causing that individual distress

Meanings

Disclosed

Includes uploading images on the internet, sharing by text or email or showing someone an actual physical image. The disclosure can equally be offline as well as online and can be shared by electronic means or a more traditional way.

Private sexual photograph/film

The photograph or film would have to be both private and sexual—this includes any individual's exposed genitals or someone who is engaged in sexual behaviour or posing in a sexually provocative way. It has to be of a kind not ordinarily seen in public and mentions the genitals and sexual behaviour to be captured as being of an essential 'intimate' nature.

The offence only applies to material which looks photographic and which originates from an original photograph or film recording.

Consent of the individual appearing in the photograph or film

Includes a general consent covering the disclosure as well as consent to the particular disclosure.

Intention to cause distress

For intention, see **9.2**.

Distress can include anxiety, pain, sorrow and embarrassment.

Explanatory notes

- The offence does not apply to computer-generated images or to digitally manipulated photographs where that manipulation is the only cause of the image becoming private and sexual.

- A person who has non-consensually disclosed a private and sexual photograph of his or her former partner in order to cause distress to that person, will not escape liability by, for example, digitally altering the colour of their hair.

- It is not an offence to disclose the photograph or film to the individual within the photograph or film.

- The transposition of the head of a former partner onto a sexual photograph of a completely different person will not be captured by this offence.

- If a person re-tweets or forwards messages which are sexual and private, they will not be guilty of the offence unless it is done with the intention to cause distress to the person depicted in the photograph or film who has not consented to the disclosure.

- It is the responsibility of the website or social media provider to remove images of this nature and it is hoped that the creation of the offence will encourage those providers to take their responsibility seriously.

Practical considerations

- Consider offences under the Malicious Communications Act or the Telecommunications Act if this offence cannot be proved.

- Ensure preservation of means of disclosure by the recovery of all equipment used in committing the offence; for example, computers, phones, etc for examination by the appropriate unit within the force.

- It will always be necessary to show that the reason for disclosing the photograph or film will be the intention to cause distress.

- Circumstantial evidence surrounding reaction to the disclosure online will be of value to show that distress.

- The offence extends to England and Wales. Where the victim and offender were physically located in England or Wales, it would be possible for the offence to be committed even if the offence was committed using a website hosted abroad.

- Consider possession of extreme pornographic images contrary to s 63 of the Criminal Justice and Immigration Act 2008 (see **8.1.4**) as an alternative—as this relates to possession only—although the definition of extreme pornographic images is more restrictive.

Defences

There are several defences provided to this offence which are as follows.

Section 33(3)

It is a defence for a person charged with an offence under this section to prove that he or she reasonably believed that the disclosure was necessary for the purposes of preventing, detecting or investigating crime.

Section 33(4)

It is a defence for a person charged with an offence under this section to show that—
(a) the disclosure was made in the course of, or with a view to the publication of journalistic material, and
(b) he or she reasonably believed that, in the particular circumstances, the publication of the journalistic material was, or would be, in the public interest.

Section 33(5)

It is a defence for a person charged with an offence under this section to show that—
(a) he or she reasonably believed that the photograph or film had previously been disclosed for reward, whether by the individual shown in the photograph or film or another person, and
(b) he or she had no reason to believe that the previous disclosure for reward was made without the consent of the individual concerned.

Section 33(6)

A person is taken to have shown the matters mentioned in subsection (4) and (5) if—
(a) sufficient evidence of the matters is adduced to raise an issue with respect to it and
(b) the contrary is not proved beyond reasonable doubt.

Defence notes

- There will occasionally be circumstances where such pictures will be evidence in a story of genuine public interest. It is not the intention of the legislature to fetter the freedom of the press to publish such stories.
- Public interest means on this occasion that the journalist had a reasonable belief in the circumstances surrounding the publication etc, that there was a legitimate need for the public to have access to that journalistic material.

- There will be occasions when people pass on images which have been previously commercially published and exploited—for example in a pornographic magazine or online (whatever the motives)—unless of course the person passing them on has some reason to believe that the person in the image had not consented when the material had originally been published for reward.
- There is a specific Schedule to the Act which addresses 'information society providers' in relation to this offence. It reflects a requirement in a European e-commerce directive that information service providers based in the European Economic Area (EEA) should usually be prosecuted for any offences which might be committed by providing services in the country where they are established.
- In rare cases where all the requirements of the offence are present, including the intention to cause distress to the victim, the Schedule does not stop an operator being guilty of an offence if it actively participates in the disclosure or fails to remove the material once it is aware of the criminal nature of the content.

 Either way offence in England and Wales

 Time limit for prosecution: none

 Summary: maximum 12 months' imprisonment and/ or fine

Indictment: maximum 2 years' imprisonment and/or fine

8.1.4 **Possession of extreme pornographic images**

Section 63 of the Criminal Justice and Immigration Act 2008 introduces the offence of possession of extreme pornographic images. There are specific definitions of what is depicted as extreme pornography but the offence was introduced to address areas where the previous legislation did not cater for those pertinent points. The offence came into force on 26 January 2009.

Offence

It is an offence for a person to be in possession of an extreme pornographic image.

Criminal Justice and Immigration Act 2008, s 63(1)

Section 65

Sets out three general defences which are the same as for the possession of indecent images of children under s 160(2) of the Criminal Justice Act 1988 (see **10.7**).

(1) Where a person is charged with an offence under section 63 it is a defence for the person to prove any of the matters mentioned in subsection (2).

(2) The matters are—

    (a) that the person had a legitimate reason for being in possession of the image concerned;

    (b) that the person had not seen the image concerned and did not know, nor had any cause to suspect, it to be an extreme pornographic image;

    (c) that the person—

        (i) was sent the image concerned without any prior request having been made by or on behalf of the person, and

        (ii) did not keep it for an unreasonable time.

Section 66

Creates an additional defence for those who participate in the creation of extreme pornographic images.

(A1) Subsection (A2) applies where in England and Wales—

    (a) a person ('D') is charged with an offence under section 63, and

    (b) the offence relates to an image that portrays an act or acts within subsection (7)(a) to (c) or (7A) of that section (but does not portray an act within subsection (7)(d) of that section).

(A2) It is a defence for D to prove—

    (a) that D directly participated in the act or any of the acts portrayed, and

    (b) that the act or acts did not involve the infliction of any non-consensual harm on any person, and

    (c) if the image portrays an act within section 63(7)(c), that what is portrayed as a human corpse was not in fact a corpse, and

    (d) if the image portrays an act within section 63(7A), that what is portrayed as non-consensual penetration was in fact consensual.

(3) For the purposes of this section harm inflicted on a person is **non-consensual** harm if—

    (a) the harm is of such a nature that the person cannot, in law, consent to it being inflicted on himself or herself; or

    (b) where the person can, in law, consent to it being so inflicted, the person does not in fact consent to it being so inflicted.

Defence notes

- An 'excluded image' is an image which forms part of a series of images contained in a recording of the whole or part of a classified work. A 'recording' is any disc, tape or other device capable of storing data electronically and from which images may be produced. This therefore includes images held on a computer.
- The effect of the exclusion is that a person who has a video recording of a film which has been classified by the British Board of Film Classification and which contains images that might otherwise be caught by the offence in s 63, could not be liable for prosecution. However, the exclusion from the scope of the offence does not apply in respect of images contained within extracts from classified films which must reasonably be assumed to have been extracted solely or principally for the purpose of sexual arousal.
- Essentially, the exemption for an image forming part of a classified work is lost where the image is extracted from that work for pornographic purposes.
- An 'extract' includes a single image. When an extracted image is one of a series of images, in establishing whether or not it is of such a nature that it must reasonably be assumed to have been extracted for the purpose of sexual arousal, regard is to be had to the image itself and to the context it which it appears in the series of images.
- In determining whether a recording is a recording of a whole or part of a classified work, alterations due to technical reasons, such as a failure in the recording system, or due to inadvertence, such as setting the wrong time for a recording, or the inclusion of extraneous material such as advertisements, are to be disregarded.
- Nothing in s 64 affects any duty of a designated authority to take into account the offence in s 63 when considering whether to issue a classification certificate in respect of a video work. Where an alteration is made to a video work in respect of which a classification certificate has been issued, the classification certificate does not apply to the altered work.
- The three general defences set out in s 65 are the same as for the possession of indecent images of children under s 160(2) of the Criminal Justice Act 1988. The definition of a legitimate reason continues not to be defined; however, it covers those who have a legitimate work reason for being in possession of the image. The burden of proof is on the defendant to show that the reason for possession falls within the defence.
- The defence provided by s 66 is limited in as much as images of bestiality and necrophilia which depict a real corpse are excluded. In order to benefit from the defence, the defendant must prove, on the

balance of probabilities, that he directly participated in the act or acts portrayed in the image and that the act(s) did not involve the infliction of non-consensual harm on any person. Where the image depicts necrophilia, the defendant must also prove that the human corpse portrayed was not in fact a corpse.

- Non-consensual harm is harm which is of such a nature that, in law, a person cannot consent to it being inflicted on him or herself, or harm to which a person can consent but did not in fact consent.

Practical considerations

- Evidence of circulation of images will help in providing aggravating features of the offence.
- Evidence of exploitation of those depicted in the images will also add credibility to the allegation.
- The larger the number of images, the more chance of a prosecution.
- Previous similar behaviour will assist in making prosecution decisions—evidence of bad character.
- Reliable experts when judging realistic images will be of assistance.
- Gather all evidence including software, hardware and associated devices, seal and forward according to local instructions.
- Consider other offences available, such as revenge porn or, where children are involved, possession of indecent images and, where the images have been made/published, consider offences under the Obscene Publications Act 1959 (see **10.9**).
- Powers of forfeiture are available under s 143 of the Powers of Criminal Courts Act 1973.

 Either way offence when relating to offences where an act threatening a person's life or which results or is likely to result in serious injury to a person's private parts

 Time limit for prosecution: none

 Summary: maximum imprisonment not exceeding the relevant period and/or fine
Indictment: maximum 3 years' imprisonment and/or fine

Either way offence when relating to all other circumstances where the activity is not as described above

🕐 **Time limit for prosecution**: none

▥ **Summary**: imprisonment not exceeding the relevant period and/or fine
Indictment: maximum 2 years' imprisonment and/or fine

8.2 Harassment/Stalking

In order to understand the specific offences of racially/religiously aggravated harassment/stalking provided for by the Crime and Disorder Act 1998 which are defined as 'hate crime', the basic offence created by the Protection from Harassment Act 1997 is explained below. It provides criminal and civil remedies to restrain conduct amounting to harassment or stalking.

8.2.1 Harassment—no violence

Section 1(1) of the Protection from Harassment Act 1997 prohibits harassment, while s 2 creates the offence of harassment.

Offences

Section 1
(1) A person must not pursue a course of conduct—
    (a) which amounts to harassment of another, and
    (b) which he knows or ought to know amounts to harassment of the other.
(1A) A person must not pursue a course of conduct—
    (a) which involves harassment of two or more persons, and
    (b) which he knows or ought to know amounts to harassment of those persons, and
    (c) by which he intends to persuade any person (whether or not one of those mentioned above)—
        (i) not to do something that he is entitled or required to do, or
        (ii) to do something that he is not under any obligation to do.

Section 2
(1) A person who pursues a course of conduct in breach of section 1(1) or (1A) is guilty of an offence.

Points to prove

✓ pursued a course of conduct

✓ on at least two occasions

✓ amounting to harassment

✓ which you knew/ought to have known amounted to
  harassment

Meanings

Course of conduct

Must involve, towards a single person under s 1(1), conduct on at
least two occasions in relation to that person or to two or more
persons under s 1(1A), conduct on at least one occasion in relation
to each of those persons.

Conduct includes speech and online communication.

Harassment

Includes causing the person(s) alarm or distress.

Explanatory notes

- If a reasonable person in possession of the same information as
  the defendant would think the course of conduct amounted to
  harassment, then the offender should have realised this as well
  (*Kellett v DPP* [2001] EWHC 107 (Admin)).

- A person may be subjected to harassment by writing (e.g.
  emails, online communication or letters), orally (e.g. in person
  or by telephone) or by conduct.

- An offender does not have to act in a malicious, threatening,
  abusive or insulting way for the basic offence; however, see **8.3.1**
  for the ingredient of a racially/religiously aggravated offence.

- The court can issue a 'restraining order' against the defendant.

Defences

Section 1(1) or (1A) does not apply to a course of conduct if the person
who pursued it shows—

(a) that it was pursued for the prevention or detection of crime,

(b) that it was pursued under any enactment or rule of law or to comply
    with any condition or requirement imposed by any person under any
    enactment, or

> (c) that in the particular circumstances the pursuit of the course of conduct was reasonable.
>
> Protection from Harassment Act 1997, s 1(3)

Defence notes

- These defences would apply to the police, customs or security services including the private sector (e.g. private detective or store detective).
- A suspect suffering from some form of obsessive behaviour or schizophrenia cannot use their mental illness as a defence because of the 'reasonable person' test.

Related cases

Hayes v Willoughby [2011] EWCA Civ 1541 If a defendant could not show that their course of conduct was pursued for the purpose of preventing or detecting crime, it was accordingly unlawful.

Buckley, Smith v DPP [2008] EWHC 136 (Admin) This case provides guidance on a continuing course of conduct over a period of time.

Daniels v Metropolitan Police Commissioner [2006] EWHC 1622 (QB) In establishing vicarious liability for harassment, there must be an established case of harassment by at least one employee who is shown on at least two occasions to have pursued a course of conduct amounting to harassment, or by more than one employee each acting on different occasions in furtherance of some joint design.

DPP v Baker [2004] EWHC 2782 (Admin) Harassment may occur either continuously or intermittently over a period of time, providing at least one of the incidents relied on by the prosecution occurred within the six-month limitation period.

Lau v DPP [2000] All ER 224, QBD During an argument, Lau hit his girlfriend across her face. Four months later he threatened violence against her new boyfriend. Held: Lau had not 'pursued a course of conduct' because of the time between the two incidents and the conduct was against two different people.

Practical considerations

- Evidence of previous complaints of harassment will help to prove continuance of the harassment on at least two separate occasions.

- Two isolated incidents do not constitute a course of conduct.
- Have any previous warnings been given to the alleged offender?
- A campaign of collective harassment applies equally to two or more people as it does to one (trolling).
- Obtain Criminal Justice Act witness statements.
- Obtain all available evidence (e.g. other witnesses, CCTV camera footage, computers if appropriate, detailed telephone bills, entries in domestic violence registers).
- Could any of the defences apply?

 Either way offence

 Time limit for prosecution: 6 months

 Summary: maximum 6 months imprisonment
Indictable: maximum 5 years' imprisonment and/or level 5 fine

8.2.2 **Harassment where violence is feared**

Section 4 of the Protection from Harassment Act 1997 relates to a course of conduct which, on two occasions or more, causes another to fear that violence will be used against them.

Offence

A person whose course of conduct causes another to fear, on at least two occasions, that violence will be used against him is guilty of an offence if he knows or ought to know that his course of conduct will cause the other so to fear on each of those occasions.

Protection from Harassment Act 1997, s 4(1)

Points to prove

✓ caused fear of violence
✓ by a course of conduct on at least two occasions
✓ which you knew/ought to have known
✓ would cause fear of violence on each occasion

Meaning

Course of conduct (see **8.2.1**)

Explanatory notes

- The person whose course of conduct is in question ought to know that it will cause another to fear that violence will be used against him on any occasion, provided that a reasonable person with the same information would think it would cause the other so to fear in the circumstances.

- A defendant found not guilty of this offence (at trial on indictment) may be convicted of s 2 harassment (see **8.2.1**) or s 2A stalking (see **8.2.3**).

- The court can issue a 'restraining order' against the defendant.

Defences

It is a defence for a person charged with an offence under this section to show that—
(a) his course of conduct was pursued for the purpose of preventing or detecting crime,
(b) his course of conduct was pursued under any enactment or rule of law or to comply with any condition or requirement imposed by any person under any enactment, or
(c) the pursuit of his course of conduct was reasonable for the protection of himself or another or for the protection of his or another's property.

Protection from Harassment Act 1997, s 4(3)

Related cases

R v Curtis [2010] EWCA Crim 123 Prosecution to establish that course of conduct amounts to harassment. The conduct has to be an oppressive, unreasonable and unacceptable campaign, to a degree that would be a criminal matter.

R v Patel [2004] EWCA Crim 3284 Incidents must be so connected in type and context that they amount to a course of conduct.

Howard v DPP [2001] EWHC 17 (Admin) Where one of the many threats made by the defendant was to kill a family's dog. This was deemed sufficient grounds for the family to fear violence being used against them.

Either way offence

 Time limit for prosecution: none

 Summary: maximum 6 months' imprisonment and/or fine
Indictment: maximum 5 years' imprisonment and/or fine

8.2.3 **Stalking**

Section 2A of the Protection from Harassment Act 1997 creates the offence of stalking which is a different offence when carried out or motivated by religion or race at which point it becomes an offence defined by the police and the CPS as a 'hate crime'. The basics of the offence are explained below.

Offences

(1) A person is guilty of an offence if—
   (a) the person pursues a course of conduct in breach of section 1(1), and
   (b) the course of conduct amounts to stalking.
(2) For the purposes of subsection (1)(b) (and section 4A(1)(a)) a person's course of conduct amounts to stalking of another person if—
   (a) it amounts to harassment of that person,
   (b) the acts or omissions involved are ones associated with stalking, and
   (c) the person whose course of conduct it is knows or ought to know that the course of conduct amounts to harassment of the other person.

Protection from Harassment Act 1997, s 2A

Points to prove

✓ pursued a course of conduct in breach of s 1(1)
✓ that conduct amounted to stalking
✓ which you knew/ought to have known
✓ amounted to harassment

Meanings

Breach of section 1(1) (see **8.1.1**)

Harassment (see **8.2.1**)

Includes causing the person(s) alarm or distress.

Acts or omissions (s 2A(3))

The following are examples which, in particular circumstances, are associated with stalking:

- following a person;
- contacting, or attempting to contact, a person by any means;
- publishing any statement or other material—whether online, via Twitter, Facebook, email or other ICT—relating or purporting to relate to a person, or purporting to originate from a person;
- monitoring the use by a person of the internet, email or any other form of electronic communication;
- loitering in any place (whether public or private);
- interfering with any property in the possession of a person;
- watching or spying on a person.

Explanatory notes

- An offender does not have to act in a malicious, threatening, abusive or insulting way; however, there has to be an element of racial or religious hatred motivation for it to be considered for the aggravated sentence.
- The court can issue a 'restraining order' against the defendant.

Practical considerations

- Section 2B allows a Justice of the Peace to issue a warrant, which authorises a constable to enter and search premises on reasonable grounds for believing that a stalking offence under s 2A has been, or is being, committed, and there is material on the premises which is likely to be of substantial value (whether by itself or together with other material) to the investigation of the offence.
- Section 4A concerns the offence of stalking involving fear of violence or serious alarm or distress (see **8.2.4**).
- Home Office Circular 18/2012 provides further details concerning the ss 2A and 4A stalking offences and power of entry under s 2B.
- If it is racially or religiously aggravated stalking, see **8.3.1**.

Summary offence

 Time limit for prosecution: 6 months

 Sentence: maximum 6 months' imprisonment and/or level 5 fine

8.2.4 **Stalking (fear of violence/serious alarm or distress)**

Section 4A relates to stalking causing another to fear, on at least two occasions, that violence will be used against them or causes them serious alarm or distress which has a substantial adverse effect on their usual day-to-day activities.

Offence

A person (A) whose course of conduct—
(a) amounts to stalking, and
(b) either—
    (i) causes another (B) to fear, on at least two occasions, that violence will be used against B, or
    (ii) causes B serious alarm or distress which has a substantial adverse effect on B's usual day-to-day activities,
is guilty of an offence if A knows or ought to know that A's course of conduct will cause B so to fear on each of those occasions or (as the case may be) will cause such alarm or distress.

Protection from Harassment Act 1997, s 4A(1)

Points to prove

✓ course of conduct that amounted to stalking
✓ caused another to fear on at least two occasions that violence would be used or
✓ caused serious alarm/distress which had a substantial adverse effect on B's usual day-to-day activities
✓ which you knew/ought to have known
✓ would cause either fear of violence on each occasion or serious alarm/distress

---

Meaning

Stalking (see **8.2.3**)

Explanatory notes

- The phrase 'substantial adverse effect' on the usual day-to-day activities' is not defined in s 4A. However, Home Office Circular 18/2012 states that evidence of a substantial adverse effect may include the victim:
  + changing their routes to work, work patterns or employment;
  + arranging for friends or family to pick up children from school;
  + installing additional security in/around their home;
  + suffering from physical or mental ill-health;
  + suffering from stress due to deterioration in performance at work;
  + moving home; or
  + stopping/changing the way they socialise.

- The person whose course of conduct is in question ought to know that it will cause another to fear that violence will be used against them on any occasion if a reasonable person in possession of the same information would think the course of conduct would cause the other to fear on that occasion.

- For the purposes of this section, the person whose course of conduct is in question ought to know that their course of conduct will cause the victim serious alarm or distress which has a substantial adverse effect on the victim's usual day-to-day activities if a reasonable person in possession of the same information would think the course of conduct would cause the victim such alarm or distress.

Defences

It is a defence for A to show that—

(a) A's course of conduct was pursued for the purpose of preventing or detecting crime,

(b) A's course of conduct was pursued under any enactment or rule of law or to comply with any condition or requirement imposed by any person under any enactment, or

(c) the pursuit of A's course of conduct was reasonable for the protection of A or another or for the protection of A's or another's property.

Protection from Harassment Act 1997, s 4A(4)

Either way offence

 Time limit for prosecution: none

 Summary: maximum 6 months' imprisonment and/or fine

Indictment: maximum 5 years' imprisonment and/or fine

The offences explained in this chapter so far are in effect aggravated by the motivation of hostility or demonstration of hostility on the basis of race or religion alone. These were introduced by the Crime and Disorder Act 1998 and those offences are explained below.

8.3 **Racially or Religiously Aggravated Harassment/ Stalking**

Offence

A person is guilty of an offence under this section if he commits—

(a) an offence under section 2 or 2A of the Protection from Harassment Act 1997 (offences of harassment and stalking); or

(b) an offence under section 4 or 4A of that Act (putting people in fear of violence and stalking involving fear of violence or serious alarm or distress),

which is racially or religiously aggravated for the purposes of this section.

Crime and Disorder Act 1998, s 32

Points to prove

✓ committed an offence

✓ contrary to s 2, 2A, 4 or 4A of the Protection from Harassment Act 1997

✓ such an offence was racially/religiously aggravated

Meaning

Racially or religiously aggravated

An offence is racially or religiously aggravated for the purposes of section 32 if—

(a)   at the time of committing the offence, or immediately before or after doing so, the offender demonstrates towards the victim of the offence hostility based on the victim's membership (or presumed membership) of a racial or religious group; or

(b)   the offence is motivated (wholly or partly) by hostility towards members of a racial or religious group based on their membership of that group.

Crime and Disorder Act 1998, s 28(1)

Membership

In relation to a racial or religious group, includes association with members of that group.

Presumed

Means presumed by the offender.

Racial group

A group of persons defined by reference to race, colour, nationality (including citizenship) or ethnic or national origins.

Religious group

A group of persons defined by reference to religious belief or lack of religious belief.

Explanatory notes

- It is immaterial for the purposes of paragraph (a) or (b) of subsection (1) whether or not the offender's hostility is also based, to any extent, on any other factor not mentioned in that paragraph.

- It will be up to the courts to define the extent of the term 'immediately'. The longer the interval between the demonstration of hostility and the offence itself, the less likely it will be that the circumstances will pass the test of racial or religious aggravation.

- The use of a broad non-inclusive term such as 'immigrant doctor', depending upon the context in which it was used, could constitute the description of a person within a racial group (*R v D; Attorney General's Reference (No 4 of 2004)*).

- A motivation by hostility towards a victim could be exampled in the cyber world by sending emails or creating a website purely on the basis of a dislike for a particular racial group.

- A demonstration of hostility to a victim could be shown by actions being taken purely on the basis of the victim belonging to a particular racial or religious group.
- Guidance can be found on racially aggravated offences in the case of *Taylor v DPP* [2006] EWHC 1202 (Admin).
- A police officer is just as entitled to protection under these provisions as anyone else.
- The court can make ancillary orders when sentencing for offences outlined in this chapter under s 5 of the Protection from Harassment Act 1997.
- Civil remedies are also available under s 3 of the same Act.

8.4 **Stirring Up of Hatred Offences**

As explained in the introduction to this chapter, there are two types of offence included within the official definition of hate crime. The following are known as the 'stirring up offences'. Again, they only address offences against a number of the protected characteristics (race, religion and sexual orientation).

The use of the internet and other networked communications in stirring up hatred against the defined racial, religious and sexual orientation protected characteristics, has become more prevalent in recent years and commands a worldwide audience.

There are distinctions between those offences directed at racial groups in contrast to those which are against religious groups or those relating to sexual orientation.

8.4.1 **Use of words/behaviour or display of written material (racial)**

Offence

A person who uses threatening, abusive or insulting words or behaviour or displays any written material which is threatening, abusive or insulting, is guilty of an offence if—

(a) he intends thereby to stir up racial hatred, or

(b) having regard to all the circumstances racial hatred is likely to be stirred up thereby.

Public Order Act 1986, s 18(1)

Points to prove

- ✓ used or displayed
- ✓ threatening/abusive/insulting
- ✓ words/behaviour/written material
- ✓ intended/likely to stir up racial hatred

Meanings

Displayed

Presented visually, including by use of online and social media.

Threatening

Includes verbal and physical threats.

Abusive

Degrading or reviling.

Insulting

Insolent or contemptuous.

Written material

Includes any reproduced image or likeness and will include there-fore electronic forms of representation.

Intention (see 9.2)

Racial hatred

Is defined by s 17 of the Act as hatred against a group of persons defined by reference to colour, race, nationality (including citizenship) or ethnic or national origins.

Explanatory notes

- Racial hatred includes hatred manifested in Great Britain but directed against a racial or religious group outside Great Britain.
- Insulting words in an email or on a website do not include those which may be irritating or which cause resentment.
- The offence may be committed in public or in private but if committed inside a dwelling then the defence provided by s 18(4) below may apply.
- If this offence relates to the display of written racial hatred material, the court may order forfeiture of the material.
- If the offence is committed by a body corporate, with the consent or connivance of a director, manager,

company secretary or other similar officer or person acting as such, then they as well as the company are guilty of the offence (s 28).

• Consider CPS Charging Standards for racial hatred offence.
• Consent of Attorney General/Solicitor General required.

Defences

(4) It is for the accused to prove that he was inside a dwelling and had no reason to believe the words or the behaviour used, or the written material displayed, would be heard or seen by a person outside that or another dwelling.

(5) A person who is not shown to have intended to stir up racial hatred is not guilty of an offence under this section if he did not intend his words or behaviour, or the written material to be and was not aware that it might be, threatening, abusive or insulting.

Public Order Act 1986, s 18

 Either way offence

 Time limit for prosecution: none

 Summary: maximum 6 months' imprisonment and/or fine
Indictment: maximum 7 years' imprisonment and/or fine

8.4.2 **Publishing/distributing written racial material**

Offence

A person who publishes or distributes written material which is threatening abusive or insulting is guilty of an offence if—

(a) he intends thereby to stir up racial hatred or,
(b) having regard to all the circumstances racial hatred is likely to be stirred up.

Public Order Act 1936, s 19(1)

Points to prove

✓ published/distributed
✓ threatening/abusive/insulting

✓ written material
✓ intended
✓ likely to stir up racial hatred

Meanings

Published/distributes

Publication or distribution to the whole or section of the public.

Written material

See **8.4.1**—wholly applicable to messages, websites, Twitter, Facebook, etc.

For all other words and phrases, see above.

Defences

It is for the accused, who is not shown to have intended to stir up racial hatred, to prove that he was not aware of the content of the material and did not suspect nor had reason to suspect that it was threatening, abusive or insulting.

Public Order Act 1986, s 19(2)

Related case

R v Sheppard [2010] EWCA Crim 65 Sheppard created and uploaded onto the internet written material which cast doubt on the holocaust and made contemptuous remarks which were racial in their content. Although uploaded within the UK, the website's server was situated in California. The court had jurisdiction as a 'substantial measure' of these activities took place in the UK. Held: that written material includes articles in electronic form and it was published over the internet for general access and consumption of the public as a whole.

Practical considerations

Other racial hatred offences do exist but are not being addressed in this Handbook and include:

• the public performance of a play—s 20;
• the distribution showing or playing of a recording—s 21;
• the broadcasting or including a programme in a programme service—s 22;
• the possession of racially inflammatory material—s 23.

Either way offence

 Time limit for prosecution: none

 Summary: maximum 6 months' imprisonment and/
or fine

Indictment: maximum 7 years' imprisonment and/or fine

8.5 **Religious or Sexual Orientation Hatred Offences**

In a similar vein, and created by Part 3 of the Public Order Act 1986, are the offences where racial hatred is replaced by an intention to stir up hatred on the grounds of religion or sexual orientation. There are two stark differences with these offences, in that the words, behaviour or displayed written material can only be threatening. The offence is not committed if they are abusive or insulting, and they can only be intended to stir up religious or sexually oriented hatred **not** likely to stir up hatred. It will, therefore, always be more difficult to prosecute these offences.

Offence

A person who uses threatening words or behaviour, or displays any written material which is threatening, is guilty of an offence if he intends thereby to stir up religious hatred or hatred on the grounds of sexual orientation.

Public Order Act 1986, s 29B(1)

Points to prove

✓ used threatening words or behaviour or

✓ written material

✓ intended to stir up religious hatred or

✓ sexual orientation hatred

Meanings

Threatening (see **8.4.1**)

221

Displays (see **8.4.1**)

Written material (see **8.4.1**)

Intention (see **9.2**)

Religious hatred

Hatred against a group of persons defined by reference to religious belief or lack of religious belief.

Hatred on the grounds of sexual orientation

Means hatred against a group of persons defined by reference to sexual orientation (whether towards persons of the same sex, the opposite sex or both).

Explanatory notes

- If the offence relates to written material, the court may under s 29I order forfeiture of the material.
- The offence may be committed in public or in private but if committed inside a dwelling then the defence provided by s 29B(4) below may apply.
- If the offence is committed by a body corporate, with the consent or connivance of a director, manager, company secretary or other similar officer or person acting as such, then they as well as the company are guilty of the offence (s 29).
- Consider CPS Charging Standards.
- Consent of Attorney General/Solicitor General required.

Defences

It is for the accused to prove that he was inside a dwelling and had no reason to believe that the words or behaviour used or the written material displayed would be heard or seen by a person outside that or another dwelling.

Public Order Act 1986, s 29B(4)

8.5.1 Protection for freedom of expression

8.5.1.1 Religious hatred

Section 29J states that:

Nothing in this part shall be read or given effect in a way which prohibits or restricts discussion, criticism or expressions of antipathy, dislike, ridicule, insult or abuse of particular religions or the beliefs or practices of their adherents, or of any other belief system or the beliefs or practices of its adherents, or proselytising or urging adherents of a different religion or belief system to cease practising their religion or belief system.

8.5.1.2 Sexual orientation hatred

Likewise, s 29JA also addresses the right to a freedom of expression by stating:

(1) In this Part, for the avoidance of doubt, the discussion or criticism of sexual conduct or practices or the urging of persons to refrain from or modify such conduct or practices shall not be taken of itself to be threatening or intended to stir up hatred

(2) In this Part, for the avoidance of doubt, any discussion or criticism of marriage which concerns the sex of the parties to marriage shall not be taken of itself to be threatening or intended to stir up hatred.

 Either way offence

 Time limit for prosecution: none

 Summary: maximum 6 months' imprisonment and/or fine
Indictment: maximum 7 years' imprisonment and/or fine

8.5.2 **Publishing or distributing written material—religious or sexual orientation hatred**

Offence

A person who publishes or distributes written material which is threatening is guilty of an offence if he intends thereby to stir up religious hatred or hatred on the grounds of sexual orientation.

Public Order Act 1986, s 29C

Points to prove

✓ published/distributed written material

✓ which was threatening

✓ intending to stir up religious hatred

✓ hatred on the grounds of sexual orientation

Meanings

Published/distributes

Publication or distribution to the whole or a section of the public.

Written material

See **8.4.1**—wholly applicable to messages, websites, Twitter, Facebook, etc.

Intention (see **9.2**)

Religious hatred (see **8.5**)

Hatred on the grounds of sexual orientation (see **8.5**)

Explanatory notes

- If the offence is committed by a body corporate, with the consent or connivance of a director, manager, company secretary or other similar officer or person acting as such, then they as well as the company are guilty of the offence (s 29).
- Consider CPS Charging Standards.
- Consent of Attorney General/Solicitor General required.
- If the offence relates to written material, the court may under s 29I order forfeiture of the material.
- Other religious or sexual orientation hatred offences under this Part of the Act which could be considered for use within the cyber arena include:
  + public performance of a play—s 29D;
  + distributing, showing or playing a recording—s 29E;
  + broadcasting or including a programme in a programme service—s 29F;
  + possession of inflammatory material—s 29G.

They are all either way offences and carry the same sentence as the offences under ss 23B and 23C.

8.6 **Encourage or Assist Crime**

In addition, and as a catch-all for those offenders where the substantive offence cannot be proved, in all chapters of this section of the book it is recommended that the offences created by the Serious Crime Act 2007 could be made use of. The Act abolished the common law offence of incitement and creates three encouraging or assisting crime offences.

Offence

A person commits an offence if—
(a) he does an act capable of encouraging or assisting the commission of an offence; and
(b) he intends to encourage or assist its commission.

Serious Crime Act 2007, s 44(1)

Points to prove

✓ did an act which was capable of encouraging or assisting

✓ in the commission of an offence, namely (detail offence)

✓ intending to

✓ encourage or assist in its commission

Meanings

Does an act

This includes a reference to a course of conduct.

Capable of encouraging or assisting

(1) A reference in this Part to a person's doing an act that is capable of encouraging the commission of an offence includes a reference to his doing so by threatening another person or otherwise putting pressure on another person to commit the offence.

(2) A reference in this Part to a person's doing an act that is capable of encouraging or assisting the commission of an offence includes a reference to his doing so by—

(a) taking steps to reduce the possibility of criminal proceedings being brought in respect of that offence;

(b) failing to take reasonable steps to discharge a duty.

(3) But a person is not to be regarded as doing an act that is capable of encouraging or assisting the commission of an offence merely because he fails to respond to a constable's request for assistance in preventing a breach of the peace.

Serious Crime Act 2007, s 65

Encouraging or assisting commission of an offence

Reference in Part 2 to encouraging or assisting the commission of an offence is to be read in accordance with s 47.

Intends (see **9.2**)

Explanatory notes

- A person is not taken to have intended to encourage or assist the commission of an offence merely because such encouragement or assistance was a foreseeable consequence of that person's act.
- If a person (D1) arranges for a person (D2) to do an act that is capable of encouraging or assisting the commission of an offence, and D2 does the act, D1 is also to be treated for the purposes of this Part as having done it.
- Section 47 provides further meanings, assumptions and, in particular, sets out what is required to prove intent or belief and whether an act would amount to the commission of an offence.

Defences of acting reasonably

(1) A person is not guilty of an offence under this Part if he proves—
   (a) that he knew certain circumstances existed; and
   (b) that it was reasonable for him to act as he did in those circumstances.

(2) A person is not guilty of an offence under this Part if he proves—
   (a) that he believed certain circumstances to exist;
   (b) that his belief was reasonable; and
   (c) that it was reasonable for him to act as he did in the circumstances as he believed them to be.

(3) Factors to be considered in determining whether it was reasonable for a person to act as he did include—
   (a) the seriousness of the anticipated offence (or, in the case of an offence under section 46, the offences specified in the indictment);
   (b) any purpose for which he claims to have been acting;
   (c) any authority by which he claims to have been acting.

Serious Crime Act 2007, s 50

Practical considerations

- Other sections worthy of note in Part 2 of the Act are as follows:
   ◆ encouraging or assisting an offence believing it will be committed—s 45;

- encouraging or assisting offences believing one or more will be committed—s 46;
- proving an offence under Part 2—s 47;
- further provision as to proving a s 46 offence—s 48;
- supplemental provisions—s 49;
- protective offences: victims not liable—s 51;
- persons who may be perpetrators or encouragers—s 56.

- A person may commit an offence under Part 2 whether or not any offence capable of being encouraged or assisted by his act is committed.

- MOJ Circular 4/2008 provides further details and guidance on Part 2 of the Act.

- Consider confiscation of cash and property for an offence under s 44, which is listed as a 'criminal lifestyle' offence under Sch 2 to the Proceeds of Crime Act 2002.

- Similarly, aiding, abetting, counselling or procuring the commission of the s 46 offence is also listed under Sch 2.

For a s 46 offence, a defendant might believe that his conduct would assist in the commission of one or more different offences by another individual without necessarily knowing, or being able to identify, the precise offence or offences which the person to whom he offered encouragement or assistance intended to commit or would actually commit (*R v Sadique* [2013] EWCA Crim 1150).

Offences in s 46

⚬ Indictable offence

🕐 **Time limit for prosecution**: none

Offences in s 44 or 45

⚬ Indictment as with anticipated offence

🕐 **Time limit for prosecution**: variable as to trial venue

Offences in ss 44–46

▥ **Sentence**: penalty per anticipated offence, subject to s 58

Chapter 9

Cyber-Enabled Fraud

9.1 **Introduction**

Cyber-enabled crimes are those traditional crimes (identified under the Home Office Counting Rules) which can be carried out and increased in their scale by the use of computers, networks or other forms of ICT. Over the past years, cyber-enabled fraud and theft have increased.

This chapter will identify, define and explain those criminal offences which can be committed using the computer and associated networks. As with many other forms of crime, there are no explicit pieces of legislation which address the specific use of the computer to commit fraud or theft. The offences continue to be addressed by the original offences which can also be committed without the computer.

A sample of instances where computers are used to enable frauds and thefts are:

- online banking frauds and internet-enabled frauds where a cardholder is not present and transactions are performed remotely from anywhere in the world;

- there are also fraudulent sales conducted through online retail, auction or bogus websites. Purchases of counterfeit products through misrepresentation are also prevalent, for example through online ticketing fraud;

- mass marketing frauds and consumer scams have become highly profitable and those most notably renowned are the inheritance frauds, online romance frauds, fake charity or disaster relief frauds and even fake lotteries. All these are conducted online by either persuading people to part with money upfront with the promise of a larger sum being returned to them on a future date, being directed to a fake website or where personal details are obtained following online 'relationships'.

Although the list of fraud types of offences appears innovative but not exhaustive, the basic criminal offences remain the same and arise from the Fraud Act 2006. Always remember that many frauds will also be theft.

For that reason, this chapter has been confined to the relevant offences under the Fraud Act 2006 and, as the criminal property that is acquired is either laundered or disposed of, the three relevant offences under the Proceeds of Crime Act 2002 are also included.

The circumstances of the offence may well also reveal other offences, such as theft, false accounting (s 17 of the Theft Act 1968), offences contrary to the Computer Misuse Act 1990 (see **7.2**) and the Forgery and Counterfeiting Act 1981.

It is important to remember that theft carries a lower minimum sentence than fraud and on occasions will be easier to prove, although the fraud offences do not require an intention to permanently deprive.

The Fraud Act 2006 provides for the offence of fraud and other fraudulent offences of which dishonesty is a constituent part. Sections 1 to 4 detail the three different ways of committing fraud, s 12 the liability of company officers and s 13 evidential matters relating to fraud.

9.2 **Fraud Offence**

Section 1 creates the general offence of fraud, and ss 2 to 4 detail three different ways of committing fraud by false representation, failing to disclose information or by abuse of position.

Offences

(1) A person is guilty of fraud if he is in breach of any of the sections listed in subsection (2) (which provide for different ways of committing the offence).

(2) The sections are—

    (a) section 2 (fraud by false representation),

    (b) section 3 (fraud by failing to disclose information), and

    (c) section 4 (fraud by abuse of position).

Fraud Act 2006, s 1

Points to prove

Section (2)(a): false representation

✓ dishonestly made a false representation

✓ intending to make a gain for yourself/another or

✓ intending to cause loss to another/expose another to risk of loss

Section (2)(b): failing to disclose information

✓ dishonestly failed to disclose to another

✓ information which you were under a legal duty to disclose

✓ intending by that failure

✓ to make a gain for yourself/another or

✓ to cause loss to another/expose another to risk of loss

Section (2)(c): fraud by abuse of position

✓ occupying a position in which you were expected

✓ to safeguard or not to act against the financial interests of another

✓ dishonestly abused that position

✓ intending to make a gain for yourself/another or

✓ intending to cause loss to another/expose another to a risk of loss

---

Meanings

Fraud by false representation (see 9.2.1)

Fraud by failing to disclose information (see 9.2.2)

Fraud by abuse of position (see 9.2.3)

Gain and loss

(1) The references to gain and loss in sections 2 to 4 are to be read in accordance with this section.

   (2) 'Gain' and 'loss'—

       (a) extend only to gain or loss in money or other property;

       (b) include any such gain or loss whether temporary or permanent; and 'property' means any property whether real or personal (including things in action and other intangible property).

(3) 'Gain' includes a gain by keeping what one has, as well as a gain by getting what one does not have.

---

(4) 'Loss' includes a loss by not getting what one might get, as well as a loss by parting with what one has.

Fraud Act 2006, s 5

Dishonestly

A court must decide what is dishonest according to the ordinary standards of reasonable and honest people and whether that person knew that what they were doing was dishonest by those standards (*R v Ghosh* [1982] 2 All ER 689).

Intention

This can be proved by drawing on various sources of information:

- admissions by the defendant in interview which reveal their state of mind at the time of the commission of the offence;
- answers given by the defendant to questions regarding their actions and intentions at the time of the offence;
- by inference from the circumstances at the time of the offence;
- evidence from witnesses;
- actions by the defendant before, during and after the event and from property found on them or under their control.

It is vital that the state of mind at the time of the offending is proved.

Explanatory notes

- Section 1 creates the general offence of fraud, and ss 2 to 4 detail three different ways of committing the fraud offence.
- All three fraud offences require an intention to make a gain for oneself or another or cause loss to another/expose another to a risk of loss.
- Similarly, in all of these fraud offences intention must be proved (see **9.2**).
- Property covers all forms of property, including intellectual property.
- If any offences are committed by a company, the company officers may also be liable under s 12.
- Section 13 deals with evidential matters under this Act, conspiracy to defraud or any other offences involving any form of fraudulent conduct or purpose.

9.2.1 **Meaning of fraud by false representation**

(1)   A person is in breach of this section if he—
   (a)   dishonestly makes a false representation and
   (b)   intends by making the representation—
      (i)   to make a gain for himself or another, or
      (ii)   to cause a loss to another or expose another to risk of a loss.

(2)   A representation is false if—
   (a)   it is untrue or misleading, and
   (b)   the person making it knows that it is, or might be untrue or misleading.

(3)   Representation means any representation as to fact or law, including a representation as to the state of mind of—
   (a)   the person making the representation, or
   (b)   any other person.

(4)   A representation may be express or implied.

(5)   For the purposes of this section a representation may be regarded as being made if it (or anything implying it) is submitted in any form to any system or device designed to receive, convey or respond to communications (with or without human intervention).

Fraud Act 2006, s 2

Gain and loss (see **9.2**)

Dishonestly (see **9.2**)

Intention (see **9.2**)

Explanatory notes

- The offence of fraud by false representation is legislated for by fraud s 1 (see **9.2**) and **not** s 2.
- The gain or loss does not actually have to take place.
- There is no restriction on the way in which the representation may be communicated. It can be spoken, written (hardcopy or electronically—e.g. email) or communicated by conduct.
- An example of a false representation by conduct is where a person dishonestly uses a credit card whether physically or online to pay for goods. By tendering the card, they are falsely representing that they have the authority to use it for that transaction. It is immaterial whether the retailer accepting the card is deceived by this representation.

- The practice of 'phishing' where an email purports to come from, for example, a legitimate financial institution in order to obtain credit card and bank account details, is an example of false representation. Online romances if made for the purpose of obtaining details, could also fall within this category.

- It could well be that the only recipient of the false statement is a machine or a piece of software, where a false statement is submitted to a system for dealing with electronic communications and not to a human being (e.g. postal or messenger systems).

9.2.2 **Meaning of fraud by failing to disclose information**

A person is in breach of this section if he—

(a) dishonestly fails to disclose to another person information which he is under a legal duty to disclose, and

(b) intends, by failing to disclose the information—

(i) to make a gain for himself or another, or

(ii) to cause loss to another or to expose another to a risk of loss.

Fraud Act 2006, s 3

Gain and loss (see **9.2**)
Dishonestly (see **9.2**)
Intention (see **9.2**)

Explanatory notes

- The offence of fraud by failing to disclose information falls under fraud s 1 (see **9.2**) and **not** s 3.

- A legal duty to disclose information may include duties under both oral and/or written contracts.

- The concept of 'legal duty' may derive from statute, a transaction that requires good faith (e.g. contract of insurance), express or implied terms of a contract, custom of a particular trade/market or a fiduciary relationship between the parties (e.g. between agent and principal).

- This legal duty to disclose information may be where the defendant's failure to disclose gives the victim a cause of action for damages, or the law gives the victim a right to set aside any change in their legal position to which they may consent as a result of the non-disclosure.

- An example of an offence under this section could be where a person intentionally failed to disclose information relating to their physical condition when making an online application for life insurance.

9.2.3 **Meaning of fraud by abuse of position**

(1)   A person is in breach of this section if he—

    (a)   occupies a position in which he is expected to safeguard, or not to act against, the financial interests of another person,

    (b)   dishonestly abuses that position, and

    (c)   intends, by means of the abuse of that position—

        (i)   to make a gain for himself or another, or

        (ii)   to cause loss to another or to expose another to a risk of loss.

(2)   A person may be regarded as having abused his position even though his conduct consisted of an omission rather than an act.

Fraud Act 2006, s 4

Gain and loss (see **9.2**)

Dishonestly (see **9.2**)

Intention (see **9.2**)

Explanatory notes

- The offence of fraud by abuse of position is actually created by s 1 fraud (see **9.2**) and **not** s 4.

- The offence of committing fraud by a person dishonestly abusing their position applies in situations where they are in a privileged position, and by virtue of this position are expected to safeguard another's financial interests or not act against those interests.

- The necessary relationship could be between trustee and beneficiary, director and company, professional person and client, agent and principal, employee and employer or even between partners. Generally, this relationship will be recognised by the civil law as importing fiduciary duties. This relationship and the existence of duty can be ruled upon by the judge or be subject of directions to the jury.

- The term 'abuse' is not defined because it is intended to cover a wide range of conduct. Furthermore, the offence can be committed by omission as well as by positive action.

- Examples of offences under this section are:
  + purposely failing to take up the chance of a crucial contract in order that an associate or rival company can take it up instead to the loss of their employer;
  + a software company employee uses their position to clone software products with the intention of selling the products to others;
  + where a carer for an elderly or disabled person has access to that person's bank account and abuses their position by transferring funds for their own gain.

All these examples could be performed by making use of online facilities and emails and have relevance to this chapter.

9.2.4 **Liability of company officers for an offence by a company**

Liability:

(1) Subsection (2) applies if an offence under this Act is committed by a body corporate.

(2) If the offence is proved to have been committed with the consent or connivance of—

(a) a director, manager, secretary or other similar officer of the body corporate, or

(b) a person who was purporting to act in any such capacity, he (as well as the body corporate) is guilty of the offence and liable to be proceeded against and punished accordingly.

(3) If the affairs of a body corporate are managed by its members, subsection (2) applies in relation to the acts and defaults of a member in connection with his functions of management as if he were a director of the body corporate.

Fraud Act 2006, s 12

Explanatory notes

- This section provides that if people who have a specified corporate role are party to the commission of an offence under the Act by their body corporate, they will be liable to be charged for the offence as well as the corporation.
- Liability for this offence applies to directors, managers, company secretaries and other similar officers of companies and other bodies corporate.

- Furthermore, if the body corporate is charged with an offence and the company is managed by its members, the members involved in management can be prosecuted too.

9.2.5 **Admissible evidence**

Evidence:

    (1)   A person is not to be excused from—

        (a)   answering any question put to him in proceedings relating to property, or

        (b)   complying with any order made in proceedings relating to property,

on the ground that doing so may incriminate him or his spouse or civil partner of an offence under this Act or a related offence.

    (2)   But, in proceedings for an offence under this Act or a related offence, a statement or admission made by the person in—

        (a)   answering such a question, or

        (b)   complying with such an order,

is not admissible in evidence against him or (unless they married or became civil partners after the making of the statement or admission) his spouse or civil partner.

    (3)   "Proceedings relating to property" means any proceedings for—

        (a)   the recovery or administration of any property,

        (b)   the execution of a trust, or

        (c)   an account of any property or dealings with property,

and "property" means money or other property whether real or personal (including things in action and other intangible property).

    (4)   "Related offence" means—

        (a)   conspiracy to defraud;

        (b)   any other offence involving any form of fraudulent conduct or purpose.

Fraud Act 2006, s 13

Explanatory notes

- This means that during any proceedings for:
  - the recovery or administration of any property;
  - the execution of a trust; or
  - an account of any property or dealings with property;

a person cannot be excused from answering any question or refuse to comply with any order made in those proceedings on the grounds of incrimination under this Act, conspiracy to defraud or an offence involving any form of fraudulent conduct or purpose.

- However, any statement or admission made in answering such a question, or complying with such an order, is not admissible in evidence against them or their spouse or civil partner (unless they married or became civil partners after the making of such a statement or admission).

- Although this section is similar to s 31(1) of the Theft Act 1968 where a person/spouse/civil partner is protected from incrimination, while nonetheless being obliged to cooperate with certain civil proceedings relating to property, it goes beyond that section by removing privilege in relation to this Act, conspiracy to defraud and any other offence involving any form of fraudulent conduct or purpose.

- A civil partnership is a relationship between two people of the same sex ('civil partners') registered as civil partners under the Civil Partnerships Act 2004 and ends only on death, dissolution or annulment.

 Either way offence

 Time limit for prosecution: none

 Summary: maximum 6 months' imprisonment and/or fine
Indictment: maximum 10 years' imprisonment and/or fine

9.3 **Articles for Use in Fraud**

The Fraud Act 2006 provides for offences which are enabling or pre-paratory to the complete offence(s)—similar to the Theft Act where there is an offence of going equipped (s 25) and the Computer Misuse Act 1990 (ss 3/3A). This offence provides an element of prevention before the full offence can be committed.

The two offences are explained below and should be considered in the context of computers, other ICT and the internet.

9.3.1 **Possess or control article for use in fraud**

Section 6 creates the offence of an offender having in their possession or under their control an article for use in fraud.

Offence

A person is guilty of an offence if he has in his possession or under his control any article for use in the course of or in connection with any fraud.

Fraud Act 2006, s 6(1)

Points to prove

✓ had in your possession/under your control

✓ an article

✓ for use in the course of/in connection with a fraud

Meanings

Possession

The mental element is addressed by showing that the person knows of the existence of the article. The physical element is much wider than actually 'having' the article with them. It can be deemed to be in their possession if it is a computer program on a computer in a vehicle over which they have control.

Article

Means an article:

• made or adapted for use in the course of or in connection with an offence of fraud; or

• intended by the person having it with them for such use by them or by some other person.

It also includes any program or data held in electronic form.

Fraud (see **9.2**)

Intention (see **9.2**)

Explanatory notes

- Having the article after the commission of the fraud is not sufficient for this offence.

- The prosecution must prove that the defendant was in possession of the article, and intended the article to be used in the course of or in connection with some future fraud. It is not necessary to prove that they intended it to be used in the course of or in connection with any specific fraud; it is enough to prove a general intention to use it for fraud.

- Similarly, it will be sufficient to prove that they had it with them with the intention that it should be used by someone else.

- Examples of electronic programs or data which could be used in fraud are a computer program that can generate credit card numbers, computer templates that can be used for producing blank utility bills, computer files containing lists of other people's credit card details or draft letters in connection with 'advance fee' frauds.

 Either way offence

 Time limit for prosecution: none

 Summary: maximum 6 months' imprisonment and/or fine

Indictment: maximum 5 years' imprisonment and/or fine

9.3.2 **Making or supplying article for use in fraud**

Section 7 deals with the offence of making or supplying an article for use in fraud.

Offence

A person is guilty of an offence if he makes, adapts, supplies or offers to supply any article—

(a) knowing that it is designed or adapted for use in the course of or in connection with fraud, or

(b) intending it to be used to commit, or assist in the commission of, fraud.

Fraud Act 2006, s 7(1)

Points to prove

- ✓ made/adapted/supplied/offered to supply
- ✓ an article
- ✓ knowing that it was designed/adapted for use in the course of/in
- ✓ connection with fraud

  or

- ✓ intending it to be used to commit/assist in the commission of fraud

---

Meanings

Article (see 9.3.1)

Fraud (see 9.2)

Intention (see 9.2)

Explanatory notes

- The offence is to make, adapt, supply or offer to supply any article, knowing that it is designed or adapted for use in the course of or in connection with fraud, or intending it to be used to commit or facilitate fraud.
- Such an example would be where a person creates programs which are sold on the internet to facilitate the obtaining of credit card details or to infiltrate systems in financial institutions.

Practical considerations

- A general intention to commit fraud will suffice rather than a specific offence in specific circumstances (e.g. credit card skimming equipment may provide evidence of such an intention).
- Proof is required that the defendant had the article for the purpose of or with the intention that it be used in the course of or in connection with fraud, and that a general intention to commit fraud will suffice.

 Either way offence

 Time limit for prosecution: none

 Summary: maximum 12 months' imprisonment and/or fine
Indictment: maximum 10 years' imprisonment and/or fine

9.4 **Proceeds of Crime Offences**

Where organised online fraud takes place, the investigation of what has happened to the proceeds of those crimes is likely to reveal money laundering offences. Money laundering is the way that these criminal proceeds would be 'cleaned' so that their origins are not easy to find. With the opportunities now afforded to online criminals, they are able to hide proceeds of crimes in safe havens and make the possession of the money appear wholly legitimate.

This can be simple and if that is the case then it is relatively easy to detect. However, with the sophistication of online movement of monies across borders that have no legal boundary these money laundering events can usually be put into three phases:

- it usually involves placement which means actually getting the money into the financial system;
- layering, where monies are purposefully moved about, even making use of offshore companies, and finally;
- integration where the proceeds or criminal monies become absorbed into the economy usually through some form of investment.

Money laundering offences were previously focused on those offences within drugs trafficking legislation but there are now three main offences provided by the Proceeds of Crime Act 2002 (ss 327 and 328) which address money laundering from crime. Section 329 is not included as it relates particularly to those involved in the regulated sector.

In addition, and also included within this chapter, are the lifestyle assumptions provided by s 75 of and Sch 2 to the Proceeds of Crime Act 2002 which apply to ss 327 and 328 of the Act.

The Proceeds of Crime Act 2002 is a complicated piece of legislation and is policed through properly trained financial investigators. For that reason, the three basic offences will be addressed in this chapter as they can be quite easily linked and facilitated by the use of the internet and other forms of ICT.

Section 327 of the Proceeds of Crime Act 2002 creates the offences of concealing, disguising, converting, transferring or removing from the jurisdiction, criminal property; that is, property which the alleged offender knows or suspects, constitutes or represents benefit from any criminal conduct.

9.4.1 **Section 327 offence—concealing criminal property etc**

Offence

A person commits an offence if he—
(a) conceals criminal property;
(b) disguises criminal property;
(c) converts criminal property;
(d) transfers criminal property;
(e) removes criminal property from England and Wales or from Scotland or Northern Ireland.

Proceeds of Crime Act 2002, s 327(1)

Points to prove

✓ conceals
✓ disguises
✓ converts
✓ transfers
✓ removes
✓ criminal property

Meanings

Conceals/disguises

Defined as concealing or disguising its nature, source, location, disposition, movement or ownership or any rights with respect to it (Proceeds of Crime Act 2002, s 327(3)).

Converts

Adapts, alters, transforms or exchanges.

Transfers

Moves, transmits, relocates.

Removes

Takes away from England and Wales or Scotland or Northern Ireland.

Criminal property

Property is criminal property if:

(a) it constitutes a person's benefit from criminal conduct or it represents such a benefit (in whole or part and whether directly or indirectly), and

(b) the alleged offender knows or suspects that it constitutes or represents such a benefit.

Proceeds of Crime Act, s 340(3)

Explanatory notes

- Criminal conduct is conduct which:
  (a) constitutes an offence in any part of the UK, or
  (b) would constitute an offence in any part of the UK if it occurred there (Proceeds of Crime Act, s 340(2)).

- For the purposes of this offence, property is all property wherever situated and includes: money; all forms of property real or personal, heritable or moveable; things in action and other intangible or incorporeal property (Proceeds of Crime Act, s 340(9)).

- If a person benefits from conduct, his benefit is the property obtained as a result of or in connection with the conduct.

- If a person obtains a pecuniary advantage as a result of or in connection with conduct, he is to be taken to obtain as a result of or in connection with the conduct a sum of money equal to the value of the pecuniary advantage.

- This offence attracts lifestyle assumptions under s 75 of and Sch 2 to the Proceeds of Crime Act 2002.

Defences

A person does not commit an offence contrary to s 327(1) of the Proceeds of Crime Act if:

(a) he makes an authorised disclosure under section 338 and (if the disclosure is made before he does the act mentioned in subsection (1)) he has the appropriate consent;

(b) he intended to make such a disclosure but had a reasonable excuse for not doing so;

(c) the act he does is done in carrying out a function he has relating to the enforcement of any provision of this Act or of any other enactment relating to criminal conduct or benefit from criminal conduct.

Proceeds of Crime Act 2002, s 327(2)

Nor does a person commit an offence under subsection (1) if:

(a) he knows, or believes on reasonable grounds, that the relevant criminal conduct occurred in a particular country or territory outside the United Kingdom, and

(b) the relevant criminal conduct—

(i) was not, at the time it occurred, unlawful under the criminal law then applying in that country or territory, and

(ii) is not of a description prescribed by an order made by the Secretary of State.

Proceeds of Crime Act 2002, s 327(2A)

Exceptions to the defences in subsection (2A) above in respect of relevant criminal conduct are now identified as conduct which would constitute an offence punishable by imprisonment for a maximum term in excess of 12 months in any part of the UK if it occurred there other than:

(a) an offence under the Gaming Act 1968;

(b) an offence under the Lotteries and Amusements Act 1976; or

(c) an offence under section 23 or 25 of the Financial Services and Markets Act 2000.

Proceeds of Crime Act 2002 (Money Laundering: Exceptions to Overseas Conduct Defence) Order 2006

Where a deposit-taking body either converts or transfers what is later identified as criminal property, it does not commit an offence under s 327(1) if it does the act in operating an account maintained with it, and the value of the criminal property concerned is less than the threshold amount determined under s 339A of the Act (£250—but which can be altered or negotiated in consultation with an officer of Her Majesty's Revenue and Customs or a constable).

(A deposit-taking body means a business which engages in the activity of accepting deposits or the National Savings Bank.)

Explanatory notes

- It is not uncommon for the police or other enforcement authorities to take possession of criminal property in the course of their official duties and to convert or transfer it, for example, into an interest-bearing account pending further investigation. Therefore subsection (2)(c) gives them the necessary exemption from the offence.

- A disclosure is authorised under s 338 of the Act if it is a disclosure to a constable, a customs officer or a nominated officer by the alleged offender that property is criminal property and the first, second or third condition set out below is satisfied.

+ First: the disclosure is made before the alleged offender does the prohibited act.

+ Second: the disclosure is made while the alleged offender is doing the prohibited act, he began to do the act at a time when, because he did not then know or suspect that the property constituted or represented a person's benefit from criminal conduct, the act was not a prohibited act, and the disclosure is made on his own initiative and as soon as is practicable after he first knows or suspects that the property constitutes or represents a person's benefit from criminal conduct.

+ Third:
  (a) the disclosure is made after the alleged offender does the prohibited act;
  (b) he has a reasonable excuse for his failure to make the disclosure before he did the act; and
  (c) the disclosure is made on his own initiative and as soon as it is practicable for him to make it.

• An authorised disclosure is not to be taken to breach any restriction on the disclosure of information (however imposed).

• A disclosure to a nominated officer is a disclosure which:
  (a) is made to a person nominated by the alleged offender's employer to receive authorised disclosures, and
  (b) is made in the course of the alleged offender's employment.

• Section 335 of the Act provides the parameters of 'appropriate consent' for the purposes of the authorised disclosure provisions. A key element of this section is the specification of time limits within which a constable or customs officer must respond to suspicious transaction reports in circumstances where a consent decision is required. It specifies that consent decisions must be made within seven working days. If nothing is heard within that time, then the person making the disclosure can go ahead with an otherwise prohibited act without an offence being committed.

• If consent is withheld within the seven working days, then the constable or customs officer has a further 31 calendar days in which to take further action, such as seeking a court order to restrain the assets in question. If nothing further is heard after the end of the 31-day period, then the person making the disclosure can proceed with the transaction and be able to make use of the defence provided under s 327(2).

Practical considerations

- Evidence of the criminal origin of proceeds may be gathered through:
  - ✦ accomplice evidence;
  - ✦ circumstantial evidence;
  - ✦ forensic evidence (e.g. contamination of cash with drugs) from which inferences can be drawn that money came from drug trafficking;
  - ✦ evidence of complex audit trails, from which an accountancy expert may be able to conclude that the complexity of the transactions indicate that the property was the proceeds of crime;
  - ✦ evidence of the unlikelihood of the property being of legitimate origin—if the offender has no legitimate explanation for possessing the property in question, a jury may be willing to draw an inference that it is proceeds of crime.
- Criminals often attempt to launder proceeds through a cash-intensive business.
- Money laundering offences are not limited to cases involving money. It only needs to be shown that the proceeds are criminal property and constitute a benefit from criminal conduct. Therefore, handling stolen goods will always be an alternative charge to consider.

 Either way offence

 Time limit for prosecution: none

 Summary: maximum 6 months' imprisonment and/or fine

Indictment: maximum 14 years' imprisonment and/or fine

9.4.2 **Section 328 offence—arrangements**

Section 328 potentially catches a wider range of involvement in money laundering offences where money is moved about within financial systems, networks and even across borders.

It takes place predominantly where others act for and on behalf of others within financial or credit institutions and even accountants where the facilitation of money laundering is at its easiest particularly through online transactions.

Offence

A person commits an offence if he enters into or becomes concerned in an arrangement which he knows or suspects facilitates (by whatever means) the acquisition, retention, use or control of criminal property by or on behalf of another person.

Proceeds of Crime Act 2002, s 328(1)

Points to prove

✓ enter into or become concerned in an arrangement
✓ knows or suspects facilitates acquisition/retention/use/control
✓ of criminal property
✓ by or on behalf of another person

Meanings

Enter into

Take part in, join in, participate in.

Become concerned in an arrangement

Become involved in.

Knows

Recognises, discerns, identifies.

Suspects

Has sufficient information to lead one to have an idea.

Acquisition/retention/control

To gain, get hold of/withhold/manipulate, manage, direct.

Criminal property (see 9.4.1)

Explanatory notes

- An offence under this section is only committed where the arrangement into which the offender enters or becomes involved, relates to property which has already become criminal property.

- If the property becomes criminal property as a result of the arrangement into which the offender has entered or become involved, then the terms of the offence are not satisfied (*Kensington International Ltd v Republic of Congo* [2008] 1 WLR 1144, CA (Civ Div)).

- An arrangement within this section where the offender has done no more than negotiate about the possible purchase of stolen property with a view to resale (but where there was no particular purchaser in mind), would not be an arrangement for the purposes of s 328 (*Dare v CPS* [2012] 7 Archbold Review 1, QBD).

- Section 328 was not intended to cover or affect the ordinary conduct of litigation by legal professionals, which included any step taken in litigation from the issue of proceedings and the securing of injunctive relief or a freezing order up to its final disposal by judgment, neither does it override legal professional privilege.

- Once a bank suspects that a customer's account contains criminal property, it is obliged to report the matter to the relevant authority and not to carry out any transactions in relation to the account. If it did so and the account actually held criminal property, it would commit an offence contrary to s 328(1). That remains the position unless and until authorised consent is given or the relevant time limit has expired (Proceeds of Crime Act 2002, s 335—(see **9.4.1** under Defences).

- This offence attracts the lifestyle assumptions under s 75 of and Sch 2 to the Proceeds of Crime Act 2002 (see **9.4.3**).

Defences

The defences against committing the offence are the same as in s 327 and are as outlined at **9.4.1**.

9.4.3 **Criminal lifestyle criteria**

The money laundering offences which have been explained so far in this chapter, among many others included within this book, attract the criminal lifestyle assumptions created by s 75 of the Proceeds of Crime Act 2002.

The question of whether a person has a criminal lifestyle is central to the operation of Part 2 (Confiscation) of the Act, because it determines whether the defendant is subject to the confiscation of benefit from his particular criminal conduct or his general criminal conduct. This section sets out in detail the criteria that govern whether or not a person has a criminal lifestyle.

Criteria

(1) A defendant has a criminal lifestyle if (and only if) the following condition is satisfied.

(2) The condition is that the offence (or any of the offences) concerned satisfies any of these tests—
  (a) it is specified in Schedule 2;
  (b) it constitutes conduct forming part of a course of criminal activity;
  (c) it is an offence committed over a period of at least six months and the defendant has benefited from the conduct which constitutes the offence.

(3) Conduct forms part of a course of criminal activity if the defendant has benefited from the conduct and—
  (a) in the proceedings in which he was convicted he was convicted of three or more other offences, each of three or more of them constituting conduct from which he has benefited, or
  (b) in the period of six years ending with the day when those proceedings were started (or, if there is more than one such day, the earliest day) he was convicted on at least two separate occasions of an offence constituting conduct from which he has benefited.

(4) But an offence does not satisfy the test in subsection (2)(b) or (c) unless the defendant obtains relevant benefit of not less than £5000.

(5) Relevant benefit for the purposes of subsection (2)(b) is—
  (a) benefit from conduct which constitutes the offence;
  (b) benefit from any other conduct which forms part of the course of criminal activity and which constitutes an offence of which the defendant has been convicted;
  (c) benefit from conduct which constitutes an offence which has been or will be taken into consideration by the court in sentencing the defendant for an offence mentioned in paragraph (a) or (b).

(6) Relevant benefit for the purposes of subsection (2)(c) is—
  (a) benefit from conduct which constitutes the offence;

(b) benefit from conduct which constitutes an offence which has been or will be taken into consideration by the court in sentencing the defendant for the offence mentioned in paragraph (a).

Proceeds of Crime Act 2002, s 75

All the criminal offences which attract the provisions of this section are identified in Sch 2 to the Proceeds of Crime Act 2002.

Explanatory notes

- The criminal lifestyle tests are designed to identify individuals who may be living off crime and make them account for their assets, which are liable to be confiscated if the person is unable to account for their lawful origin.

- The first test is that he is convicted of an offence specified in Sch 2.

- The second test is that the defendant is convicted of an offence of any description, provided that it was committed over a period of at least six months, and obtained not less than £5,000 from that offence and/or any others taken into consideration by the court on the same occasion.

- The third test is that the defendant is convicted of a combination of offences amounting to 'a course of criminal activity'.

- This third test is more complicated than the other two. The defendant satisfies it if he has been convicted in the current proceedings of four or more offences of any description from which he has benefitted; or any one such offence and has other convictions for any such offences on at least two separate occasions in the last six years.

- In addition, the total benefit from the offence(s), and/or any others taken into consideration by the court, must be not less than £5,000.

- The purpose of confiscation proceedings under s 6 is to recover the financial benefit that the offender has obtained from his criminal conduct. Proceedings are conducted according to the civil standard of proof, being on the balance of probabilities.

- In certain circumstances, the court is empowered to assume that the defendant's assets, and his income and expenditure during the period of six years before proceedings were brought, have been derived from criminal conduct and to calculate the confiscation order accordingly.

- Confiscation orders may be made in the Crown Court following conviction. Where the conviction takes place in the magistrates' court, a confiscation order can only be made if the defendant is either committed to the Crown Court for sentence or for sentence and confiscation under s 70.

Chapter 10

Cyber-Enabled Child Protection Offences

10.1 Introduction

This chapter will look at the key criminal offences which relate to sexual offending against children which can be, and quite often are, cyber-enabled. They fall into two categories and are potentially damaging and dangerous in their effect. The key categories are online grooming and the proliferation of indecent images of children.

10.1.1 Online grooming

Online grooming offences are catered for by the Sexual Offences Act 2003. These offences relate to the use of digital technology to facilitate online or offline sexual contact with children. The online scenarios range from the use of chat rooms, social networking sites and gaming sites where the opportunities to befriend children are many. This type of activity falls within the category of child exploitation and provides the offender with a fulfilment of their sexual motivations without necessarily meeting the child. Offenders often take on the persona of a child/peer and will then move on to make threats and even blackmail to achieve their aims.

Linked to this area of offending is the offence of voyeurism, created again by the Sexual Offences Act 2003. With the advances of online communication, recording facilities and the subsequent invasion of privacy, voyeurism in itself can quite often be a precursor to other criminal offences both on- and offline.

10.1.2 **Proliferation of indecent images of children**

There are a variety of offences which address the increase in type and quantity of images online. It is important to be able to distinguish between the offences which are available to address a variety of different situations. The Protection of Children Act 1978 was precise in its original intentions and was developed by s 160 of the Criminal Justice Act 1988 to address a loophole relating to pure possession of the images. Most recently, s 62 of the Coroners and Justice Act 2009 brought the context of the legislation up to date, to deal with the glut of what were described as prohibited images online, such as avatars (which were not photographs).

The precursor to all these pieces of legislation was the Obscene Publications Act 1959 which once again has been brought up to date and includes data stored in any form. It is more precise in what it has to offer but comes with many safeguards as it does not purely deal with children. The relevant offence(s) are included in this chapter so that all options relating to the protection of children are available.

10.2 **Arrange/Facilitate Commission of a Child Sex Offence**

This offence is created by s 14 of the Sexual Offences Act 2003.

Offence

A person commits an offence if—
(a) he intentionally arranges or facilitates something that he intends to do, intends another person to do, or believes that another person will do, in any part of the world, and
(b) doing it will involve the commission of an offence under any of sections 9 to 13.

Sexual Offences Act 2003, s 14(1)

Points to prove

✓ intentionally
✓ arranged/facilitated
✓ an act which the defendant
✓ intended to do or
✓ intended/believed another person would do
✓ in any part of the world
✓ and doing it will involve the commission of an offence
✓ under s 9, 10, 11, 12 or 13

Meanings

Intentionally

This is the defendant's aim or purpose in pursuing a particular course of action. If the defendant intended to commit the act but was physically unable to do so or he admitted that it was his intent, then the law states that he still had the necessary intent.

Arranges

Organise or plan, reach agreement about an action or event in advance.

Facilitates

Make it happen, make it easier to achieve or promote.

Explanatory notes

- The defendant does not have to be the one who will commit the sexual offence; it will be enough if they intended/believed that they or another person will commit the relevant offence in any part of the world.

- The offence covers a situation where the defendant takes a person to a place where there is a child in the belief that the person is likely to engage in sexual activity with that child.

- It also caters for situations whereby the defendant arranges for them or another the procurement of a child, with whom they propose to engage in sexual activity. For example, the defendant is going on holiday and plans to engage in sexual activity with children whilst there and so arranges through an agency to meet children.

- The sexual activity does not have to occur for the offence to be committed.

- The relevant offences are:
  - ✦ sexual activity with a child—s 9;
  - ✦ causing or inciting a child to engage in sexual activity—s 10;
  - ✦ engaging in sexual activity in the presence of a child—s 11;
  - ✦ causing a child to watch a sexual act—s 12;
  - ✦ child sex offences committed by children or young persons—s 13.

Defences

(2) A person does not commit an offence under this section if—
  (a) he arranges or facilitates something that he believes another person will do, but that he does not intend to do or intend another person to do, and
  (b) any offence within subsection (1)(b) would be an offence against a child for whose **protection** he acts.

(3) For the purposes of subsection (2), a person acts for the **protection** of a child if he acts for the purposes of—
  (a) protecting the child from sexually transmitted infection,
  (b) protecting the physical safety of the child,
  (c) preventing the child from becoming pregnant, or
  (d) promoting the child's emotional well-being by the giving of advice, and not for the purpose of obtaining sexual gratification or for the purpose of causing or encouraging the activity constituting the offence within subsection (1)(b) or the child's participation in it.

Sexual Offences Act 2003, s 14

Defence note

This is intended to protect those people, such as health-care workers, who are aware that a person is having sex with a child under 16 and gives them condoms as they believe that if they do not, the child will have unprotected sex. It appears as if the health-care worker must warn the person that what they are doing is illegal, but is allowed to give the condoms without committing an offence under this section.

Practical considerations

- The specified offence (under ss 9 to 13) does not have to take place. If it does occur or would have occurred if it were not for there being facts which made the commission of the offence impossible, then it may be easier to prove the above offence.
- Obtain any evidence which proves the links (e.g. advertisement, emails, bookings for hotels).

- Seize mobile phone, computer hard drive and any other physical evidence relevant to the offence.
- This offence is listed as a 'criminal lifestyle' offence under Sch 2 to the Proceeds of Crime Act 2002.
- The Child Sex Offender (CSO) disclosure scheme is operated by CEOP. For further guidance and details about this matter, see Home Office Circular 7/2010.

 Either way offence

 Time limit for prosecution: none

Summary: maximum 6 months' imprisonment and/or fine
Indictment: maximum 14 years' imprisonment

10.3 Meeting a Child Following Sexual Grooming

This offence is created by s 15 of the Sexual Offences Act 2003.

Offences

A person aged 18 or over (A) commits an offence if—
(a) A has met or communicated with another person (B) on one or more occasions and subsequently—
  (i) A intentionally meets B,
  (ii) A travels with the intention of meeting B in any part of the world or arranges to meet B in any part of the world, or
  (iii) B travels with the intention of meeting A in any part of the world,
(b) A intends to do anything to or in respect of B, during or after the meeting mentioned in paragraph (a)(i) to (iii) and in any part of the world, which if done will involve the commission by A of a relevant offence,
(c) B is under 16, and
(d) A does not reasonably believe that B is 16 or over.

Sexual Offences Act 2003, s 15(1)

Points to prove

- ✓ being a person 18 or over (A)
- ✓ has on at least one or more earlier occasions met/ communicated
- ✓ with a person under 16 (B)
- ✓ not reasonably believing that person to be 16 or over
- ✓ intentionally met **or** travelled intending to meet **or** arranged to meet that person **or** that person has travelled with the intention of meeting A
- ✓ in any part of the world
- ✓ intending to do anything to/in respect of that person
- ✓ during/after the meeting and in any part of the world
- ✓ which if done would involve commission by A
- ✓ of a relevant offence

Meanings

Has met or communicated

The reference to A having met or communicated with B is a reference to A having met B in any part of the world or having communicated with B by any means from, to or in any part of the world.

Intentionally (see 10.2)

Relevant offence

Means an offence under Part 1 (ss 1 to 79 of the Sexual Offences Act 2003 inclusive) and anything done outside England and Wales being an offence within Part 1.

Reasonably believe (see 'Defence' below)

Explanatory notes

- Recent changes have been implemented to lower the number of occasions a defendant must have communicated with the person. It now is only one or more occasions that the offender must have communicated or met with the person. The communication could be by telephone, texting, Twitter or email. These communications do not have to contain sexually explicit language or pornography but could, for example, be something as seemingly innocuous as the offender giving the victim swimming lessons or meeting them incidentally through a friend.

- They must intentionally meet or travel with the intention of meeting or arranging to meet each other. This meeting can take place anywhere in the world as long as some part of the journey took place in England, Wales or Northern Ireland.
- The meeting itself does not have to take place, arranging will suffice, although the intent to commit the relevant offence (in any part of the world) will have to be proved.
- This offence is intended to deal with predators who groom young children by gaining their trust and lying about their age, then arranging to meet them in order to sexually abuse them. This offence is preventative, in that the relevant sexual offence does not have to occur in order for the offence to be committed.

Defence

Reasonable belief that the victim is 16 or over.

Defence notes

- If the victim is aged between 13 and 15, the prosecution must provide evidence that the defendant's belief was not reasonable. For example, that the defendant knew that a girl attended school and had not yet taken her GCSE examinations.
- However, if the defendant and the complainant met for the first time over the internet, the complainant provided photographs of her in which she looked much older than she in fact was and if she told the defendant that she was 18 and looked 18, then the belief may be reasonable.
- If the prosecution can provide such evidence, it is open to the defendant to rebut it, if he can show on the balance of probabilities that his belief was reasonably held.

Related cases

R v G [2010] EWCA Crim 1693   There is no requirement that either communication be sexual in nature. A sexual intent must exist at the time of arranging the meeting, but the meeting does not have to take place.

R v Mohammed [2006] EWCA Crim 1107   M sent intimate text messages to a vulnerable 13-year-old girl, with severe learning difficulties and behavioural problems. Both were found together 8 miles from her foster home. M confirmed she had visited his home; the abduction was short-lived, with the girl being willing and initiating contact, but no sexual act had taken place. M's motivation was sexual and he had blatantly taken her from the control of carers. Convicted of child abduction and s 15(1).

R v Mansfield [2005] EWCA Crim 927 'The law is there to protect young girls against their own immature sexual experimentation and to punish older men who take advantage of them.'

Practical considerations

- Prove that the victim is under 16. Only a suitably trained or qualified person should be used to take a statement or obtain evidence from the victim.
- Any articles in the defendant's possession such as condoms, pornography, rope and lubricant could help to prove intent.
- The Children Act 2004 makes specific provision for the police and other agencies to protect the welfare and safety of children.
- Offence applies to all offences in Part 1 of the Act (ss 1 to 79).
- All evidence in relation to the grooming should be seized (e.g. any communications, bookings or other documents which link the defendant and victim).
- Consider CCTV evidence.
- Seize any computer and mobile phone that could have been used.
- Section 72 allows sexual offences committed outside the UK to be dealt with in England and Wales, as if the person had committed the act in the UK provided certain conditions are met. The conditions are that the defendant is a UK national or resident who commits an act in a country outside the UK, and the act, if committed in England and Wales, would constitute a sexual offence given in Sch 2.

 Either way offence

 Time limit for prosecution: none

 Summary: maximum 6 months' imprisonment and/or fine
Indictment: maximum 10 years' imprisonment

10.4 **Voyeurism**

This offence is created by s 67 of the Sexual Offences Act 2003 and would be and can be demonstrated within the cyber world by, for example, a landlord setting up a webcam in rooms he rents out, without the knowledge of the tenants and linking up the product to the internet. One point which needs to be stressed is that the whole point of conducting things this way would be for his sexual gratification or that of another third person.

Offences

(1) A person commits an offence if—
  (a) for the purpose of obtaining sexual gratification, he observes another person doing a private act, and
  (b) he knows that the other person does not consent to being observed for his sexual gratification.
(2) A person commits an offence if—
  (a) he operates equipment with the intention of enabling another person to observe, for the purpose of obtaining sexual gratification, a third person (B) doing a private act, and
  (b) he knows that B does not consent to his operating equipment with that intention.
(3) A person commits an offence if—
  (a) he records another person (B) doing a private act,
  (b) he does so with the intention that he or a third person will, for the purpose of obtaining sexual gratification, look at an image of B doing the act, and
  (c) he knows that B does not consent to his recording the act with that intention.
(4) A person commits an offence if he installs equipment, or constructs or adapts a structure or part of a structure, with the intention of enabling himself or another person to commit an offence under subsection (1).

Sexual Offences Act 2003, s 67

Points to prove

Observing (s 67(1))

✓ for purpose of obtaining sexual gratification
✓ observed another person
✓ doing a private act

✓ knowing that the person
✓ does not consent to being observed
✓ for defendant's sexual gratification

Operating equipment to observe (s 67(2))

✓ operated equipment
✓ with the intention of enabling another person
✓ for the purpose of obtaining sexual gratification
✓ to observe a third person doing a private act
✓ knowing that person does not consent
✓ to defendant operating equipment for that intention

Recording a private act (s 67(3))

✓ recorded another person doing a private act
✓ with intention that
✓ defendant or a third person
✓ would for the purpose of obtaining sexual gratification
✓ look at an image of that other person doing the act
✓ knowing that the other person does not consent
✓ to defendant recording the act with that intention

Install equipment/construct/adapt a structure (s 67(4))

✓ installed equipment **or**
✓ constructed/adapted a structure/part of a structure
✓ with intent
✓ to enable defendant or third person
✓ to commit an offence under s 67(1)

Meanings
Private act

A person is doing a private act if they are in a place where they could reasonably expect privacy and their genitals, breasts or buttocks are exposed or covered only by underwear, they are using the toilet, or doing a sexual act that is not normally done in public.

Consent

Defendant must **know** that the person does not consent to being observed for **sexual gratification**. They may have consented to being observed for some other reason.

Sexual gratification

In s 67(1), the sexual gratification must be for the defendant; in the other subsections it could be for a third party's sexual gratification.

Structure

Includes a tent, vehicle or vessel, or other temporary or movable structure.

Explanatory notes

- Previously it was not an offence to watch someone for sexual gratification. This will cater for such situations involving unsolicited webcams filming innocent parties.
- For s 67(2)–(4), it is irrelevant whether or not any third parties knew that the person did not consent.
- Section 67(2) is aimed at those who install webcams or other recording equipment for their own gratification or for that of others. An image is defined as 'a moving or still image and includes an image produced by any means and, where the context permits, a three-dimensional image'.
- Section 67(4) would cover a person who installed a two-way mirror or a spy-hole in a hotel room. The offender would commit the offence even if the peephole or mirror was discovered before it was ever used.

Related case

R v Bassett [2008] EWCA Crim 1174 Whether a person had a reasonable expectation of privacy would depend on the facts in each case and would be closely related to the nature of the observation taking place. Some parts of the body are those which people would expect privacy for (e.g. female breasts as opposed to the bare male chest).

Practical considerations

- Any equipment used requires seizing.
- CCTV footage may be of use.
- Search for films made and evidence of equipment hire.
- Medium/equipment used for recording/storing image can be seized for examination and evidence.

 Either way offence

 Time limit for prosecution: none

Summary: maximum 6 months' imprisonment and/or fine

Indictment: maximum 2 years' imprisonment

10.5 **Possession of Prohibited Image of a Person Under 18**

This offence is created by s 62 of the Coroners and Justice Act 2009.

Offence

It is an offence for a person to be in possession of a prohibited image of a child.

Coroners and Justice Act 2009, s 62(1)

Points to prove

✓ in possession

✓ prohibited image

✓ of a child

Meanings

Prohibited image

- The image is pornographic;
- the image is grossly offensive, disgusting or otherwise of an obscene character;
- the image focuses solely or principally on a child's genitals or anal region or portrays any of the following acts:
  + the performance by a person of an act of intercourse or oral sex with or in the presence of a child;
  + an act of masturbation by, of, involving or in the presence of a child;
  + an act which involves penetration of the vagina or anus of a child with a part of a person's body or with anything else;
  + an act of penetration, in the presence of a child, of a vagina or anus of a person with a part of a person's body or with anything else;

* the performance by a child of an act of intercourse or oral sex with an animal (whether dead or alive or imaginary);
* the performance by a person of an act of intercourse or oral sex with an animal (whether dead or alive or imaginary) in the presence of a child.

Pornographic

The image has to have been produced solely or principally for the purpose of sexual arousal—not necessarily of the defendant.

Grossly offensive

Disgusting or otherwise of an obscene character.

All the terms are to be read in line with their dictionary definitions.

Child

A person under the age of 18 years.

Explanatory notes

* Where an individual image is held in a person's possession as part of a larger series of images. The question of whether the image is pornographic must be determined by reference both to the image itself and also the context in which it appears in the larger series of images. Take, for example, the circumstances where an image is integral to a narrative such as a documentary film which, if taken as a whole, could not reasonably be assumed to be pornographic. That image itself may be taken not to be pornographic, even if were it considered in isolation, a contrary conclusion would have been reached.

* Should the images be part of a British Board of Film Classification classified film then they are taken outside the scope of the offence. However, these are not deemed to be so should they have been removed in isolation principally for the purposes of sexual arousal where the benefit of context has been lost and the image is kept on its own or with other images. The legitimacy of the extraction of the image will be for a court to decide.

* An image includes a moving or still image (produced by any means), or data stored (by any means) which is capable of conversion into an 'image'. For the purpose of the offence an 'image' does not include an indecent photograph, or indecent pseudo-photograph of a child, because such images are covered by existing legislation, as outlined below.

* In normal circumstances, deleting images held on a computer is sufficient to get rid of them, i.e. not to be in possession of

them. There is case law to provide an exception to this (see
Porter in 'Related cases' in **10.7**).

- The offence was not created for those who accidentally find
  prohibited images while searching for legal material on the
  internet. As with the position regarding deleted images, the
  main issue will be whether the person has control and custody
  and therefore possession of that image.

- Offenders aged 18 or above who receive a sentence of two years'
  imprisonment or more shall automatically be made subject to
  notification requirements under Part 2 of the Sexual Offences
  Act 2003.

- This covers material available on computers, mobile phones or
  any other electronic device.

Defences

Section 64 of the Coroners and Justice Act 2009 provides defences for
the offence under s 62.

(1) Where a person is charged with an offence under section 62(1), it is
    a defence for the person to prove any of the following matters—
    (a) that the person had a legitimate reason for being in possession of
        the image concerned;
    (b) that the person had not seen the image concerned and did not
        know, nor had any cause to suspect, it to be a prohibited image of
        a child;
    (c) that the person—
        (i) was sent the image concerned without any prior request hav-
            ing been made by or on behalf of the person, and
        (ii) did not keep it for an unreasonable time.

(2) In this section prohibited image has the same meaning as in
    section 62.

Coroners and Justice Act 2009, s 64

Defence notes

- The defence provided at s 64(1)(a) relates to those who are able to
  show that their legitimate business means that they have a reason for
  possessing the image. This would include, for example, the police and
  the prosecuting authorities, those involved in the classification of films,
  those dealing with complaints from the public about content in the
  mobile and internet industries, such as the Internet Watch Foundation,
  and those creating security software to block such images.

- The defence provided in s 64(1)(b) caters for situations where, for example, a person is in possession of an image which had been inadvertently downloaded from the internet, which was as far as they were concerned deleted but which, due to a lack of IT skills, they did not realise was still being stored as a back-up copy or in the system's 'History'.
- The defence provided in s 64(1)(c) covers those who are sent unsolicited material by any means and who act quickly to delete it or otherwise get rid of it. What constitutes an unreasonable amount of time depends on all the circumstances of the case.
- In a Crown Court case the 'Trojan Horse' virus defence was successful. In short, expert evidence confirmed the likelihood of this virus being responsible for 14 depraved images saved on the defendant's personal computer. It was accepted that these could have been sent remotely, without the defendant's knowledge. Although this case is not binding on other courts, and each case will be determined according to its own particular facts, officers should be aware of the possibility of this defence being raised.

Related case

R v Steven Freeman In 2011, the Metropolitan Police secured a first conviction under s 62 of the Coroners and Justice Act 2009. It was seen as a landmark decision as it captured indecent drawings of children which were not photographic. Over 3,000 drawings were found at Freeman's home which he traded with other members of the Paedophile Information Exchange. Freeman was sentenced to prison for an indeterminate length of time but a minimum of 30 months. Albeit the case was not internet-based, it shows that indecent drawings do fall within the ambit of this Act.

Practical considerations

- Proceedings for this offence require the consent of the DPP.
- If the offender receives more than 2 years' imprisonment, then they are to be made subject of notification requirements under the Sexual Offences Act 2003.
- Seize all computer equipment as evidence under s 20 of PACE.
- Schedule 11 to the Protection of Children Act 1978 permits forfeiture of indecent images of children and the devices that hold them without the involvement of a court, unless the owner or other person with an interest in the material objects, gives notice of a legitimate claim to the property.
- Any such image found in possession of a school pupil by a member of staff at the school can be given to a police constable

(Schools Specification and Disposal of Articles Regulations 2012, reg 550ZA).

- There are some authoritative factors in deciding whether or not a defence may apply, depending on whether the person(s):

  - acted reasonably in all the circumstances;
  - reported the images as soon as was practicable and to the appropriate authority;
  - stored the images in a secure and safe manner;
  - inappropriately copied or distributed the images unnecessarily.

 Either way offence

 Time limit for prosecution: none

 Summary: maximum 12 months' imprisonment and/or fine
Indictment: maximum 3 years' imprisonment

10.6 **Take, Distribute, Publish Indecent Photograph(s) of Person Under 18**

This offence is created by s 1 of the Protection of Children Act 1978.

Offences

Subject to sections 1A and 1B [defences], it is an offence for a person—

(a) to take, or permit to be taken, or to make, any indecent photograph or pseudo-photograph of a child; or

(b) to distribute or show such indecent photographs or pseudo-photographs; or

(c) to have in his possession such indecent photographs or pseudo-photographs, with a view to their being distributed or shown by himself and others; or

(d) to publish or cause to be published any advertisement likely to be understood as conveying that the advertiser distributes or shows such indecent photographs or pseudo-photographs or intends to do so.

Protection of Children Act 1978, s 1(1)

Points to prove

Section 1(1)(a), (b)

✓ made/permitted to be taken/took/showed/distributed
✓ indecent photograph(s)/pseudo-photograph(s)
✓ of a child/children

Section 1(1)(c)

✓ possessed
✓ indecent photograph(s)/pseudo-photograph(s)
✓ of child/children
✓ with a view to it (them) being distributed/shown to another

Section 1(1)(d)

✓ published/caused to be published
✓ an advertisement which is likely to convey or be understood
✓ that the advertiser
✓ distributes/shows or intends to distribute/show
✓ indecent photograph(s)/pseudo-photograph(s)
✓ of child/children

Meanings

Make

Includes downloading images from the internet and storing or printing them (*R v Bowden* [2000] 1 WLR 1427).

Indecent photographs

- Includes indecent film, a copy of an indecent **photograph** or **film** and an indecent photograph comprised in a film.
- Photographs (including those comprised in a film) shall, if they show children and are indecent, be treated for all purposes of this Act as indecent photographs of children and so as respects pseudo-photographs.

Photograph

References to a photograph include:

- the negative as well as the positive version; and
- data stored on a computer disc or by other electronic means which is capable of conversion into a photograph;

- a tracing or other image, whether made by electronic or other means (of whatever nature)—

  - which is not itself a photograph or pseudo-photograph; but
  - which is derived from the whole or part of a photograph or pseudo-photograph (or a combination of either or both);

and data stored on a computer disc or by other electronic means which is capable of conversion into the above tracing or image.

Note: if the impression conveyed by a pseudo-photograph is that of a child, the pseudo-photograph shall be treated as showing a child and so shall a pseudo-photograph where the predominant impression conveyed is that the person shown is a child notwithstanding that some of the physical characteristics shown are those of an adult.

Film

This includes any form of video recording.

Pseudo-photograph

Means an image, whether made by computer graphics or otherwise howsoever, which appears to be a photograph.

Indecent pseudo-photograph

This includes a copy of an indecent pseudo-photograph; and data stored on a computer disc or by other electronic means which is capable of conversion into an indecent pseudo-photograph.

Child (see **10.5**)

Distribute

Means to part with possession to another person, or exposes or offers for acquisition by another person.

Shown by himself

Means shown by the defendant to other people.

Explanatory notes

- The image does not have to be stored in a way that allows it to be retrieved. However, the image must be made deliberately. Innocently opening a file from the internet may not be an offence, see s 1(4)(b) in '**Defences**' below.
- The attendant circumstances of the way in which the images have been downloaded, stored, labelled and filed will be important in demonstrating the extent to which the defendant

was or should have been aware of their indecent nature. Other correspondence (by email or otherwise) with the defendant will also be useful here, as will any evidence of a general interest in paedophilia (*R v Mould* [2001] 2 Crim App R (S) 8).

Defences

Section 1

(4) Where a person is charged with an offence under subsection 1(b) or (c), it shall be a defence for him to prove—

  (a) that he had a legitimate reason for distributing or showing the photographs or pseudo-photographs or (as the case may be) having them in his possession; or

  (b) that he had not himself seen the photographs or pseudo-photographs and did not know, nor had any cause to suspect, them to be indecent.

Section 1A: marriage and partnership

(1) This section applies where, in proceedings for an offence under s 1(1)(a) of taking or making an indecent photograph or pseudo-photograph of a child, or for an offence under s 1(1)(b) or (c) relating to an indecent photograph or pseudo-photograph of a child, the defendant proves that the photograph or pseudo-photograph was of the child aged 16 or over, and that at the time of the offence charged the child and he—

  (a) were married or civil partners of each other, or

  (b) lived together as partners in an enduring family relationship.

(2) Subsections (5) and (6) also apply where, in proceedings for an offence under s 1(1)(b) or (c) relating to an indecent photograph or pseudo-photograph of a child, the defendant proves that the photograph or pseudo-photograph was of the child aged 16 or over, and that at the time when he obtained it the child and he—

  (a) were married or civil partners of each other, or

  (b) lived together as partners in an enduring family relationship.

(3) This section applies whether the photograph or pseudo-photograph showed the child alone or with the defendant, but not if it showed any other person.

(4) In the case of an offence under s 1(1)(a), if sufficient evidence is adduced to raise an issue as to whether the child consented to the photograph or pseudo-photograph being taken or made, or as to whether the defendant reasonably believed that the child so consented, the defendant is not guilty of the offence unless it is proved that the child did not so consent and that the defendant did not reasonably believe that the child so consented.

(5) In the case of an offence under s 1(1)(b), the defendant is not guilty of the offence unless it is proved that the showing or distributing was to a person other than the child.

(6) In the case of an offence under s 1(1)(c), if sufficient evidence is adduced to raise an issue both—

(a) as to whether the child consented to the photograph or pseudo-photograph being in the defendant's possession, or as to whether the defendant reasonably believed that the child so consented, and

(b) as to whether the defendant had the photograph or pseudo-photograph in his possession with a view to its being distributed or shown to anyone other than the child,

the defendant is not guilty of the offence unless it is proved either that the child did not so consent and that the defendant did not reasonably believe that the child so consented, or that the defendant had the photograph or pseudo-photograph in his possession with a view to its being distributed or shown to a person other than the child.

Section 1B: instances when defendant is not guilty of the offence

(1) In proceedings for an offence under s 1(1)(a) of making an indecent photograph or pseudo-photograph of a child, the defendant is not guilty of the offence if he proves that—

(a) it was necessary for him to make the photograph or pseudo-photograph for the purposes of the prevention, detection or investigation of crime, or for the purposes of criminal proceedings, in any part of the world,

(b) at the time of the offence charged he was a member of the Security Service or the Secret Intelligence Service, and it was necessary for him to make the photograph or pseudo-photograph for the exercise of any of the functions of that Service, or

(c) at the time of the offence charged he was a member of GCHQ, and it was necessary for him to make the photograph or pseudo-photograph for the exercise of any of the functions of GCHQ.

(2) In this section 'GCHQ' has the same meaning as in the Intelligence Services Act 1994.

Protection of Children Act 1978, ss 1(4), 1A and 1B

Defence notes

• The defence given in s 1(4)(b) as to 'not seeing and did not know, nor had any cause to suspect, them to be indecent' would cater for situations where an email attachment was opened innocently and not subsequently deleted owing to a genuine lack of IT skills (e.g. may still be in a 'deleted' directory, 'recycle bin' or other 'temporary' directory) or innocently downloading an image from the web, then immediately deleting the image without realising that it was also stored as a back-up copy in a temporary internet directory.

- In a Crown Court case the 'Trojan Horse' virus defence was successful. In short, expert evidence confirmed the likelihood of this virus being responsible for 14 depraved images saved on the defendant's personal computer. It was accepted that these could have been sent remotely, without the defendant's knowledge. Although this case is not binding on other courts, and each case will be determined according to its own particular facts, officers should be aware of the possibility of this defence being raised.

Related cases

R v Dooley [2005] EWCA Crim 3093 If downloaded material was accessible to all club members then it is downloaded with a view to its distribution or showing to others.

R v T (1999) 163 JP 349, CA Courts will **not** accept an intention by the offender to show photographs to himself as sufficient to prove the offence under s 1(1)(c).

R v Smith and Jayson [2002] 1 Cr App R 13, CA Deliberately opening an indecent computer email attachment or downloading an indecent image from the internet, so that it can be viewed on a screen, is making a photograph.

R v Bowden [2001] 1 WLR 1427, CA Downloading would come within s 1 'to make' as a file is created when the photograph is downloaded.

Practical considerations

- It is not an offence under this Act to possess photographs to show to yourself, although this is an offence under s 160 of the Criminal Justice Act 1988 (see **10.7**).
- MOJ Circular 6/2010 provides guidelines about extending the 'marriage/other relationships' provisions to offences relating to indecent pseudo-photographs of persons under 18.
- Proceedings for this offence require the consent of the DPP.
- Ascertain how the photographs or pseudo-photographs were made, discovered and whether stored.
- Seize all computer equipment as evidence under s 20 of PACE.
- The Schedule to the 1978 Act permits forfeiture of indecent images of children and the devices that hold them without the

involvement of a court, unless the owner or other person with an interest in the material objects gives notice of a legitimate claim to the property.

- There are some authoritative factors in deciding whether or not a defence may apply, depending on whether the person(s):
  + acted reasonably in all the circumstances;
  + reported the photographs or pseudo-photographs as soon as was practicable and to the appropriate authority;
  + stored the photographs or pseudo-photographs in a secure and safe manner;
  + copied or distributed the photographs or pseudo-photographs unnecessarily.

 Either way offence

 Time limit for prosecution: none

 Summary: maximum 6 months' imprisonment and/or fine
Indictment: maximum 10 years' imprisonment

10.7 **Possession of Indecent Photograph(s) of Person Under 18**

Section 160 of the Criminal Justice Act 1988 concerns the offence of simple possession of indecent photographs or pseudo-photographs of a person under 18.

Offence

Subject to section 160A it is an offence for a person to have any indecent photograph or pseudo-photograph of a child in his possession.

Criminal Justice Act 1988, s 160(1)

Points to prove

✓ possessed
✓ indecent photo(s)/pseudo-photograph(s)
✓ of a child/children

10 Cyber-Enabled Child Protection Offences

Meanings

Section 160A (see 'Defences' below)

Photographs (see **10.6**)

Indecent photograph (see **10.6**)

Pseudo-photograph (see **10.6**)

Child (see **10.5**)

Explanatory note

Where there is evidence of intent to distribute or show then the offence under s 1 of the Protection of Children Act 1978 should be used.

Defences

Section 160

(2) Where a person is charged with an offence under subsection (1) above it shall be a defence for him to prove—

  (a) that he had a legitimate reason for having the photograph or pseudo-photograph in his possession; or

  (b) that he had not himself seen the photograph or pseudo-photograph and did not know, nor had any cause to suspect, it to be indecent; or

  (c) that the photograph or pseudo-photograph was sent to him without any prior request made by him or on his behalf and that he did not keep it for an unreasonable time.

Section 160A

(1) This section applies where, in proceedings for an offence under section 160 relating to an indecent photograph or pseudo-photograph of a child, the defendant proves that the photograph or pseudo-photograph was of the child aged 16 or over, and that at the time of the offence charged the child and he—

  (a) were married or civil partners of each other, or

  (b) lived together as partners in an enduring family relationship.

(2) This section also applies where, in proceedings for an offence under section 160 relating to an indecent photograph or pseudo-photograph of a child, the defendant proves that the photograph or pseudo-photograph was of the child aged 16 or over, and that at the time when he obtained it the child and he—

  (a) were married or civil partners of each other, or

  (b) lived together as partners in an enduring family relationship.

(3) This section applies whether the photograph or pseudo-photograph showed the child alone or with the defendant, but not if it showed any other person.

(4) If sufficient evidence is adduced to raise an issue as to whether the child consented to the photograph or pseudo-photograph being in the defendant's possession, or as to whether the defendant reasonably believed that the child so consented, the defendant is not guilty of the offence unless it is proved that the child did not so consent and that the defendant did not reasonably believe that the child so consented.

Criminal Justice Act 1988, ss 160 and 160A

Defence note

The conditions for the defence are listed under s 160A(1)–(4) as outlined above. If any of these conditions are not satisfied, the prosecution need only prove the offence as set out in s 160. But if the three conditions are satisfied, the defendant is not guilty of the offence unless the prosecution proves that the child did not consent and that the defendant did not reasonably believe that the child consented.

Related cases

R v Porter [2006] EWCA Crim 560 The computer hard drives of P were found to contain deleted images which could only be retrieved using specialist software, which P did not have. If a person cannot access deleted images on a computer then he is no longer in custody, control or possession of those images. The jury must decide on this issue having regard to all the relevant circumstances and the defendant's knowledge at the time.

R v Matrix [1997] Crim LR 901, CA A shop assistant may possess indecent photographs as well as the shop owner.

Atkins v DPP and Goodland v DPP [2000] 2 All ER 425, QBD Atkins: images stored in a temporary directory unbeknown to the defendant did not amount to possession, knowledge was required.

Practical considerations

- Ensure that the photographs or pseudo-photographs are seized.
- Seize the computer or storage mechanism as evidence under s 20 of PACE.

- The Schedule to the 1978 Protection of Children Act also permits forfeiture of indecent images of children and the devices that hold them without the involvement of a court, unless the owner or other person with an interest in the material objects gives notice of a legitimate claim to the property.
- Check on the audit chain for the photograph and documents relating to them to ensure possession is the only suitable charge.
- Consent of the DPP required.
- MOJ Circular 6/2010 provides guidelines about extending the 'marriage/other relationships' provisions to offences relating to indecent pseudo-photographs of persons under 18.

 Either way offence

 Time limit for prosecution: none

 Summary: maximum 6 months' imprisonment and/or level 5 fine
Indictment: maximum 5 years' imprisonment and/or fine

10.8 **Possession of a Paedophile Manual**

Section 69 of the Serious Crime Act 2015 creates an offence of possessing a paedophile manual. As shown previously in this chapter, there are already a number of criminal offences which seek to prevent the possession, creation and distribution of indecent images of children and dissemination of that material.

These offences do not criminalise mere possession of material containing advice and guidance about grooming and abusing a child sexually. This offence plugs that gap in the law.

Offence

It is an offence to be in possession of any item that contains advice or guidance about abusing children sexually.

Serious Crime Act 2015, s 69

Points to prove

✓ possession

✓ item

✓ abusing children sexually

Meanings

Possession

The state of having, owning or controlling something.

Item

Includes anything in which any information is recorded. This should be interpreted widely and includes both physical and electronic documents (e.g. emails and information downloaded from a computer/internet).

Abusing children sexually

Means doing anything that constitutes:

(a) an offence under Part 1 of the Sexual Offences Act 2003, against a person under 16, or

(b) an offence under s 1 of the Protection of Children Act 1978, involving indecent photographs (but not pseudo-photographs), or doing anything outside England and Wales or Northern Ireland that would constitute such an offence if done in England and Wales or Northern Ireland.

Defences

- That the person had a legitimate reason for being in possession of the item. This would be a question of fact for the jury to decide and each case should be treated on its own merit—for example, where possession is through work requirements;
- that the person had not seen (or listened to) the item in his possession and therefore neither knew, nor had cause to suspect, that it contained advice or guidance about abusing children sexually; and
- that the person had not asked for the item—it having been sent without request—and that he had not kept it for an unreasonable period of time; this will cover those who are sent unsolicited material and who act quickly to delete it or otherwise get rid of it.

Serious Crime Act 2015, s 69(2)

Defence note

The standard of proof with all these defences is that based on the balance of probabilities.

Practical considerations

- The offence allows for broad powers of forfeiture to be applied—under s 143 of the Powers of Criminal Courts Act 1973—which allows the court to make an order depriving an offender of his rights to articles used and conferring powers on the police to take possession of the property.
- In addition, the power under s 5 and the Schedule to the Protection of Children Act 1978 confers the power to seize, retain and destroy any indecent photograph or pseudo-photograph of a child and any property which it is not reasonably practicable to separate from that property following lawful seizure.
- These powers will apply to paedophile manuals.
- If possession of photographs and films or pseudo-photographs are also revealed then consider offences under:
  + Obscene Publications Act 1959, s 2;
  + Protection of Children Act 1978, s 1;
  + Criminal Justice Act 1988, s 160;
  + Criminal Justice Act 2008, s 63;
  + Coroners and Justice Act 2009, s 62.
- Remember to seize all equipment and materials. Electronic and IT equipment to be sealed and forwarded to Hi-Tech Crime Units or as appropriate. For computers etc, use s 20 of PACE.
- DPP's consent required.

 Either way offence

 Time limit for prosecution: none

 Summary: maximum 6 months' imprisonment, a fine or both
Indictment: maximum 3 years' imprisonment, a fine or both

10.9 **Publishing Obscene Articles**

This offence is created by s 2 of the Obscene Publications Act 1959.

Offence

Subject as hereinafter provided any person who, whether for gain or not, publishes an obscene article, or who has an obscene article for publication for gain (whether to gain for himself or gain to another) commits an offence.

Obscene Publications Act 1959, s 2(1)

Points to prove

Publishing

✓ publishes
✓ obscene
✓ article

To have an article for publication

✓ has/have
✓ obscene
✓ article

Meanings
Publishes

Distributes, circulates, sells, lets on hire, gives or lends the article, or offers it for sale or for letting on hire or in the case of an article containing or embodying matter to be looked at or a record, shows, plays or projects it, or, where the matter is data stored electronically, transmits that data.

Obscene

For the purposes of this Act, an article shall be deemed to be obscene if its effect or (where the article comprises two or more distinct items) the effect of any one of its items is, if taken as a whole, such as to tend to deprave and corrupt persons who are likely, having regard to all relevant circumstances, to read, see or hear the matter contained or embodied in it.

Article

In this Act 'article' means any description of article containing or embodying matter to be read or looked at or both, any sound record, and any film or other record of a picture or pictures.

Has/have

For the purpose of any proceedings for an offence under s 2 (of the 1959 Act), a person shall be deemed to have an obscene article for publication for gain if with a view to such publication he has the article in his ownership, possession or control.

Explanatory notes

- Section 72 of the Sexual Offences Act 2003 confers extra-territorial jurisdiction on the courts of England and Wales in respect of a number of offences contrary to that Act along with the Protection of Children Act 1978 and s 160 of the Criminal Justice Act 1988. Case law (*R v Perrin*) also ensures that the Obscene Publications Act 1959 is embraced by the territorial jurisdiction and states that the mere transmission of data constitutes publication.

- Prosecution for an offence shall not be commenced without the DPP's consent or more than two years after the commission of the offence.

- The CPS indicate within their charging practice the acts portrayed which will be included in the definition of 'obscene' and they include a sexual act with an animal, realistic portrayals of rape, torture with instruments, bondage, graphic mutilation, perversion/degradation such as drinking urine, excretion or vomiting on the body and fisting.

- Insofar as prosecuting under s 2 of the Obscene Publications Act 1959 is concerned, the CPS will not normally do so for articles portraying consensual sexual intercourse (vaginal or anal), oral sex, masturbation, mild bondage, simulated intercourse or buggery fetishes which do not encourage physical abuse.

- There are principal factors influencing whether a prosecution under s 2 is required and these include:
  + the degree and type of obscenity—pictures speak louder than words;

- ✦ the type and scale of commercial venture should be taken into account;
- ✦ whether publication was made to a vulnerable adult or child, or the possibility that such publication would take place.

- Where children are likely to access material of a degree of sexual explicitness the same as what is available to those aged 18 or over in a licensed sex shop, the material may be considered to be obscene. This applies to the front page of a pornography website, for example, where it is not behind a suitable payment barrier.
- Where publication took place especially if material can readily be seen by the general public, for example on websites easily accessible to children.
- Article 10 relating to Convention rights to freedom of expression has not been infringed by the Obscene Publications Act as it has an aim that is legitimate in protecting the morals in a democratic society.
- Section 1(3) of the Obscene Publications Act 1959 was amended to ensure that electronically stored data or the transmission of such data was included within the Act.
- Alternative offences where the protection of children is at issue will be those defined under the Protection of Children Act 1978, s 166 of the Criminal Justice Act 1988 and s 62 of the Coroners and Justice Act 2009.

Defences

A person shall not be convicted of an offence against this section if he proves that he had not examined the article in respect of which he is charged and had no reasonable cause to suspect that it was such that his publication of it would make him liable to be convicted of an offence contrary to this section.

Obscene Publications Act 1959, s 2(5)

10.10 **Obscene Publications Act 1959, s 2(5)**

Subject to subsection (1A) of this section, a person will not be convicted of an offence against s 2 of this Act if it is proved that publication of the article in question is justified as being for the public good on the grounds that it is in the interests of science, literature, art or learning, or of other objects of general concern.

> Subsection (1) of this section shall not apply where the article in question is a moving picture film or soundtrack, but
>
> (a) a person shall not be convicted of an offence against section 2 of this Act in relation to any such film or soundtrack, and
>
> (b) an order for forfeiture of any such film or soundtrack shall not be made under section 3 of this Act, if it is proved that publication of the film or soundtrack is justified as being for the public good on the ground that it is in the interests of drama, opera, ballet or any other art, or of literature or learning.

Obscene Publications Act 1959, s 4(1A)

Defence notes

- If the defendant avails himself of the statutory defence provided by s 2(5), the onus of proof is on him, but the standard of that proof is less than the prosecution, which is one of beyond reasonable doubt. The standard of proof for the defence is the lower requirement of 'on the balance of probabilities'.
- The defence provided by s 4 is known as one of 'public good'. In this case, the accused has to prove that the publication of the article in question is justified as being for the public good on the ground that it is, for example, in the interests of science, literature, art or learning.

Related cases

Handyside v United Kingdom, 1976, European Court of Human Rights The Obscene Publications Act has an aim that is legitimate under Article 10(2) namely, the protection of morals in a democratic society.

R v Perrin [2002] EWCA Crim 747 This case is specifically concerned with the 'publishing' of electronic data and indicates that the mere transmission of data constitutes publication.

R v Waddon, 6 April 2000, unreported Makes it clear that along with the above stated case that there is publication both when the images are uploaded and when they are downloaded. This case also confirmed that the content of US websites would fall under British jurisdiction when downloaded in the UK.

DPP v Whyte [1972] AC 849 The words 'deprave' and 'corrupt' refer to the effect on the mind including the emotions and it is not necessary that any physical or obvious sexual activity should result.

Practical considerations

- Any equipment used requires seizing.
- Warrant may be issued under Obscene Publications Act 1959 to search, seize and forfeit films and any other data without prosecution (see the following section).
- The courts are slow to accept that police officers can themselves become depraved or be corrupted. Therefore, there is a need to discover the nature of the audience or likely audience aside from themselves.
- Media/equipment used for recording/storing the image can also be seized for examination and evidence.

 Either way offence

 Time limit for prosecution: none

 Summary: maximum 6 months' imprisonment and/or fine
Indictment: maximum 5 years' imprisonment and/or fine

10.10.1 Warrant to search and seize— leading to forfeiture of obscene articles

(1) If a justice of the peace is satisfied by information on oath that there are reasonable grounds for suspecting that, in any premises in that area, or on any stall or vehicle in that area, being premises or a stall or vehicle specified in the information, obscene articles are, or are from time to time, kept for publication for gain, the justice may issue a warrant under his hand empowering any constable to enter (if need be by force) and search the premises, or to search the stall or vehicle, and to seize and remove any articles found therein or thereon which the constable has reason to believe to be obscene articles and to be kept for publication for gain.

(2) A warrant under the foregoing subsection shall, if any obscene articles are seized under the warrant, also empower the seizure and removal of any documents found in the premises or, as the case may be, on the stall or vehicle which relate to a trade or business carried on at the premises or from the stall or vehicle.

(3) Subject to subsection (3A) of this section any articles seized under subsection (1) of this section shall be brought before a justice of the peace acting for the same petty session area as the justice who issued the warrant, and the justice before whom the articles are brought may thereupon issue a summons to the occupier of the premises or, as the case may be, the user of the stall or vehicle to appear on a day specified in the summons before a magistrates' court for that petty sessions area to show cause why the articles or any of them should not be forfeited; and if the court is satisfied as respects any of the articles, that at the time when they were seized they were obscene articles kept for publication for gain, the court shall order those articles to be forfeited.

Obscene Publications Act 1958, s 3

Meanings

Obscene (see **10.9**)

Article (see **10.9**)

Publication (see **10.9**)

Explanatory notes

- Care should be taken to ensure that the wording of a warrant under s 3 is not too wide. It has been held that a warrant authorising a search for 'any other material of a sexually explicit nature' was not lawful. Such articles are not necessarily obscene. (*Darbo v DPP* [1991] CLR 56.)

- The issue of warrants and any subsequent search must be conducted in accordance with the provisions of PACE and Code B to that Act.

- Where the articles were intended for publication outside the jurisdiction of the English courts, the court remains competent and entitled to hold that those articles are obscene.

- If no successful prosecution results, the courts can order forfeiture under s 3.

- Where orders for forfeiture of articles are made on conviction where the proceedings have been made with the DPP's consent, then the warrant under which the article was seized has to have been issued on an information laid by or on behalf of the DPP.

- Owners of premises, makers of articles and persons through whose hands the articles have passed, can appear at court to explain why articles should not be forfeited.

10.11 **Cyber Management and Facilitation of Human Trafficking**

Human trafficking is a topical area and once again the ability to initiate and control the progress of the crime without any recognition of geographical borders has made the use of the internet and the networks it provides more prevalent in relation to exploitation and sexual exploitation.

Some trafficking cases start with the offender contacting the potential victims on social networking sites such as Facebook and MySpace or even on the darknet. After befriending the victim, there are a variety of techniques used to gain their trust including promising to make the victim a star, or the attraction of an exceptional job in another country then providing a ticket to that new location away from the victim's home.

Other trafficking efforts have started with the targeting of victims through online employment searches and end in a possibly naive victim relocating from his or her home on the promise of an unbelievably good job. After the victim has succumbed to the offender's offers, the victim is restricted from contacting family, friends or the outside world by the use of physical punishment and threats to both their own and their family's safety unless the victim complies with the trafficker's demands.

Human trafficking has several definitions but the one most accepted and used in Europe is that created by the Palermo Protocol of 15 December 2000 which supplemented the United Nations Convention against Transnational Organised Crime.

> Trafficking in persons shall mean the recruitment, transportation, transfer, harbouring or receipt of persons, by means of the threat or use of force or other forms of coercion, of abduction, of fraud, of deception, of abuse of power or of a position of vulnerability or of the giving or receiving of payments or benefits to achieve the consent of a person having control over another person, for the purpose of exploitation.
>
> Exploitation shall include, at a minimum, the exploitation of the prostitution of others or other forms of sexual exploitation, forced labour or services, slavery or practices similar to slavery, servitude or removal of organs.

The legislation in England and Wales which is provided to combat human trafficking for sexual exploitation is by s 59A of the Sexual Offences Act 2003, and human trafficking for exploitation contrary to s 4(1A) of the Asylum and Immigration (Treatment of Claimants, etc) Act 2004 where exploitation is defined as contravening Article 4 of the European Convention on Human Rights.

10.11.1 **Trafficking for sexual exploitation**

Offence

(1) A person ('A') commits an offence if A intentionally arranges or facilitates—

   (a) the arrival in, or entry into, the United Kingdom or another country of another person ('B'),

   (b) the travel of B within the United Kingdom or another country, or

   (c) the departure of B from the United Kingdom or another country, with a view to the sexual exploitation of B.

Sexual Offences Act 2003, s 59A

Points to prove

Subsection (1)(a)

✓ intentionally

✓ arranged/facilitated

✓ the arrival in/entry into

✓ the UK/another country

✓ of another person

✓ intending to do anything to **or**

✓ believing that another person is likely to do something

✓ in respect of that other person

✓ after the journey and in any part of the world

✓ which if done would have involved the commission of a relevant offence

Subsection (1)(b)

✓ intentionally

✓ arranged/facilitated

✓ the travel within the UK/another country

- ✓ of another person
- ✓ intending to do anything to **or**
- ✓ believing that another person is likely to do something
- ✓ in respect of that other person
- ✓ after the journey and in any part of the world
- ✓ which if done would have involved the commission of a relevant offence

Subsection (1)(c)

- ✓ intentionally
- ✓ arranged/facilitated
- ✓ departure from the UK/another country
- ✓ by another person
- ✓ intending to do anything to **or**
- ✓ believing that another person is likely to do something to or
- ✓ in respect of that other person during/after the journey and in any part of the world
- ✓ which if done would have involved the commission of a relevant offence

---

Meanings

Intentionally (see 10.2)

Arranged/facilitated

Take in hand, smooth the progress of, make things happen.

United Kingdom

England, Northern Ireland, Scotland and Wales.

Another country

Includes any territory or other part of the world.

Sexual exploitation

Involves the commission of a relevant offence which means any offence under Part 1 of the Sexual Offences Act 2003, or an offence under s 1(1)(a) of the Protection of Children Act 1978 or anything done outside England and Wales which is not an offence within para (a) but would be if done in England and Wales.

Explanatory notes

- For the purposes of subsection (1)(a) and (c), A's arranging or facilitating is with a view to the sexual exploitation of B if, and only if:
  - (i) A intends to do anything to or in respect of B, after B's arrival, entry or departure but in any part of the world, which if done will involve the commission of a relevant offence; or
  - (ii) A believes that another person is likely to do something to or in respect of B, after B's arrival, entry or departure but in any part of the world, which if done will involve the commission of a relevant offence.

- For the purposes of subsection (1)(b), A's arranging or facilitating is with a view to the sexual exploitation of B if, and only if:
  - (i) A intends to do anything to or in respect of B, during or after the journey and in any part of the world, which if done will involve the commission of a relevant offence; or
  - (ii) A believes that another person is likely to do something to or in respect of B, during or after the journey and in any part of the world, which if done will involve the commission of a relevant offence.

- A person who is a UK national commits an offence under this section regardless of:
  - (i) where the arranging or facilitating takes place; or
  - (ii) which country is the country of arrival, entry, travel to or departure.

- A person who is not a UK national commits an offence under this section if:
  - (i) any part of the arranging or facilitating takes place in the UK; or
  - (ii) the UK is the country of arrival, entry, travel or departure.

- Under ss 60A to 60C of the Sexual Offences Act 2003, a court can order the forfeiture of a vehicle, ship or aircraft used by a person convicted of this offence.

- Immigration officers have a power of arrest for trafficking for sexual exploitation offences (see s 14 of the Asylum and Immigration (Treatment of Claimants, etc) Act 2004). This power is available to an immigration officer who uncovers evidence of this (and other named offences) whilst in the course of their usual duties (investigating immigration matters).

- This offence is also a 'lifestyle offence' for the purposes of Sch 2 to the Proceeds of Crime Act 2002.

    Either way offence

🕐   **Time limit for prosecution**: none

▥▥   **Summary**: maximum 12 months' imprisonment
    Indictment: maximum 14 years' imprisonment

10.11.2 Trafficking people for exploitation

Offence

(1A) A person ('A') commits an offence if A intentionally arranges or facilitates—
(a) the arrival in, or entry into, the United Kingdom or another country of another person ('B'),
(b) the travel of B within the United Kingdom or another country, or
(c) the departure of B from the United Kingdom or another country, with a view to the exploitation of B.

    Asylum and Immigration (Treatment of Claimants, etc) Act 2004, s 4

Points to prove

Section 4(1A)(a)

✓ intentionally
✓ arranged/facilitated
✓ the arrival in the UK/another country
✓ of an individual
✓ intending to/believing that another person was likely to
✓ exploit him/her
✓ in the UK/elsewhere

Section 4(1A)(b)

✓ intentionally
✓ arranged/facilitated
✓ travel within the UK/another country
✓ of an individual
✓ intending to/believing that another person was likely to
✓ exploit him/her

✓ during/after the journey

✓ in any part of the world

Section 4(1A)(c)

✓ intentionally

✓ arranged/facilitated

✓ the departure from the UK/another country

✓ of an individual

✓ intending to/believing that another person was likely to

✓ exploit him/her after departure

✓ in the UK/elsewhere

Meanings

Intentionally (see **10.2**)

Arranged/facilitated (see **10.2**)

United Kingdom (see **10.11.1**)

Another country (see **10.11.1**)

Exploitation

A person is exploited when they are (would be): subject to slavery/forced labour; involved in an offence concerning organ removal; subject to force, threats or deception for providing services/benefits or to enable another person to acquire benefits; or requested/induced to do something (chosen because that person is vulnerable, either because they are ill, disabled, young or related to a person, in circumstances where any other person would be likely to refuse or resist).

UK national

A person who is either a British citizen; a person who is a British subject by virtue of Part 4 of the British Nationality Act 1981 and who has the right of abode in the UK; or a person who is a British overseas territories citizen by virtue of a connection with Gibraltar.

Explanatory notes

- Providing services for sexual exploitation is catered for under s 59A of the Sexual Offences Act 2003 (see **10.11.1**)

- Under subsection (1A)(a) and (c), A's arranging or facilitating is with a view to the exploitation of B if (and only if):

  (a) A intends to exploit B, after B's arrival, entry or (as the case may be) departure but in any part of the world; or
  (b) A believes that another person is likely to exploit B, after B's arrival, entry or (as the case may be) departure but in any part of the world.

- Under subsection (1A)(b), A's arranging or facilitating is with a view to the exploitation of B if (and only if):
  (a) A intends to exploit B, during or after the journey and in any part of the world; or
  (b) A believes that another person is likely to exploit B, during or after the journey and in any part of the world.

- A person who is a UK national commits an offence under this section regardless of:
  (a) where the arranging or facilitating takes place; or
  (b) which country is the country of arrival, entry, travel or (as the case may be) departure.

- A person who is not a UK national commits an offence under this section if:
  (a) any part of the arranging or facilitating takes place in the UK; or
  (b) the UK is the country of arrival, entry, travel or (as the case may be) departure.

- Immigration officers have a power of arrest for offences under this section. This power is available to an immigration officer who uncovers evidence of this (and other named offences) whilst in the course of their usual duties (investigating immigration matters).

- This offence is also a 'lifestyle offence' for the purposes of the Proceeds of Crime Act 2002.

- Under s 25D of the Immigration Act 1971, a senior immigration officer or constable can authorise detention of a vehicle, ship or aircraft used by a person arrested for this offence until he is charged and then until a court directs otherwise (a court can order forfeiture on conviction under s 25C of the same Act).

 Either way offence

 Time limit for prosecution: none

 Summary: maximum 12 months' imprisonment
Indictment: maximum 14 years' imprisonment

Chapter 11
Cyber-Enabled Terrorism

11.1 **Introduction**

The internet has transformed the way in which terrorist organisations operate, providing them with an easy-to-access international communications platform previously only available to states. It has enabled the concept of global jihad. Without the internet, terrorists would find it much more difficult to reach a global audience and to plan specific operations. Terrorists use the internet for the following.

- **Propaganda**: with a dynamic series of messages circumventing censorship laws, they are able to host material on sites which are unlikely to be removed. A network of influential propagandists for terrorism in this country and elsewhere make use of the internet and target specific personal vulnerabilities and local factors which make certain ideologies seem both attractive and compelling. There has been the opportunity to make particular use of some 'free speech' legislation to call for the murder of innocent people.

- **Radicalisation and recruitment**: the use of the internet has provided a limitless source of material for those who carry out radicalisation. Radicalisation refers to the process by which people come to support and, in some cases, to participate in terrorism. It has created isolated private communities who then share and expand on extremist ideas. It has provided a conduit for ideologies from overseas to infiltrate the UK to preach to vulnerable groups and sometimes reinforce fundamental commitment to violence as a lawful means to an end.

- **Communication and planning**: the internet has provided a wide expanse of avenues to allow interaction between what might previously have been considered to be disparate groups; for example, email, web chats within forums, and social networking, whilst researching targets and techniques. Like many others, they will use the internet for voice calls which means it can be more difficult to trace.

- **Carrying out a cyber attack** is now within the reach of terrorists whether by malware, DDoS or other techniques. The motives may well differ from those which have been carried out in the past (e.g. financial) but the principles and effects of such an attack remain constant.

The Terrorism Act 2000 and Terrorism Act 2006 provide the offences which have the potential to involve the use of the internet and other cyber provisions. Those sections will be defined and explained in the rest of this chapter and include along with others:

- s 1 of the Terrorism Act 2006—encouragement of terrorism;
- s 2 of the Terrorism Act 2006—dissemination of terrorist publications;
- s 57 of the Terrorism Act 2000—possess an article for terrorist purposes;
- s 58 of the Terrorism Act 2000—collect, record or possess without reasonable excuse, information which is likely to be useful to a person committing or preparing an act of terrorism;
- s 3 of the Terrorism Act 2006—provides that those served with notices who fail to remove, without reasonable excuse, the material that is unlawful and terrorism-related within a specified period, are treated as endorsing it.

Where material crosses the threshold of illegality and is hosted in the UK, the Counter Terrorism Internet Referral Unit (CTIRU) will work with the CPS to prosecute wherever possible and work with the internet industry to remove it. If the material is hosted abroad, the CTIRU will try to work with international law enforcement and the private sector to effect its removal.

11.1.1 **Encouragement of terrorism**

Section 1 of the Terrorism Act 2006 creates the offence of encouragement of terrorism which caters for direct encouragement and indirect encouragement, including glorification of terrorism.

Offence

(1) This section applies to a statement that is likely to be understood by some or all of the members of the public to whom it is published as a direct or indirect encouragement or other inducement to them to the commission, preparation or instigation of acts of terrorism or Convention offences.

> (2) A person commits an offence if—
>   (a) he publishes a statement to which this section applies or causes another to publish such a statement; and
>   (b) at the time he publishes it or causes it to be published, he—
>   (i) intends members of the public to be directly or indirectly encouraged or otherwise induced by the statement to commit, prepare or instigate acts of terrorism or Convention offences; or
>   (ii) is reckless as to whether members of the public will be directly or indirectly encouraged or otherwise induced by the statement to commit, prepare or instigate such acts or offences.
>
> Terrorism Act 2006, s 1(1) and (2)

Points to prove

- ✓ date and location
- ✓ publish/cause another to publish
- ✓ statement that is likely to be understood
- ✓ by some/all members of the public to whom it was published
- ✓ as direct/indirect encouragement/other inducement
- ✓ to commit/prepare/instigate acts of terrorism/Convention offences
- ✓ intending/being reckless as to
- ✓ direct/indirect encouragement/other inducement by the statement
- ✓ to commit/prepare/instigate acts of terrorism/Convention offences

Meanings
Statement

References to a statement are references to a communication of any description, including a communication without words consisting of sounds or images or both (Terrorism Act 2006, s 20(6)). This means that it also includes images such as videos and within digital files.

The public

References to the public:

(a) are references to the public of any part of the UK or of a country or territory outside the UK, or any section of the public; and

(b) also include references to a meeting or other group of persons
which is open to the public (whether unconditionally or
on the making of a payment or the satisfaction of other
conditions) (Terrorism Act 2006, s 20(3)).

Publishing a statement

References to a person's publishing a statement are references to:

(a) his publishing it in any manner to the public;
(b) his providing electronically any service by means of which
the public have access to the statement; or
(c) his using a service provided to him electronically by another
so as to enable or to facilitate access by the public to the
statement (Terrorism Act 2006, 20(4)).

The definition in s 20(4)(b) includes ISPs.

The definition in s 20(4)(c) includes those who run websites that
contain message boards and those who post messages on such
message boards.

Terrorism/act of terrorism

Terrorism in s 1(1) and (2) of the Terrorism Act 2000 means the use
or threat of actions where:

- the action:
  + involves serious violence against a person, or
  + involves serious damage to property, or
  + endangers a person's life, other than that of the person
    committing the action, or
  + creates a serious risk to the health or safety of the public or
    a section of the public, or is designed seriously to interfere
    with or seriously to disrupt an electronic system; and
- the use or threat is designed to influence the government or an
  international governmental organisation or to intimidate the
  public or a section of the public or involves the use of firearms
  or explosives; and
- the use or threat is made for the purpose of advancing a
  political, religious, racial or ideological cause (Terrorism Act
  2000, s 1(1) and (2)).

It is worth emphasising the definition of terrorism as it is very wide
and it needs to be proved before any action can be taken with any
offence under the relevant Acts.

It therefore basically includes any use or threat of violence for political, religious, racial or ideological reasons.

It also covers acts that are not in themselves violent, but which may nevertheless have a devastating impact, such as disrupting key computer systems or interfering with the supply of water or power where life, health or safety may be put at risk. Some acts will also constitute criminal offences; other acts, such as those involving 'endangering another person's life' or 'creating a serious risk to the health or safety of the public or a section of the public', may involve conduct that would not itself be a criminal offence.

The consent of the DPP or the Attorney General is required for some offences which rely on the definition of terrorism, because it is so broad.

The use or threat of action amounts to terrorism if it meets three elements:

(i)   the action involves serious violence, damage, risk to the public, etc;
(ii) the use or threat of action has a certain purpose: to influence the government or intimidate the public (this does not have to be met if the action involves the use of firearms or explosives); and
(iii) the purpose of the threat is to advance a political, religious, racial or ideological cause.

The definition of terrorism is not restricted to 'domestic' terrorism; it extends to terrorist activities in the UK and abroad. This reflects the international nature of terrorism, and perhaps also the fact that the UK wants to avoid becoming or appearing to be a safe haven for foreign terrorists wherever they want to or have committed their acts.

Action against terrorism within a country's borders is also required by international law under UN Security Council Resolution 1373 of 2001. Many terrorism offences cover acts carried out abroad. There is no distinction made between those regimes which are seen as 'friendly' and those which, at least in the past, have been seen as a source of terrorism.

Campaigns using firearms or explosives are deemed to be terrorism whether or not the action is designed to influence the government or intimidate the public.

Acts of terrorism

Acts of terrorism include anything constituting an action taken for the purposes of terrorism, within the meaning of the Terrorism Act 2000 (Terrorism Act 2006, s 20(2)).

Convention offence
Means an offence listed in Sch 1 to the Terrorism Act 2006 or an equivalent offence under the law of a country or territory outside the UK and includes offences such as causing explosions, hostage-taking or terrorist fundraising.

Explanatory notes

- This offence has three elements:
  + the defendant must publish a statement or cause another to publish a statement (Terrorism Act 2006, s 1(2)(a));
  + the statement must be likely to be understood by some or all members of the public to whom it is published as a direct or indirect encouragement to them to commit or prepare or instigate acts of terrorism or Convention offences (Terrorism Act 2006, s 1(1)); and
  + the defendant must have the necessary state of mind when publishing the statement/causing it to be published, and must act intentionally or recklessly (Terrorism Act 2006, s 1(2)(b)).

- **'Members of the public'** means that statements made in private are not covered by this offence. However, if the statement is in writing, consider the offence of dissemination of terrorist publication (see **11.1.2**).

- Indirect encouragement/glorification—statements that are likely to be understood by members of the public as indirectly encouraging the commission or preparation of acts of terrorism or Convention offences include every statement which glorifies the commission or preparation (whether in the past, in the future, or generally) of such acts or offences, and is a statement from which those members of the public could reasonably be expected to infer that what is being glorified is being glorified as conduct that should be emulated by them in existing circumstances (Terrorism Act 2006, s 1(3)).

- Section 1(3) gives an example of statements that indirectly encourage terrorism and those that glorify acts of terrorism, but it does not restrict indirect encouragement to glorification. What else might be covered is not explained, and there will, therefore, be a danger that too wide an interpretation will breach rights to free expression under Article 10 as not being 'in accordance with the law'. The offence can be committed by indirectly encouraging terrorism, either by glorifying terrorism or by indirectly encouraging terrorism in any other way, even if the statement does not fall within s 1(3).

- In addition, s 1(3)(b) limits indirect encouragement to those statements from which the intended audience would draw a conclusion to do something that is similar to what has been glorified. It must be possible for them to carry out such conduct in the current circumstances. Consequently, not every statement that glorifies terrorism will automatically be regarded as indirect encouragement. Glorification of historical events is therefore unlikely to be caught, although it can be committed by making reference to past acts as long as they resonate with the present.

- The inclusion of the expression 'to glorify' was criticised when the Act was created; it has been regarded as too wide and too vague which leaves the offence not being clearly defined. Some argue that the offence might infringe the freedom of expression and therefore be incompatible with the Human Rights Act 1998.

- When determining how a statement is likely to be understood and what members of the public could reasonably be expected to infer from it, both the content of the statement as a whole and the circumstances and manner of its publication have to be considered (Terrorism Act 2006, s 1(4)). This ensures that the context of a statement is taken into account. It will therefore make a difference when considering a specific issue whether it is dealt with in an online academic thesis or in an inflammatory page on a website or Facebook page.

- It is irrelevant whether the encouragement relates to specific acts of terrorism or Convention offences or to such acts or offences generally and whether anyone is in fact encouraged or induced by the statement (Terrorism Act 2006, s 1(5)). This means that the statement, or how it is likely to be understood, need not relate to specific acts of terrorism or Convention offences and the offence is committed even if no such act or offence has actually taken place.

- The offence can be committed intentionally or recklessly (s 1(2)(b)). Intention requires that the defendant intends members of the public to be encouraged to commit, prepare or instigate acts of terrorism or Convention offences. Recklessness requires that the defendant is reckless as to the possibility that the statement will have the effect of members of the public being encouraged. 'Reckless' should be interpreted in accordance with current case law on the meaning of recklessness. That means that in order to be reckless, the defendant has to be shown to be aware of the risk that an effect of the statement would be to encourage terrorism or Convention offences, and in the circumstances known to him, it was unreasonable for him to take that risk (*R v G and R* [2003] UKHL 50).

- Extra-territorial jurisdiction: this offence applies to acts done outside the UK regardless of the nationality of the offender, insofar as the act is committed in relation to the commission, preparation or instigation of one or more Convention offences, in respect of acts of terrorism (Terrorism Act 2006, s 17). Where an ISP established in the UK provides information society services in an EEA state (the EU states, plus Iceland, Liechtenstein and Norway) other than the UK, refer to the Electronic Commerce Directive (Terrorism Act 2006) Regulations 2007 (SI 2007/1550).

- This offence can be tried anywhere in the UK if it was committed in the UK (Counter-Terrorism Act 2008, s 28).

- Notification requirements apply. Sections 40 to 61 of and Schs 4 to 6 to the Counter-Terrorism Act 2008 provide a notification scheme that applies to all offenders sentenced or even made subject of a hospital order if convicted of a terrorist offence or offences having a terrorist connection. They are similar to those for sex offenders in ss 80 to 92 of the Sexual Offences Act 2003. They address, for example, foreign travel and refusal of entry to the UK and it is an offence to fail to comply.

- Corporate liability: for the liability of company directors etc, see s 18 of the Terrorism Act 2006.

Defence

In proceedings for an offence under this section against a person in whose case it is not proved that he intended the statement directly or indirectly to encourage or otherwise induce the commission, preparation or instigation of acts of terrorism or Convention offences, it is a defence for him to show—

(a) that the statement neither expressed his views nor had his endorsement (whether by virtue of s 3 or otherwise); and

(b) that it was clear, in all the circumstances of the statement's publication, that it did not express his views and (apart from the possibility of his having been given and failed to comply with a notice under subsection (3) of that section) did not have his endorsement.

Terrorism Act 2006, s 1(6)

The defence applies only if the defendant is alleged to have acted recklessly. The defence is intended, for example, to cover television companies, news broadcasters and publishers. It imposes an evidential burden on the defendant. The defendant only has to adduce sufficient evidence to raise this defence and it then remains for the prosecution to prove or disprove it. However, the defence does not apply if a person has received a notice under s 3 (e.g. the ISP has been required to modify a terrorism-related article) and has failed to comply with it, because this is regarded as endorsement of the statement.

 Either way offence

 Time limit for prosecution: none

 Summary: maximum 6 months' imprisonment and/or fine not exceeding the statutory maximum
Indictment: maximum 7 years' imprisonment and/or fine

11.1.2 **Dissemination of terrorist publication**

Section 2 of the Terrorism Act 2006 creates the offence of dissemination of terrorist publications.

Offences

(1) A person commits an offence if he engages in conduct falling within subsection (2) and, at the time he does so—
  (a) he intends an effect of his conduct to be a direct or indirect encouragement or other inducement to the commission, preparation or instigation of acts of terrorism;
  (b) he intends an effect of his conduct to be the provision of assistance in the commission or preparation of such acts; or
  (c) he is reckless as to whether his conduct has an effect mentioned in paragraph (a) or (b).
(2) For the purposes of this section a person engages in conduct falling within this subsection if he—
  (a) distributes or circulates a terrorist publication;
  (b) gives, sells or lends such a publication;
  (c) offers such a publication for sale or loan;
  (d) provides a service to others that enables them to obtain, read, listen to or look at such a publication, or to acquire it by means of a gift, sale or loan;
  (e) transmits the contents of such a publication electronically; or
  (f) has such a publication in his possession with a view to its becoming the subject of conduct falling within any of paragraphs (a) to (e).
Terrorism Act 2006, s 2(1) and (2)

Points to prove

✓ distributed/circulated or
✓ gave/sold/lent/offered for sale/loan or
✓ provided a service to others that enabled them to obtain/
  read/listen to/look at or to acquire by means of gift/sale/
  loan or
✓ transmitted electronically the contents of or
✓ possessed with a view to it being distributed/circulated/
  given/sold/lent/offered for sale/loan/being part of a service/
  being transmitted electronically a terrorist publication
✓ at the time of doing so intended/reckless as to
✓ effect of conduct being direct/indirect encouragement/other
✓ inducement to the commission/preparation/instigation of
  acts of terrorism or
✓ effect of conduct being the provision of assistance in the
✓ commission/preparation of acts of terrorism

Meanings

Acts of terrorism (see **11.1.1**)

Publication

Means an article or record of any description that contains any of
the following, or any combination of them:

(a) matter to be read;
(b) matter to be listened to;
(c) matter to be looked at or watched (Terrorism Act 2006,
    s 2(13)).

This means that as well as books this section also covers, amongst
other things, films and videos (with or without sound), cassette
tapes, electronic books, material contained on CDs and photographs. This definition of publication is different from that provided in s 20 of the Act which applies to s 1 (encouragement of
terrorism, see **11.1.1**).

Article

Includes anything for storing data (Terrorism Act 2006, s 20(2)).

Record

Means a record so far as not comprised in an article, including a temporary record created electronically and existing solely in the course of, and for the purposes of, the transmission of the whole or a part of its contents (Terrorism Act 2006, s 20(2)).

Terrorist publication

A publication is a terrorist publication, in relation to conduct falling within subsection (2), if matter contained in it is likely:

(a) to be understood by some or all of the persons to whom it is or may become available as a consequence of that conduct, as a direct or indirect encouragement or other inducement to them to the commission, preparation or instigation of acts of terrorism; or
(b) to be useful in the commission or preparation of such acts and to be understood, by some or all of those persons, as contained in the publication, or made available to them, wholly or mainly for the purpose of being so useful to them (Terrorism Act 2006, s 2(3)).

Matter that is likely to be understood by a person as indirectly encouraging the commission or preparation of acts of terrorism includes any matter which:

(a) glorifies the commission or preparation (whether in the past, in the future or generally) of such acts; and
(b) is matter from which that person could reasonably be expected to infer that what is being glorified is being glorified as conduct that should be emulated by him in existing circumstances (Terrorism Act 2006, s 2(4)).

Glorification, glorify, etc includes any form of praise or celebration (Terrorism Act 2006, s 20(1)).

Lend/loan

Lend includes let on hire, and loan is to be construed accordingly (Terrorism Act 2006, s 2(13)).

Explanatory notes

- The offence has three elements:
  (i) there must be a terrorist publication (s 2(3));
  (ii) the person must engage in a specific conduct (s 2(2)); and
  (iii) the person must have the necessary state of mind; and the offence can be committed recklessly or intentionally (s 2(1)).

- For the purposes of this section, the question whether a publication is a terrorist publication in relation to particular conduct must be determined as at the time of that conduct; and having regard both to the contents of the publication as a whole and to the circumstances in which that conduct occurs (s 2(5)). This means that account can be taken of the nature of the bookseller or other disseminator of the publication.

- In s 2(1), references to the effect of a person's conduct in relation to a terrorist publication include references to an effect of the publication on one or more persons to whom it is or may become available as a consequence of that conduct (s 2(6)).

- This means that the effect of a person holding/storing a publication intending to disseminate it later, for example by way of online sale, will include the effect on the audience to whom it is intended it will be made available by a later act of dissemination—that is, the release or sale itself. This is intended to cater for the situation where a person, for example, only holds a publication with the intention of disseminating it, the effect of that conduct is not to encourage terrorism or to be useful to terrorists, because only once the publication is disseminated can it have one of those effects.

- The offence covers not only bookshops but also those who sell books and publications over the internet, whether the publication is in hard copy or electronic. The offence covers commercial and non-commercial transactions.

- The purpose mentioned in s 2(1) (encouragement or inducement to commit, prepare or instigate acts of terrorism or provision of assistance to commit or prepare such acts) may be one of several. A person may, for example, say that his main purpose is to make money or to help his friend, but at the same time be reckless as to whether his conduct also encourages the commission of acts of terrorism. In that event, he still commits the offence. (Compare *R v Dooley* [2005] EWCA Crim 3093, para 14: in this case, on the possession of indecent photographs of a child with a view to their being distributed, it was held to be sufficient that one of the purposes of the defendant's actions was the distribution of the photographs.)

- The offence is not committed where a person simply possesses a terrorist publication, but under certain circumstances he might commit an offence of 'possession of articles for terrorist purposes' (see **11.1.5**).

- Only part of the publication needs to satisfy the test in s 2(3) for the publication to be a terrorist publication.

- It is also irrelevant, in relation to matter contained in any article, whether any person is in fact encouraged or induced by that matter to commit, prepare or instigate acts of terrorism; or in fact makes use of it in the commission or preparation of such acts (s 2(8)).

- This offence can be committed intentionally or recklessly (s 1(2)(b)). 'Reckless' should be interpreted in accordance with current case law on the meaning of recklessness (*R v G and R* [2003] UKHL 50). Whether the offence is committed intentionally or recklessly is a matter of importance to sentence.

- Many cases of dissemination of terrorist publications will also fall under s 1 'encouragement of terrorism' ('publishing a statement' in s 1 includes 'publishing it in any manner to the public', see **11.1.1**).

- For the application of this section to internet activity, etc (see **11.1.3**).

- The provisions on post-charge questioning apply to this offence.

- The offence applies to conduct in the UK. It also applies where an ISP established in the UK provides information society services in an EEA state other than the UK; refer to the Electronic Commerce Directive (Terrorism Act 2006) Regulations 2007 (SI 2007/1550).

- Forfeiture: s 23A of the Terrorism Act 2000 provides that the court can order the forfeiture of money or other property, on conviction for this and other offences, if the money or property was in the possession or control of the person convicted and it had been used for terrorism purposes, was intended for that use or the court believed it would be used for that purpose unless forfeited.

Defence

In proceedings for an offence under this section against a person in respect of conduct to which subsection (10) applies, it is a defence for him to show—

(a) that the matter by reference to which the publication in question was a terrorist publication neither expressed his views nor had his endorsement (whether by virtue of section 3 or otherwise); and

(b) that it was clear, in all the circumstances of the conduct, that that matter did not express his views and (apart from the possibility of

his having been given and failed to comply with a notice under
subsection (3) of that section) did not have his endorsement.

Terrorism Act 2006, s 2(9)

Conduct to which subsection (10) applies

(10) This subsection applies to the conduct of a person to the
extent that—
  (a) the publication to which his conduct related contained matter by reference to which it was a terrorist publication by virtue of subsection (3)(a) [i.e. matter contained in it was likely
  to be understood, by some or all of the persons to whom it is
  or may become available as a consequence of that conduct,
  as a direct or indirect encouragement or other inducement to
  them to the commission, preparation or instigation of acts of
  terrorism]; and
  (b) that person is not proved to have engaged in that conduct with
  the intention specified in subsection (1)(a) [i.e. he intends an
  effect of his conduct to be a direct or indirect encouragement or
  other inducement to the commission, preparation or instigation
  of acts of terrorism].

Terrorism Act 2006, s 2(10)

This means that the defence does not apply to an offence committed intentionally under s 2(3)(a) (publication is likely to be
understood as encouragement or inducement to prepare, instigate
or commit acts of terrorism) or to any offence under s 2(3)(b) (publication is likely to be useful for the commission or preparation of
such acts).

In relation to the defence in s 2(9), the defendant need only show
that the part of the publication which satisfies the test of terrorist
publication in s 2(3) did not express his views or have endorsement
in order to establish part (a) of the defence.

Related cases

R v Rahman; R v Mohammed [2008] EWCA Crim 1465 The
Court of Appeal recognised that the circumstances in which s 2
can be committed vary widely and that factors relevant to sentence
include not only the quality and quantity of publications but also
all other circumstances, whether the defendant had intended dissemination of terrorist publications to encourage the commission,
preparation or instigation of acts of terrorism or was merely reckless as to such consequences.

R v Iqbal (Abbas Niazi), R v Iqbal (Ilyas Niazi) [2010] EWCA Crim 3215 AI was arrested at Manchester airport, intending to travel to Finland. He was found in possession of material in the UK with the relevant *mens rea* set out in s 2(1)—that the ultimate distribution may have taken place outside the UK is beside the point. The court noted that under s 2(8) it is irrelevant to subsection (2) whether or not anyone was actually encouraged by the material to commit, prepare or instigate acts of terrorism. The prosecution did not have to prove actual distribution, only the possession of the material with the relevant intent. All of that activity occurred in the UK.

R v Brown [2011] EWCA Crim 2751 B was collecting material on bomb-making and poisoning from the internet and compiling CDs for sale. The CDs were called the 'Anarchist Cookbook' and contained the largest collection of its kind which had yet come to light—contained in two CDs, the printed form would have covered thousands of pages. It was not disputed that the information accumulated would be of practical assistance to a terrorist. Prosecution of the offence did not violate B's right to freedom of expression.

11.1.3 Use of internet for encouragement of terrorism

Section 3 of the Terrorism Act 2006 contains additional provisions concerning the offences of encouragement of terrorism (see **11.1.1**) and dissemination of terrorist publications (see **11.1.2**) applying to the internet and other electronic services. It allows for the service of a notice by a constable, where he believes illegal terrorism-related material is available on a website. The person or persons responsible for that material may be required to secure that the material is not made available to the public or is modified. The effect of the notice is that if the person does not comply, he cannot use the statutory defence and claim that the publication did not have his endorsement (see **11.1.2**). Non-compliance with this section does not create an offence.

Police powers provided by the section:

(1) This section applies for the purposes of sections 1 and 2 in relation to cases where—

(a) a statement is published or caused to be published in the course of, or in connection with, the provision or use of a service provided electronically; or

(b) conduct falling within section 2(2) was in the course of, or in connection with, the provision or use of such a service.

(2)   The cases in which the statement, or the article or record to which the conduct relates, is to be regarded as having the endorsement of a person ("the relevant person") at any time include a case in which:

    (a)   a constable has given him a notice under subsection (3);

    (b)   that time falls more than 2 working days after the day on which the notice was given; and

    (c)   the relevant person has failed, without reasonable excuse, to comply with the notice.

(3)   A notice under this subsection is a notice which—

    (a)   declares that, in the opinion of the constable giving it, the statement or the article or record is unlawfully terrorism-related;

    (b)   requires the relevant person to secure that the statement or the article or record, so far as it is so related, is not available to the public or is modified so as no longer to be so related;

    (c)   warns the relevant person that a failure to comply with the notice within 2 working days will result in the statement, or the article or record, being regarded as having his endorsement; and

    (d)   explains how, under subsection (4), he may become liable by virtue of the notice if the statement, or the article or record, becomes available to the public after he has complied with the notice.

Terrorism Act 2006, s 3(1)–(3)

Meanings

Record (see **11.1.2**)

Working day

Means any day other than a Saturday or a Sunday; Christmas Day or Good Friday; or a day which is a bank holiday under the Banking and Financial Dealings Act 1971 in any part of the UK (Terrorism Act 2006, s 3(9)).

Unlawfully terrorism-related

(7)   For the purposes of this section a statement or an article or record is unlawfully terrorism-related if it constitutes, or if matter contained in the article or record constitutes—

    (a)   something that is likely to be understood, by any one or more of the persons to whom it has or may become available, as a direct or indirect encouragement or other inducement to the commission, preparation, or instigation of acts of terrorism or Convention offences; or

(b) information which—

    (i) is likely to be useful to any one or more of those persons in the commission or preparation of such acts; and

    (ii) is in a form or context in which it is likely to be understood by any one or more of those persons as being wholly or mainly for the purpose of being so useful.

Terrorism Act 2006, s 3(7)

The reference in subsection (7) to something that is likely to be understood as an indirect encouragement to the commission or preparation of acts of terrorism or Convention offences includes anything which is likely to be understood as—

(a) the glorification of the commission or preparation (whether in the past, in the future, or generally) of such acts or such offences; and

(b) a suggestion that what is being glorified is being glorified as conduct that should be emulated in existing circumstances.

Terrorism Act 2006, s 3(8)

Glorification, glorify etc

Includes any form of praise or celebration (Terrorism Act 2006, s 20(2)). For indirect encouragement and glorification, see also **11.1.2**).

The public (see **11.1.1**)

Explanatory notes

- The purpose of serving a notice is to achieve the quick removal or modification of unlawful terrorism-related content from the internet. The consequence of non-compliance with the notice is that the person cannot use the statutory defence because the statement or publication is regarded as having his endorsement.

- The power to serve a notice is only available to police officers. It can be initiated by any constable, but in practice (pursuant to the 'Guidance on Notices Issued Under Section 3 of the Terrorism Act 2006') it will normally be an officer of the Metropolitan Police Service Counter Terrorist Command. The notice should be authorised by an officer of Superintendent rank or above after consultation with the ACPO Terrorism & Allied Matters (TAM) police lead, the National Co-ordinator of the Counter Terrorism Unit (CTU), special branch of any force that might have a direct interest, and also the intelligence services.

- The notice must declare that the statement, article or record in question is unlawfully terrorism-related (s 3(7)) in the view of the constable. This notice requires the relevant person, for example a webmaster, to ensure that the statement, article or record is removed from public view or amended to ensure that it is no longer unlawfully terrorism-related. The notice must warn the person that he has two working days to comply with the notice, and that failure to do so will lead to that person being regarded as having endorsed the statement, article or record.

- Such a notice will also explain how the relevant person may be liable if the statement, article or record becomes available to the public again, following compliance with the notice. This final element relates to repeat statements (see below).

- Notices can be served on any person who is involved in the provision or use of electronic services, such as a content provider, hosting ISP, webmaster, forum moderator, etc.

- The notices should mainly be used where material is not removed voluntarily.

- Where material might be removed voluntarily and there is no suspicion that the potential subject of the s 3 notice is involved in encouraging publication of the material, one should in the first place try to achieve voluntary removal, in particular where the material breaches the terms and conditions under which a service is provided (eg chat room rules, Acceptable Use Policy).

- The procedure for giving notices to persons, bodies corporate, firms and unincorporated bodies or associations is set out in s 4 of the Terrorism Act 2006. There is further 'Guidance on Notices Issued Under Section 3 of the Terrorism Act 2006' agreed between ACPO and the Internet Service Providers Association. This guidance should be consulted before any notice is issued.

- Repeat statements: where a notice has been served and the person has complied with it, but subsequently publishes or causes to be published a so-called 'repeat statement' which is (practically) the same, the repeat statement is deemed to have the person's endorsement (s 3(4)). It is not necessary to serve another notice on that person in respect of a repeat statement.

- As provided in s 3(5)–(6) of the Terrorism Act 2006, a person is not deemed to have endorsed the statement under two conditions:
  (1) If he shows that before the publication of the repeat statement, he had taken every step he reasonably could to prevent it from becoming available to the public and to ascertain whether it did; and,
  (2) If he was not aware of the publication of the repeat statement, or having become aware of its publication, had taken every step that he reasonably could to secure that it either ceased to be available to the public or was modified so as to be no longer unlawfully terrorism-related.

- Where a service provider established in the UK provides information society services in an EEA state other than the UK, refer to the Electronic Commerce Directive (Terrorism Act 2006) Regulations 2007 (SI 2007/1550) and to the Home Office Guidance.

11.1.4 Search and seizure of terrorist publications

To be able to conduct investigations effectively within the arena of counter-terrorism, s 28 of the Terrorism Act 2006 provides powers for the search, seizure and forfeiture of terrorist publications. As this book relates to cyber investigations, the measures should be related to publications stored as data on devices and capable of being transmitted over networks. The objective insight of these powers are focused on forfeiture rather than evidence gathering.

Police power

(1) If a justice of the peace is satisfied that there are reasonable grounds for suspecting that articles to which this section applies are likely to be found on any premises, he may issue a warrant authorising a constable—

(a) to enter and search the premises; and

(b) to seize anything found there which the constable has reason to believe is such an article.

(2) This section applies to an article if—

(a) it is likely to be the subject of conduct falling within subsection (2)(a) to (e) of section 2 [offence of dissemination of a terrorist publication]; and

(b) it would fall for the purposes of that section to be treated, in the context of the conduct to which it is likely to be subject, as a terrorist publication.

(4)   An article seized under the authority of a warrant issued under this section—

(a)   may be removed by a constable to such place as he thinks fit; and

(b)   must be retained there in the custody of a constable until returned or otherwise disposed of in accordance with this Act.

Terrorism Act 2006, s 28(1), (2) and (4)

Meanings

Article (see **11.1.2**)

Premises

Includes any place and in particular, includes:

(a)   any vehicle, vessel, aircraft, or hovercraft;
(b)   any offshore installation;
(ba) any renewable energy installation; and
(c)   any tent or movable structure.

see *Police and Criminal Evidence Act 1984, s 23*

Explanatory notes

- For the meaning of 'terrorist publication' and details on the offence of dissemination of terrorist publications, see **11.1.2**.
- Where an article is seized under this power under the authority of a warrant issued on an information laid by or on behalf of the DPP it is liable to forfeiture; and, if forfeited, may be destroyed or otherwise disposed of by a constable in whatever manner he thinks fit (Terrorism Act 2006, s 28(5)).
- A person exercising the power conferred by a warrant may use such force as is reasonable in the circumstances for exercising the power (Terrorism Act 2006, s 28(3)).
- The power to seize articles attracts additional powers under ss 51 and 55 of the Criminal Justice and Police Act 2001. This enables a bulk of material to be taken away to be read, rather than being examined on the premises, to see if it should be seized. This is needed for cases where large numbers of publications are held at a set of premises.
- Sections 1 to 9 of the Counter-Terrorism Act 2008 provide further powers to remove documents for examination etc.

There are other offences which could be deemed to be capable of being cyber-enabled but will not be covered in this Handbook and can be found in full in *Blackstone's Counter-Terrorism Handbook* published by Oxford University Press. These include inciting terrorism overseas (Terrorism Act 2006, s 59) and the preparation of/for terrorist acts (Terrorism Act 2006, s 5). The internet and other forms of media could also be made use of in committing the offences of training for terrorist acts and weapons training (Terrorism Act 2006, ss 6 and 54).

11.1.5 **Possession of articles for terrorist purposes**

Section 57 of the Terrorism Act 2000 makes it an offence to possess articles connected with an act of terrorism.

Offence

A person commits an offence if he possesses an article in circumstances which give rise to a reasonable suspicion that his possession is for a purpose connected with the commission, preparation or instigation of an act of terrorism.

Terrorism Act 2000, s 57(1)

Points to prove

✓ possess article

✓ in suspicious circumstances

✓ purpose of the commission/preparation/instigation of act of

✓ terrorism

Meanings

Article

Includes substance and any other thing (Terrorism Act 2000, s 121).

For a purpose connected with terrorism

Requires a direct connection between the article and the act of terrorism.

Act of terrorism (see **11.1.1**)

Explanatory notes

Burden of proof—there is a special provision regarding the burden of proof for some elements of this offence.

- In proceedings for an offence under this section, if it is proved that an article was on any premises at the same time as the accused, or was on premises of which the accused was the occupier or which he habitually used otherwise than as a member of the public, the court may assume that the accused possessed the article, unless he proves that he did not know of its presence on the premises or that he had no control over it (Terrorism Act 2000, s 57(3)).

- Where the prosecution adduces evidence regarding the article being on premises, the court may make the assumption that the accused possessed the article unless the accused proves that he did not know of its presence or had no control over it.

- However, the accused then only has to adduce evidence which is sufficient to raise the issue of whether he knew of the presence of the article or had control over it; it is then for the prosecution to disprove this beyond reasonable doubt (Terrorism Act 2000, s 118(4)).

- The issue remains for the prosecution to prove or disprove. This eases the evidential burden placed on the accused. He is simply required to raise the issue; this negates the presumption in the statute unless the prosecution can prove otherwise.

- Extra-territorial jurisdiction: this offence applies to acts done outside the UK if committed by a UK national or a UK resident (Terrorism Act 2000, s 63A(1)).

- The possession of documentation may also fall within s 58 of the Terrorism Act 2000, to 'make/possess records or information useful to an act of terrorism' (see *R v Rowe* in 'Related cases'). Actions that might have been prosecuted under this offence might now be prosecuted under the Terrorism Act 2006, for example 'publishing statements to encourage terrorism' (see **11.1.2**).

- The courts accept that there is overlap between ss 57 and 58, although there are important differences in wording between them.

- Forfeiture: s 120A of the Terrorism Act 2000 provides that the court may order the forfeiture of any article that is the subject matter of the offence.

Defences

It is a defence for a person charged with an offence under this section to prove that his possession of the article was not for a purpose connected with the commission, preparation or instigation of an act of terrorism.

Terrorism Act 2000, s 57(2)

Section 118 of the Terrorism Act 2000 shifts the burden of proof to the prosecution where the defendant adduces evidence that is sufficient to raise this defence. It imposes an evidential burden on the accused.

If the person adduces evidence which is sufficient to raise an issue with respect to the matter, the court or jury shall assume that the defence is satisfied unless the prosecution proves beyond reasonable doubt that it is not (Terrorism Act 2000, s 118(2)).

The effect of this section is that, if a defendant adduces evidence to raise this defence, the burden of proof shifts to the prosecution.

Related cases

R v Zafar, Butt, Iqbal, Raja and Malik [2008] EWCA Crim 184 The connection between the article and the intended acts of terrorism is very important. The phrase 'for a purpose in connection with' is so imprecise that it could lead to uncertainty of the law, therefore it has to be interpreted in a way that requires a direct connection between the article and the act of terrorism. Section 57(1) should be read: 'A person commits an offence if he possesses an article in circumstances which give rise to a reasonable suspicion that he intends it to be used for the purpose of the commission, preparation, or instigation of an act of terrorism.' An example where there is a direct and obvious connection is an article that is intended to be incorporated in a bomb or used as an ingredient of explosives designed for an act of terrorism.

Possessing a document for the purpose of inciting other persons to commit an act of terrorism is sufficient; an indirect connection between possession of the item and potential terrorist acts is not. (An article could be a memory stick where the contents relate directly to an act of terrorism.)

R v Rowe [2007] EWCA Crim 635 Documents and records, such as books and computer discs, can be 'articles' for the purpose of this offence. The court held that there is an overlap between this offence in s 57 and the offence in s 58 of the Terrorism Act 2000 but they deal with different characteristics of terrorist-related activities. Section 57 deals with the possession of articles for the purpose of terrorist acts and s 58 with the collection or keeping of information of a kind likely to be useful to those involved in acts of terrorism. Only s 57 requires specific intent.

R v G, R v J [2009] UKHL 13 The House of Lords explained several issues regarding the offences in ss 57 and 58. For the offence in s 58(1), it must be proved that the defendant had control of a record which contained information which by its very nature was likely to provide practical assistance to a person committing or preparing an act of terrorism, knew that he had the record and knew the kind of information which it contained. The offence in s 57(1) ('any article') covers far more items than s 58 ('a record'). It must be proved that the defendant possessed the article in question: that means he knew he had the article and that he had control of it. Section 57(3) allows assumptions to be made about the possession, unless the defendant adduces evidence to show that he did not know of the presence of the article or had no control over it. Further, it must be proved that the circumstances in which the defendant possessed the article gave rise to reasonable suspicion that his possession was for a purpose connected with the commission, preparation or instigation of an act of terrorism. In contrast to s 58(1), the circumstances of the possession are a crucial element of the offence.

The defendant is then given a defence under s 57(2). Most people will not have a lawful reason for possessing an explosive as such, but some may have a perfectly good reason for having a bag of fertiliser. There is an overlap between s 57(1) and s 58(1) and the difference lies in the scope of the offences (s 57—possession; s 58—collecting or making record) with s 57 applying to any 'article', widely defined, and s 58 to information of a certain kind contained in 'documents and records'.

Because s 57 is so wide, it only applies to possession in certain circumstances; by contrast, s 58 covers information of a particular kind, therefore the nature of the information is the important element. The decision in *R v Rowe* (above) is correct.

 DPP/AG Consent required: Terrorism Act 2000, s 117

 Time limit for prosecution: none

 Summary: maximum 6 months' imprisonment and/or fine not exceeding the statutory maximum
Indictment: maximum 15 years' imprisonment and/or fine. For offences committed before 13 April 2006: maximum 10 years' imprisonment and/or fine

11.1.6 **Collection of information**

Section 58 of the Terrorism Act 2006 creates offences relating to the collection of information which may be useful to someone who commits or prepares acts of terrorism. There is overlap between this offence and the offence contrary to s 57 of the same Act.

Offences

A person commits an offence if—
(a) he collects or makes a record of information of a kind likely to be useful to a person committing or preparing an act of terrorism, or
(b) he possesses a document or record containing information of that kind.

Terrorism Act 2000, s 58(1)

Points to prove

✓ collect/make record of or possess document/record containing

✓ information likely to be useful to a person committing/preparing an act of terrorism

---

Meanings
Record

Includes a photographic or electronic record (Terrorism Act 2000, s 58(2)).

Act of terrorism (see **11.1.1**)

Explanatory notes

- Extra-territorial jurisdiction: this offence applies to acts done outside the UK if committed by a UK national or a UK resident (Terrorism Act 2000, s 63A(1)).

- This offence can be tried anywhere in the UK if it was committed in the UK (Counter-Terrorism Act 2008, s 28).

- The provisions on post-charge questioning apply to this offence.

- Forfeiture: s 120A of the Terrorism Act 2000 makes provision regarding forfeiture. It provides that the court may order the

---

forfeiture of any document or record containing information of the kind mentioned in subsection (1)(a).

- Consider also the offence of possessing articles in connection with an act of terrorism in s 57 of the Terrorism Act 2000 (see **11.1.5**).
- Where documents encourage the commission of acts of terrorism, consider the offence of encouragement of terrorism (see **11.1.1**) and the offence of dissemination of terrorist publications (see **11.1.2**).

Defence

It is a defence for a person charged with an offence under this section to prove that he had a reasonable excuse for his action or possession.

Terrorism Act 2000, s 58(3)

Section 118 of the Terrorism Act 2000 shifts the burden of proof to the prosecution where the defendant adduces evidence that is sufficient to raise this defence (for details, see **11.1.5**).

Related cases

R v K [2008] EWCA Crim 185 This case interpreted the meaning of 'information of a kind likely to be useful to persons committing or preparing acts of terrorism'. The literature must be, on the face of the document, wholly or mainly useful to terrorism. Section 58 could not catch, for example, the *A–Z of London* even if it might be used by suicide bombers. The literature must be intrinsically relevant to the commission or preparation of terrorism.

R v F [2007] EWCA Crim 243 It is not a reasonable excuse for the possession of documents for the purposes of s 58(3) that the documents originated as part of an effort to change an illegal or undemocratic regime.

R v Rowe [2007] EWCA Crim 635 Guidance on prosecutions under ss 57 and 58 of the Terrorism Act 2000 (see **11.1.5**).

R v G, R v J [2009] UKHL 13 Interpretation of ss 57 and 58 of the Terrorism Act 2000 (see **11.1.5**).

R v Muhammed [2010] EWCA Crim 227 The submission that there should be a narrow interpretation of the words 'information of a kind likely to be useful to a person committing or preparing an act of terrorism' in s 58(1)(a) was rejected. Trying to draw distinctions between the various stages of preparation would bring an unnecessary and unjustified complication into cases under s 58. Nor did the fact that the document might be useful to persons other than terrorists mean that it fell outside s 58. The relevant information had to be such as to call for an explanation pursuant to s 58(3).

R v AY [2010] EWCA Crim 762 A defence of reasonable excuse advanced under s 58(3) had to be left to the jury unless it was quite plain that it was incapable of being held by any jury to be reasonable.

R v Brown [2011] EWCA Crim 2751 B was collecting material on bomb-making and poisoning from the internet and compiling CDs for sale. For details, see **11.1.2**. The question whether B had a reasonable excuse on the basis of the exercise of the right to freedom of speech or freedom of expression, may be left to the jury.

 DPP/AG consent required: Terrorism Act 2006, s 117

 Time limit for prosecution: none

 Summary: maximum 6 months' imprisonment and/or fine not exceeding the statutory maximum
Indictment: maximum 10 years' imprisonment and/or fine

11.1.7 Eliciting, publishing or communicating information about members of armed forces, etc

Section 58A of the Terrorism Act 2000 makes it an offence to elicit, publish or communicate information about members of the armed forces or the intelligence services or constables. It was inserted by s 76(1) of the Counter-Terrorism Act 2008.

Offences

A person commits an offence who—
   (a) elicits or attempts to elicit information about an individual who is or has been—
      (i) a member of Her Majesty's forces,
      (ii) a member of any of the intelligence services, or
      (iii) a constable,
      which is of a kind likely to be useful to a person committing or preparing an act of terrorism, or
   (b) publishes or communicates any such information.

Terrorism Act 2000, s 58A(1)

Points to prove

✓ elicited/attempted to elicit/published/communicated

✓ information about

✓ an individual who is/has been a member of Her Majesty's forces/member of any of the intelligence services/constable

✓ which was of a kind likely to be useful to a person committing/preparing an act of terrorism

---

Meanings

Intelligence services

Means the Security Service, the Secret Intelligence Service and GCHQ (within the meaning of s 3 of the Intelligence Services Act 1994) (Terrorism Act 2000, s 58A(4)).

Act of terrorism (see **11.1.1**)

Explanatory notes

• The offence was not created to capture journalists, whistle-blowers or plane spotters; they would normally be covered by the defence in s 58A(2). It is designed to catch those who are taking steps to target police and security officers, for example by gathering information about a person's house, car, routes to work and other movements. One reason for introducing the offence was the Birmingham plots to kidnap and murder members of the armed forces. This could quite easily be collected through the internet, chat rooms and social media as well as other legitimate sources.

• Home Office Circular 12/2009 'Photography and Counter-Terrorism Legislation' provides additional information with regard to photography and using the powers under this section. It states that 'legitimate' journalistic activity (e.g. covering a demonstration for a newspaper) is likely to constitute such an excuse. Similarly, an innocent tourist or other sightseer taking a photograph of a police officer is likely to have a reasonable excuse.

• Extra-territorial jurisdiction: this offence applies to acts done outside the UK if they are committed by a UK national or a UK resident (Terrorism Act 2000, s 63A(1)).

• This offence can be tried anywhere in the UK if it was committed in the UK (Counter-Terrorism Act 2008, s 28).

- Forfeiture: s 120A of the Terrorism Act 2000 makes provision regarding forfeiture. It provides that the court may order the forfeiture of any document or record containing information of the kind mentioned in subsection (1)(a).

Defence

It is a defence for a person charged with an offence under this section to prove that they had a reasonable excuse for their action.

Terrorism Act 2000, s 58A(2)

The defence in s 58A(2) must be read with s 118, the effect of which is to limit the burden on the accused to an evidential burden, so that if that person adduces evidence sufficient to raise an issue with respect to this defence, the prosecution must then prove beyond reasonable doubt that there is no such defence.

 DPP/AG consent required: Terrorism Act 2006, s 117

 Time limit for prosecution: none

 Summary: maximum 6 months' imprisonment and/or fine not exceeding the statutory maximum
Indictment: maximum 10 years' imprisonment and/or fine

Appendix 1
Cyber Crime Glossary of Terms

Address The term address is used in several ways:

- an internet address or Internet Protocol (IP) address is a unique computer (host) location on the internet;
- a web page address is expressed as the defining directory path to the file on a particular server;
- a web page address is also called a Uniform Resource Locator, or URL;
- an email address is the location of an email user (expressed by the user's email name followed by an @ followed by the user's server domain name).

Advanced fee frauds Fraudulent tactics that deceive victims into paying fees to facilitate a transaction which purportedly benefits them. Nigerian, or 419, frauds (after the Nigerian penal code which criminalises them) deceive recipients into allowing the use of their bank account to help fraudsters allegedly to remove money out of their country. Once involved in the scam, the victim is required to pay a series of advance fees to facilitate the transaction, which never takes place. Variations use internet auctions or online dating forums to obtain advance fees.

Advanced persistent threat (APT) APT is a set of stealthy and continuous computer hacking processes, often orchestrated by human(s) targeting a specific entity. APT usually targets organisations and/or nations for business or political motives. APT processes require a high degree of covertness over a long period of time. As the name implies, APT consists of three major components/processes: advanced, persistent and threat. The advanced process signifies sophisticated techniques using malware to exploit vulnerabilities in systems. The persistent process suggests that an external command and control is continuously monitoring and extracting data off a specific target. The threat process indicates human involvement in orchestrating the attack.

Adware The common name used to describe software that is given to the user with advertisements embedded in the application.

Appendix 1: Cyber Crime Glossary of Terms

Adware is considered a legitimate alternative offered to consumers who do not wish to pay for software. There are many ad-supported programs, games or utilities that are distributed as adware (or freeware).

Algorithm A formula or set of steps for solving a particular problem. To be an algorithm, a set of rules must be unambiguous and have a clear stopping point.

Allocated space An area of a storage device that is currently being used by the operating system or the user to store data.

Ambient technology Joins devices together to create a wireless informational environment that links domestic household, business and leisure devices to assist the individual and improve their quality of life by automating many routine chores.

Anti virus (AV) Antivirus, anti-virus or AV software is computer software used to prevent, detect and remove malicious computer viruses.

AOL (America Online) An online information service based in the US that provides email, news, educational and entertainment services, and computer support by means of a graphical user interface. America Online is one of the largest US internet access providers.

Arbitrage/parallel imports The exploitation of pricing differentials between different markets.

Archive file A file that contains other files (usually compressed files). It is used to store files that are not used often or files that may be downloaded from a file library by internet users.

Asynchronicity Describes communications that take place outside conventional time frames, e.g. 'chose-time', chosen by the end-users in an email communication stream.

Attachment A file carried with an email.

Auction frauds The use of internet auction sites to commit fraudulent acts, usually luring bidders into a transaction outside the auction site.

Automated vending carts Web e-commerce software that allows criminals to quickly sell large volumes of credit card and banking account data.

Backdoor Malware that enables an attacker to bypass normal authentification to gain access to a computerised device/system.

Backup A copy taken of all information held on a computer in case something goes wrong with the original copy.

Banner grabbing A method used by hackers in order to identify the type of applications or operating system running on a victim's server. This method contains a request bypassing a firewall such as Telnet in order to reach a victim's server.

Basic Input Output System (BIOS) A program stored on the motherboard that controls interaction between the various components of the computer.

Black hackers A type of hacker who uses their skills for illegitimate and malicious purposes (e.g. to circumvent security and commit computer crimes).

Black hat A name to describe a hacker who uses their skills for illegitimate and malicious purposes (e.g. to circumvent security and commit computer crimes).

Blog Internet diaries or personal online journals shared with an online audience.

Blogosphere When individual blogs are interlinked to create a network of blogs forming an interconnected blog environment.

Blogstorm When information and debate in a blogosphere escalates rapidly and virally, creating a frenzy of, sometimes heated, discussion.

Boface A type of worm that tricks users of Facebook into purchasing fake anti-virus programs after downloading and installing malware to their computer

Boot To start a computer, more frequently used as 're-boot'.

Boot disk A disk that contains the files needed to start an operating system.

Bootkit A kernel-mode rootkit variant called a bootkit which can infect startup code like Master Boot Record (MBR), Volume Boor Record (VBR) or boot sector, and in this way, can be used to attack full disk encryption systems.

Bootloader Bootloaders are programs that are executed before the operating system of a device starts.

Bot A targeted machine that is infected by malware and is part of a botnet.

Botnet A botnet (also known as a Zombie) is often a compromised computer that can be controlled remotely by a third party for the purpose of sending spam or participating in a coordinated DDoS attack. Botnets can also be used for legitimate applications such as internet relay chat.

Appendix 1: Cyber Crime Glossary of Terms

Broadband A high bandwidth internet connection, e.g. ADSL or cable.

Browser A browser is a program that provides a way to look at, read and even hear all the information on the World Wide Web. Common examples are Firefox, Netscape and Internet Explorer.

Buffer An area of memory used to speed up access to devices. It is used for temporary storage of the data read from or waiting to be sent to a device such as a hard disk, CD-ROM, printer or tape drive.

Buffer overflow Refers to a condition where an application is bombarded by a high volume of data more than allocated capacity in its memory.

Bulletin Board Service (BBS) A BBS is like an electronic corkboard. It is a computer system equipped for network access that serves as an information and message passing centre for remote users. BBSs are generally focused on special interests, such as science fiction, movies, Windows software or Mac systems. Some are free, some are fee-based access and some are a combination.

Bullet-proof hosting Bullet-proof hosting providers actively turn a blind eye to cyber crime activities conducted by their users, whereas responsible hosting providers would shut them down. These providers are often located in countries where it is difficult to close such operations.

Byte In most computer systems, a byte is a unit of data consisting of 8 bits. A byte can represent a single character, such as a letter, a digit or a punctuation mark.

C4All An enscript used to extend the capabilities of encase for carving and classifying images and videos. Comprised of C4P (images) and C4M (movies).

Cache A cache (pronounced CASH) is a place to store something more or less temporarily. Web pages you browse are stored in your browser's cache directory on your hard disk. When you return to a page you've recently browsed, the browser can get it from the cache rather than the original server, saving you time and the network the burden of some additional traffic. Two common types of cache are: cache memory and a disk cache.

Central processing unit (CPU) The computational and control unit of a computer. Located inside a computer, it is the 'brain' that performs all arithmetic, logic and control functions in the computer.

Channel Data Format (CDF) A system used to prepare information for webcasting.

Chat room A virtual room on the internet where individuals chat to fellow members in real time. Generally, chat rooms have topics or themes.

Chatting On the internet, chatting is talking to other people who are using the internet at the same time as you. This 'talking' is the exchange of typed-in messages by a group of users who take part from anywhere on the internet. In some cases, a private chat can be arranged between two parties who meet initially in a group chat. Chats can be ongoing or scheduled for a particular time and duration. Most chats are focused on a particular topic of interest. Some involve special guests such as celebrities, athletes and politicians who 'talk' to anyone joining the chat.

Chilling effect Describes the way that a fear of legal or economic action encourages self-censorship.

Click fraud/bogus click syndrome Defrauds the internet advertising billing systems by bulk clicking advertisements either by low-wage labour or automated scripts.

Code Grants owners access to a secure environment for colloquial term for software programming language.

Compact Disk—Read Only Memory or Media (CD-ROM) CD-ROM technology is a format and system for recording, storing and retrieving electronic information on a compact disk that is read using laser optics rather than magnetic means.

Compact Disk—Recordable (CDR) A disk to which data can be written but not erased.

Compact Disk—Rewritable (CDRW) A disk to which data can be written and erased.

Compact flash card A form of storage media, commonly used in digital personal organisers and cameras but can be used in other electronic devices including computers.

Complementary Metal Oxide Semi-Conductor (CMOS) It commonly holds the BIOS preference of the computer through power off with the aid of a battery.

Computer Emergency Response Team (CERT) Also known as CSIRT, CERT are a national body used to report incidents to raise awareness about security threats, response to incidents and conduct research into potential security threats.

Computer Security Incident Response (CSIRT) Also known as CERT, CSIRT are a national body used to report incidents to raise awareness about security threats, response to incidents and conduct research into potential security threats.

Appendix 1: Cyber Crime Glossary of Terms

Cookie A piece of information or message sent by a website server to a web browser, where it is stored on the local computer. Each time someone on that computer goes back to the particular web page, the message is sent back to the server. Depending on the type of cookie used, and the browser's settings, the browser may or may not accept the cookie, and may save the cookie for either a short time or a long time. Cookies might contain information such as login or registration information, online 'shopping cart' information, user preferences, etc.

Cracker A computer expert who uses their skill to break into computer systems with malicious intent or motives. The term was coined by hackers to differentiate themselves from those who damage systems or steal information.

Crime harvest Refers to the criminal gain made by an offender during the period between the opening of a window of criminal opportunity and its closure, by, e.g., security 'patches' or public information.

Cryptography The process of securing private information sent through public networks by encrypting it in a way that makes it unreadable to anyone except the person or persons holding the mathematical key/knowledge to decrypt the information.

Cyber crime wave Describes the very quick and almost 'viral' proliferation of cyber crimes across globalised networks.

Cyber space The mentally constructed virtual environment within which networked computer activity takes place.

Cyber-terrorism Use of computers by terrorists to attack the physical infrastructure to generate mass fear and anxiety and, in theory, manipulate the political agenda.

Cyber-tsunamis Describes the very quick and almost 'viral' proliferation of cyber crimes across globalised networks.

Cyber warfare A term used when attempts sponsored by government or governments against other nations will be made in order to damage their computer and network systems.

Cyclic Redundancy Check (CRC) A common technique for detecting data transmission errors.

Darkside hackers Evolve from the inexperienced 'script kiddies' hackers and are driven by financial or other types of gain.

Database Structured collection of data that can be accessed in many ways. Common database programs are: Dbase, Paradox, Access. Uses: various including, address links, invoicing information, etc.

Data doubling Refers to the comparing of an individual's access codes with data already held by the computer system to verify his or her access rights and identity.

Data encryption key Used for the encryption of message text and for the computation of message integrity checks (signatures).

Data mining The practice of examining large pre-existing databases in order to generate new information.

Data trails Trails left by the informational transactions required to secure access to, and navigate around, the internet.

Decode The converting of encoded data to its original form.

Decryption The reverse of encryption, a method of unscrambling encrypted information so that it becomes legible again.

Defacement A technique involving compromising the web server in order to modify a victim's website content.

Deleted files If a subject knows there are incriminating files on the computer, he or she may delete them in an effort to eliminate evidence. Many computer users think that this actually eliminates the information. However, depending on how the files are deleted, in many instances a forensic examiner is able to recover all or part of the original data.

Denial of Service attacks and Distributed Denial of Service attacks (DOS and DDOS) DOS attacks are aimed at specific websites. The attacker floods the web server with messages endlessly repeated. This ties up the system and denies access to legitimate users. DOS attacks which are carried out by someone attacking from multiple computers are known as Distributed Denial of Service attacks.

Dictionary attacks The attacker uses a program that continuously tries different common words to see if one matches a password to the system or programs.

Digital bomb A program that lies dormant, waiting to be activated by a certain date or action.

Digital evidence Information stored or transmitted in binary form that may be relied upon in court.

Digital piracy The unauthorised copying and resale of digital goods (e.g. software, music files).

Digital signature A code which is used to guarantee that an email was sent by a particular sender.

Digital Versatile Disk (DVD) Similar in appearance to a compact disk, but can store larger amounts of data.

Appendix 1: Cyber Crime Glossary of Terms

Discussion group An online forum in which people communicate about subjects of common interest. Forums for discussion groups include electronic mailing lists, internet newsgroups.

Disk cache A portion of memory set aside for temporarily holding information read from a disk.

Docking station A device to which a laptop or notebook computer can be attached for use as a desktop computer, usually having a connector for externally connected devices such as hard drives, scanners, keyboards, monitors and printers.

Domain name A domain name locates an organisation or other entity on the internet; it allows you to reference internet sites without knowing the true numerical address.

Domain Name Service (DNS) The Domain Name Service is one of the core internet protocols and mechanisms. DNS is what translates human readable names (e.g. 'www.microsoft.com') into the binary IP addresses that are actually used to move data packets around on the internet.

Dongle A term for a small external hardware device that connects to a computer, often via a USB port, to authenticate a piece of software; e.g. proof that a computer actually has a licence for the software being used.

Download To transfer data from a remote server to your local system.

Drive-by-download A term used to describe software, often malware downloaded onto a computer from the internet without the user's knowledge or permission.

EC3 (European Cyber Crime Centre) EC3, located at Europol, commenced operations on 1 January 2014. The centre will be the focal point in the EU's fight against cyber crime, contributing to faster reactions in the event of online crime. It supports member states and the EU's institutions in building operational and analytical capacity for investigations and cooperation with international partners.

Ecash Money that is used in transactions entirely electronically.

E-commerce A term used to describe the buying or selling of goods or services over the internet. Usually, payment is made by using a credit or debit card.

Email bombs To flood an email account or server with mail.

Email header Emails come in two parts—the body and the header. Normal header information gives the recipient details of time, date, sender and subject. All emails also come with (usually hidden) extended headers—information that is added by email programs and transmitting devices—which shows more information about the sender that is in many circumstances traceable to an individual computer on the internet.

EnCase A very popular forensic toolkit used for analysing storage media. Recent versions also provide some support for mobile phones.

Encryption The process of scrambling, or encoding, information in an effort to guarantee that only the intended recipient can read the information.

Encryption algorithm A formula or set of steps for solving a particular problem. To be an algorithm, a set of rules must be unambiguous and have a clear stopping point.

EnScript A programming language that is used to create plug-ins for EnCase.

Ethernet address Also known as a MAC (Media Access Control) address. Every device that communicates on a network has a MAC address. MAC addresses are used to communicate with other devices on the same network, whereas IP addresses are used to communicate with other network devices.

Extended headers Information that is added by email programs and transmitting devices—which shows more information about the sender that is in many circumstances traceable to an individual computer on the internet.

Extranet An intranet that is accessible to computers that are not actually part of a company's own private network, but that is not accessible to the general public.

Faraday box/rag/room An enclosure that blocks external electric fields. It is often used in forensics for blocking signals from reaching mobile phones to protect the data that is stored on them.

File carving The process of recovering or extracting files from an allocated or unallocated space.

File Transfer Protocol (FTP) FTP is used to send whole documents or collections of documents stored in one computer to another through the internet.

Firewall Software typically run on a dedicated server that blocks transmission of certain classes of traffic to secure internal LANs from the outside world.

First responder With regards to digital forensics, first responders are responsible for identifying and securing evidence at a search site and transporting it to the forensic lab. Experienced first responders may also be responsible for conducting live data forensics on machines that are powered-on.

Floppy disk These are disks that hold information magnetically. They come in two main types: 3½ inch and 5½ inch. The 5½-inch disks which are now rarely seen, are flexible and easily damaged, the 3½-inch disks are in a stiff case. Both are square and flat. Older machines may use larger or smaller sizes of disks.

Foot printing A method used by hackers in order to identify weaknesses and vulnerabilities of a targeted system.

Free space File clusters that are not currently used for the storage of live files, but which may contain data which has been deleted by the operating system. In such cases, whole or part files may be recoverable unless the user has used specialised disk-cleaning software.

Frequently Asked Questions (FAQs) FAQs are used in email and newsgroups and is an acronym that generally refers to a list of frequently asked questions and their answers, or a question from the list. Many USENET newsgroups and some non-USENET mailing lists maintain FAQ lists so that participants don't spend a lot of time answering the same questions. It's a good idea to look at a FAQ file for a newsgroup or mailing list before participating in it.

Gateway A computer system that transfers data between normally incompatible applications or networks. It reformats the data so that it is acceptable for the new network (or application) before passing it on.

Gigabyte (Gb) 1 Gigabyte = 1024 Megabytes. A gigabyte is a measure of memory capacity and is roughly one thousand megabytes or a billion bytes. It is pronounced GIGabite with hard Gs.

Gray hackers A type of hacker who uses their skills for both defensive and offensive purposes.

Hacker Persons who are experts with computer systems and software and enjoy pushing the limits of software or hardware. To the public and the media, they can be good or bad. Some hackers come up with good ideas this way and share their ideas with others to make computing more efficient. However, some hackers intentionally use their expertise for malicious purposes (e.g. to circumvent security and commit computer crimes), these are known as 'black hat' hackers. Also see **Cracker**.

Hacking The process of exploiting the vulnerabilities of software or infrastructures for the purpose of exposing vulnerabilities or gaining access to a system or data.

Hacktivism Sometimes spelled hactivism, is a politically or ideologically motivated vandalism. Defacing a website for no particular reason is vandalism; the same defacement to post political propaganda or to cause harm to an ideological opponent is hacktivism.

Hard disk The hard disk is usually inside the PC. It stores information in the same way as floppy disks but can hold far more of it.

Hardware The physical parts of a computer. If it can be picked up it is hardware as opposed to software.

Hash sets A collection of hashes that are used to identify specific files.

History list A list of web documents that were seen during a session.

Home page The first page presented to a user when he or she selects a site or presence on the World Wide Web. It serves as a starting point for browsing the website.

Honeypot Commonly intended for gathering intelligence about potential attacks and attackers. It helps security experts to identify hackers and their offensive methods to inform the provision of countermeasures.

Host On the internet, a host is any computer that has full two-way access to other computers on the internet. A host has a specific local or host number that, together with the network number, forms its unique Internet Protocol address. If you use Point to Point Protocols (PPP) to get access to your Internet Service Provider (ISP), you have a unique IP address for the duration of any connection you make to the internet and your computer is a host for that period. In this context, a host is a node in a network.

Host machine For the purpose of this document, a host machine is one which is used to accept a target hard drive for the purpose of forensically processing.

Hotline Hotlines on the web are usually similar to a telephone hotline. Instead of dialling, you go to the hotline website, type the details you wish to report and a message is transmitted to the hotline organisation over the internet.

Hub A central connection for all the computers in a network which is usually Ethernet based. Information sent to the hub can flow to any other computer on the network.

Hypertext link Any text or graphic that contains links to other documents. Clicking on a link automatically displays the second document.

Appendix 1: Cyber Crime Glossary of Terms

Hypertext Mark up Language (HTML) HTML is the evolving standard for creating hypertext documents published on the World Wide Web. It not only formats documents, but also links text and images to documents residing on other web servers.

Hypertext Transfer Protocol Documents (HTTP) HTTP are formatted with hypertext links sent and received using HyperText Transmission Protocol. In order for hypertext documents to be sent and displayed properly, and to have active hypertext links, software on both the sending and receiving end must use HTTP.

ICQ ('I Seek You') A program that alerts users in real time when friends and colleagues sign on. Users can create a Contact List containing only people they want to have there, chat with them, send messages and files, play games or use it as a business tool to find and contact associates in real time through the internet.

Image Taking of an exact copy of the data from a digital device for examination.

Imaging The process used to obtain all of the data present on a storage media (e.g. hard disk), whether it is active data or data in free space, in such a way as to allow it to be examined as if it were the original data.

Instant messaging Technology similar to that of a chat room, it notifies a user when a friend is online allowing them to exchange messages.

Integrated Circuit Card Identifier (ICCID) A number that is used to uniquely identify SIM cards.

Integrated Services Digital Network (ISDO) ISDO is a standard for transmitting voice, video and data over digital lines.

International Mobile Equipment Identifier (IMEI) A unique 15-digit number that serves as the serial number of a GSM handset.

International Mobile Equipment Identity (IMEI) An IMEI number is used to uniquely identify mobile telephones. Usually printed in the battery compartment of a mobile phone or by typing *#06# on the devices keypad. IMEI numbers can be used to identify valid devices on a mobile network and to prevent stolen devices from being used.

International Mobile Subscriber Identity (IMSI) IMSI is a globally unique code that identifies a Global System for Mobiles (GSM) handset subscriber to the network.

Internet Access Provider (IAP) Internet access provider, also known as an Internet Service Provider.

Internet Message Access Protocol (IMAP) IMAP is gradually replacing POP as the main protocols used by email clients in communicating with email servers. Using IMAP on an email client program cannot only retrieve email but can also manipulate messages stored on the server, without having to actually retrieve the messages.

Internet Protocol (IP) address Each computer connected to the internet is addressed using a unique 32bit number called an IP address. These addresses are usually written in Dotted Quad notation, as a series of four 8bit numbers, written in decimal and separated by full stops. For example: 151.196.75.10. Each number in the IP address falls between 0 and 255. So, if you ever see something that looks like an IP address with numbers outside those ranges, it is not a real address. For example, a computer running virtual websites will have an IP address for each website it hosts. In addition, a pool of IP addresses may be shared between a number of computers. For example, on a dynamic-IP dialup connection your computer will be allocated a different IP address each time you connect.

Internet protocol spoofing A technique used to gain unauthorised access to computers.

Internet Relay Chat (IRC) A virtual meeting place where people from all over the world can meet and talk about a diversity of human interests, ideas and issues. Participants are able to take part in group discussions on one of the many thousands of IRC channels, or just talk in private to family or friends, wherever they are in the world.

Internet Service Provider (ISP) A company that sells access to the internet via telephone or cable line to your home or office. This will normally be free where the user pays for the telephone charge of a local call or by subscription—where a set monthly fee is paid and the calls are either free or at minimal cost.

InterNIC (Internet Network Information Centre) InterNIC is the organisation responsible for registering and maintaining the com, edu, gov, net and org domain names on the World Wide Web. If you are creating or already have a website, you must register the domain name with InterNIC.

Intranet An intranet is a network of networks designed for information processing within a company or organisation. Intranets are used for such services as document distribution, software distribution, access to databases and training.

Appendix 1: Cyber Crime Glossary of Terms

Jaz disk A high capacity proprietary removable hard disk system from a company named Iomega.

Joint Photographic Experts Group (JPEG) An acronym which refers to a standards committee, a method of file compression and a graphics file format. The committee originated from within the International Standards Organisation (ISO) to research and develop standards for the transmission of image data over networks. The results were a highly successful method of data compression and several closely associated file formats to store the data. JPEG files typically contain photographs, video stills or other complex images.

Key logger Refers to a piece of software or hardware designed to covertly record computer key strokes.

Keyring A pair of keys that consist of both a public key and its corresponding private key. Keyrings are used in public key encryption systems such as Pretty Good Privacy (PGP). Data encrypted with someone's public key can only be decrypted with the corresponding private key, and vice versa.

Keyword A word you might use to search for a website.

Kilobyte (KB) 1 Kilobyte = 1024 bytes.

Latency The period during which a time bomb, logic bomb, virus or worm refrains from overt activity or damage (delivery of the payload). Long latency coupled with vigorous reproduction can result in severe consequences for infected or otherwise compromised systems.

Latent Present, although not visible, but capable of becoming visible.

Link Any text or graphic coded and formatted so that clicking on it automatically displays a second document or image.

Linux An operating system popular with enthusiasts and used by some businesses.

Live data forensics The process of analysing the contents and running the process of a computer which is turned on. Traditional forensics involves creating an image or a powered-off device and analysing the image so that the original cannot be altered. Live data forensics is often used where potential evidence can be lost when the device is powered off.

Local Area Network (LAN) A computer network that covers only a small area (often a single office or building).

Logic bomb A piece of code intentionally inserted into a software system that will set off a malicious function when specified conditions are met. For example, a programmer may hide a piece of code that starts deleting files (e.g. a salary database trigger), should they ever be terminated from the company.

Logical acquisition The process of acquiring data from a device that the operating system considers is available. This is similar to the copy and paste method of extracting files from live machines and will not recover the same volume of data that a physical extraction can retrieve, since the deleted files, e.g., will not be recovered.

Login Noun: the account name used to gain access to a computer system. Not a secret (contrast with password). Verb: the act of connecting to a computer system by giving your credentials (usually your username and password).

Lurking To receive and read articles or messages in a newsgroup or other online conference without contributing anything to the ongoing exchange.

MAC (Media Access Control) address Also known as an Ethernet address. Every device that communicates on a network has a MAC address. MAC addresses are used to communicate with other devices on the same network, whereas IP addresses are used to communicate with other network devices.

Macrovirus A virus attached to instructions (called macros) which are executed automatically when a document is opened.

Magneticmedia A disk, tape, cartridge, diskette or cassette that is used to store data magnetically.

Mail Abuse Prevention System (MAPS) An organisation and system set up to defend the internet's email system from abuse by spammers through their RBL (Realtime Blackhouse List).

Mailbox Directory on a host computer where your email messages are stored. With some systems you can elect to keep saved messages either on the server or your local computer as you prefer.

Malware Malicious software or code that usually takes control, disables or steals information from a computer system. These take the forms of viruses, worms, Trojan Horses, logic bombs, rootkits, bootkits, backdoors, spyware and adware.

Man in the middle A type of attack when the attacker can monitor, change or inject messages or data into communication channels between two or more nodes.

MD5 hash An algorithm used to create digital fingerprints of storage media such as a computer hard drive, but is also commonly used to check the integrity of computer files. When this algorithm is applied to a file, it creates a unique value, typically expressed as a 32-digit hexadecimal number. Changing the data on the disk in any way will change the MD5 value.

Mediacards Small-sized data storage media that are more commonly found in other digital devices such as cameras, PDAs (Personal Digital Assistants) and music players. They can also be used for the storage of normal data files, which can be accessed and written to by computers. There are a number of different formats including: Smartmedia card, SD Expansion card, Ultra Compact Flash, Compact Flash, Multimedia Card, memory stick. The cards are non-volatile—they retain their data when power to their device is stopped—and they can be exchanged between devices.

Megabyte (Mb) 1 Megabyte = 1024 Kilobytes.

Memory Often used as a shorter synonym for random access memory (RAM). Memory is the electronic holding place for instructions and data that a computer's microprocessor can reach quickly. RAM is located on one or more microchips installed in a computer.

Memory stick A USB storage medium. See **USB storage devices**

Message ID A unique number assigned to a message.

MHz (megahertz) MHz is a unit of alternating current (AC) or electromagnetic (EM) wave frequency equal to one million hertz (1,000,000 Hz). It is commonly used to express microprocessor clock speed.

Microsoft Disk Operating System (MDOS) MDOS is an operating system marketed by Microsoft. This was once the most common operating system in use on desktop PCs, which automatically loads into the computer memory by the act of switching the computer on. Often only referred to as DOS.

Modem Modulator/Demodulator: a device that connects a computer to a data transmission line (typically a telephone line). Most people use modems that transfer data at speeds ranging from 1200 bits per second (bps) to 56 Kbps. There are also modems providing higher speeds and supporting other media. These are used for special purposes, e.g. to connect a large local network to its network provider over a leased line.

Mouse droppings Refers to the data trails left by the informational transactions required to secure access to, and navigate around, the internet.

Multimedia Documents that include different kinds of formats for information or data. For example, text, audio and video, may be included in one document.

Netscape An application used to browse the World Wide Web.

Network A group of computers and associated devices that are interconnected by communication paths. A network can involve permanent connections, such as cables, or temporary connections made through telephone or other communication links. A network can be as small as a few computers, printers and other devices, or it can consist of many small and large computers distributed over a vast geographic area.

Newsgroup An electronic discussion surrounding a particular subject. It consists of messages posted on a central internet site and redistributed through Usenet, a worldwide network of news discussion groups.

Node Any single computer connected to a network. The processing location within a network. The processing location, node, can be a computer, printer, scanner or other type of device within a network.

Offline Not connected.

Online Having access to the internet.

Operating system This software is usually loaded into the computer memory when the machine is switched on and is a prerequisite for the operation of any other software. Examples include the Microsoft Windows family of operating systems (including 3.x, NT, 2000, XP and Vista) and UNIX operating systems and their variants like Linux, HPUX, Solaris and Apple's Mac OSX and BSD.

ORB A high-capacity removable hard disk system. ORB drives use magneto resistive (MR) read/write head technology.

Packet A bundle of data that is routed between an origin and a destination on the internet. When information such as files, email messages, HTML documents, web pages, etc are sent from one place to another on the internet, TCP/IP divides the information into chunks of an efficient size for routing. Each of these packets includes the internet address of the destination. The individual packets of the information being routed may travel different routes through the internet. When they have all arrived, they are reassembled into the original file by TCP/IP.

Palmtops A portable personal computer that fits into the palm of your hand. See **Personal Organiser/Personal Digital Assistant (PDA)**.

Password A word, phrase or combination of keystrokes used as a security measure to limit access to computers or software.

Password cracker A type of tool designed to decode passwords.

Appendix 1: Cyber Crime Glossary of Terms

PCMCIA cards Similar in size to credit cards, but thicker. These cards are inserted into slots in a laptop or palmtop computer and provide many functions not normally available to the machine (modems, adapters, hard disks, etc).

Peer-to-peer (P2P) On the internet, P2P is a type of transient internet network or protocol that allows a group of computer users with the same networking program to connect with each other and directly access files from one another's hard disk drives. There are a wide variety of these networks, including Kazaa, Bit Torrent, eDonkey and Gnutella. Typically the most commonly shared files include pictures, movies, music and software programs.

Pen drive A small USB storage medium. See **USB storage devices**.

Penetration testing Refers to simulated methods used by white hackers to gain unauthorised access to a system in order to examine, evaluate and improve security standards.

Peripherals Devices external to a computer, e.g. printer, monitor, external disk.

Personal Organiser/ Personal Digital Assistant (PDA) These are pocket-sized machines and address lists and diaries. They often also contain other information. Modern PDAs take many forms and a convergent personal organiser or PDA usually holding a phone may best be described as a device capable of carrying out the functions of a multitude of devices.

Personal Unlock Key (PUK) The code to unlock a GSM SIM card that has disabled itself after an incorrect PIN was entered three times in a row.

Phishing and pharming Phishing attacks use 'spoofed' emails and fraudulent websites designed to fool recipients into divulging personal data such as credit card numbers, account user names and passwords, social security numbers, etc. Pharming uses the same malware/spyware to redirect users from real websites to the fraudulent sites (typically DNS hijacking). By hijacking the trusted brands of well-known banks, online retailers and credit card companies, phishers are able to convince recipients to respond to them.

Phrase list A list of pass phrases used by password cracker tools in order to decode passwords.

Phreaking Telephone hacking, usually to obtain free calls, by generating illicit administrative commands to the network computer.

Physical acquisition Allows the retrieval of hidden, deleted and corrupted data from a storage medium.

Pick list A list of relevant items/processes for choice.

Pirate software Software that has been illegally copied.

Point to Point Protocol (PPP) A protocol for communication between two computers using a serial interface, typically a personal computer connected by phone line to a server.

Port The word port has three meanings:

- where information goes into or out of a computer, e.g. the serial port on a personal computer is where a modem would be attached;
- in the TCP and UDP protocols used in computer networking, a port is a number present in the header of a data packet. Ports are typically used to map data to a particular process running on a computer. For example, port 25 is commonly associated with SMTP, port 80 with HTTP and port 443 with HTPPS;
- it also refers to translating a piece of software to bring it from one type of computer system to another, e.g. to translate a Windows program so that it will work on a Mac.

Program A prewritten sequence of computer commands designed to perform a specific task, e.g. word processing, accounting, inventory management, or accessing the internet and World Wide Web.

Proxy server In an enterprise that uses the internet, this is a server that acts as an intermediary between a workstation user and the internet so that the enterprise can ensure security, administrative control and caching service. A proxy server can improve performance by supplying frequently requested data, such as a popular web page, and can filter and discard requests that the owner does not consider appropriate, such as requests for unauthorised access to proprietary files.

Public domain software Any program that is not copyrighted.

Python A popular programming language that is supported by forensic tools such as UFED and XRY.

Query To search or ask. In particular, to request information in a search engine, index directory or database.

Quicktime A multimedia development, storage and playback technology developed by Apple Computers. Quicktime files combine audio, video, text and animation into a single file played with a Quicktime Player that either comes with a web browser or that can be downloaded from Apple. Quicktime files have one of the following extensions: qt, mov or moov.

Random Access Memory (RAM) RAM is a computer's short-term memory. It provides working space for the PC to work with data at high speeds. Information stored in the RAM is lost when the PC is turned off ('volatile data').

RealAudio A continuous streaming audio technology developed by Progressive Networks. RealAudio files are played with a RealAudio Player that either comes with a web browser or can be downloaded from Apple. RealAudio files have one of the following extensions: ra, ram.

Registry An important part of the Windows operating system and can be a useful resource for finding evidential data such as typed URLs and recently connected devices.

Remote Access Service (RAS) Refers to any combination of hardware and software to enable the remote access tools or information that typically reside on a network of IT devices. RAS connects a client to a host computer, known as a remote access server.

Remote exploit An exploit is a piece of software, a chunk of data or a sequence of commands that takes advantage of a bug, glitch or vulnerability in order to cause unintended or unanticipated behaviour. Frequently includes things like gaining control of a computer system, allowing privilege escalation or a DOS attack.

Removable media Items such as floppy disks, CDs, DVDs, cartridges or tape that store data and can be easily removed.

Removable media cards Small-sized data storage media which are more commonly found in other digital devices such as cameras, PDAs (Personal Digital Assistants) and music players. They can also be used for the storage of normal data files, which can be accessed and written to by computers. There are a number of these including: Smartmedia card, SD Expansion card, Ultra Compact Flash, Compact Flash, Multimedia card, memory stick. The cards are non-volatile—they retain their data when power to their device is stopped—and they can be exchanged between devices.

Rootkit A stealthy type of software, typically malicious, designed to provide privileged 'root level access' to a computer and hide the existence of certain processes or programs from normal methods of detection and enable this continued privileged access to a computer.

Router A system that transfers data between two networks that use the same protocols.

Safe boot To start a computer in a controlled manner so as not to change any stored data.

Script Small program to automate simple repetitive tasks.

Search engine A program used on the internet that performs searches for keywords in files and documents found on the World Wide Web, newsgroups, Gopher menus and FTP archives. Some search engines search only within a single internet site. Others search across many sites, using such agents as spiders to gather lists of available files and documents and store these lists in databases that users can search by keyword. Examples include Alta Vista, Metacrawler, Yahoo, Dogpile, Lycos and Excite.

Secure wipe Overwriting all material on a disk so as to destroy, as far as possible, all data stored upon it.

Security firewall A system that isolates an organisation's computers from external access, as through the internet. The firewall is intended to protect other machines at the site from potential tampering from the internet.

Server Specific to the web, a web server is the computer program running on a computer that serves requested HTML pages or files. A web client is the requesting program associated with the user. A web browser is a client that requests HTML files from web servers.

Service Provider (ISP) A person, organisation or company that provides access to the internet. In addition to internet access, many ISPs provide other services such as web hosting, Domain Name Service and other proprietary services.

Session hijacking A technique which hackers use to get control of an active session between two computers.

Shareware Software that is distributed free on a trial basis with the understanding that, if it is used beyond the trial period, the user will pay. Some shareware versions are programmed with a built-in expiration date.

Signature A personal tag automatically appended to an email message.

Slackspace The unused space in a disk cluster. The DOS and Windows file systems use fixed-sized clusters. Even if the actual data being stored requires less storage than the cluster size, an entire cluster is reserved for the file. The unused space is called the slack space.

Slimeware A slang term used to describe software that interferes with the user experience by changing key settings in order to gain profit. A type of adware.

Smartcard Plastic cards, typically with an electronic chip embedded, that contain electronic value tokens. Such value is disposable at both physical retail outlets and online shopping locations.

Appendix 1: Cyber Crime Glossary of Terms

Sniffer A program that displays the contents of all packets passing through a particular network. Originally developed to test the performance of internet connections by reading all of the information passing through a network. They can be used to trace private information such as credit card numbers and passwords.

Social engineering Attacks basically by wit, guile or outright lies, aimed at conning a user to divulge passwords or other confidential information.

Software The prewritten programs designed to assist in the performance of a specific task, such as network management, web development, file management, word processing, accounting or inventory management.

Software cracking The removal of copyright protection routines from software.

Software piracy The unauthorised copying and resale of software programs.

Solid State Driver (SSD) SSD is a storage device, also known as a solid state disk or electronic disk. It contains no actual disk but is a data storage device using integrated circuit assemblies as memory to store data persistently.

Spam/spamming The same article (or essentially the same article) posted an unacceptably high number of times to one or more newsgroups. Spam is also uninvited email sent to many people or unsolicited email advertising and can also be referred to as junk mail.

Spear phishing A targeted phishing attempt that seems more credible to its victims and thus has a higher probability of success.

Spim Spam over instant messenger.

Spit Spam over internet telephony.

Spyware Software that aids in gathering information about a person or organisation without their knowledge and that may send such information to another entity without the consumer's consent, or that asserts control over a computer without the consumer's knowledge. Spyware is mostly classified into four types: system monitors, Trojans, adware and tracking cookies. Spyware is mostly used for the purposes of tracking and storing internet users' movements on the web and serving up pop-up advertisements to internet users.

SQL injection A method used by cyber attackers to retrieve information by compromising the security of a database.

Steganography The art and science of communicating in a way that hides the existence of the communication. It is used to hide a file inside another. For example, child pornography image can be hidden inside another graphic, image file, audio file or other file format.

Streaming audio/video Listening or viewing media files from the internet in real time as opposed to saving the file and playing it later. See **RealAudio**.

Subscriber Identity Module (SIM) A smartcard which is inserted into a cellular phone, identifying the user account to the network and providing storage for data.

Suicide hackers A type of cybercriminal who will try to take down critical infrastructures for malicious purposes. They are also known as cyber terrorists.

Superzapping Using powerful utility software (originally the superzap utility on IBM mainframes) to access secure information while bypassing normal controls. Debug programs and disk editors are examples of tools used for superzapping.

Surf/surfing Exploring the internet by moving from one website to another as the whim of the user dictates.

Switch Typically a small, flat box with 4 to 8 Ethernet ports. These ports can connect to computers, cable or DSL modems and other switches. A switch directs network communications between specific systems on the network as opposed to broadcasting information to all networked connections.

System unit Usually the largest part of a PC, the system unit is a box that contains the major components. It usually has the drives at the front and the ports for connecting the keyboard, mouse, printer and other devices at the back.

Tape A long strip of magnetic coated plastic. Usually held in cartridges (looking similar to video, audio or camcorder tapes), but can also be held on spools (like reel-to-reel audio tape). Used to record computer data, usually a backup of the information on the computer.

Telnet A verb that means to log on to a distant computer and use it as a local user. The software utility allows persons to access and use a remote computer. In effect, the user's machine becomes a terminal for the other computer. Unlike FTP, Telnet does not allow users to transfer and save files to their own computers.

Temporary or swap files Many computers use operating systems and applications that store data temporarily on the hard drive. These files, which are generally hidden and inaccessible, may contain information that the investigator finds useful.

Appendix 1: Cyber Crime Glossary of Terms

Terminal A device that allows you to send commands to a computer somewhere else. At a minimum, this usually means a keyboard and a display screen and some simple circuitry.

Time bomb A program or batch file waits for a specific time before causing damage. Often used by disgruntled and dishonest employees who find out they are to be fired or by dishonest consultants who put unauthorised time-outs into their programs without notifying their clients. Logic bombs and time bombs are Trojan Horse programs; time bombs are a type of logic bomb.

Tools disk Hard disk upon which is stored software programs used for data examination and analysis.

Top Level Domain (TLD) A name such as .com, .org, .net, etc.

Transmission Control Protocol/Internet Protocol (TCP/IP) TCP/IP is the basic communication language or protocol of the internet.

Trojan Horse Often just referred to as a 'Trojan', this is a computer program that hides or disguises another program. The victim starts what they think is a safe program and instead willingly accepts something also designed to do harm to the system on which it runs.

UFED A very popular mobile forensic tool kit produced by Cellbrite.

Unallocated space Area of the disk available for use, contains deleted files and remnants of other previously stored or unused data. Data in this area can often be retrieved by a forensic examiner.

Uniform Resource Identifier (URI) An address for a resource available on the internet. The first part of the URI is called the 'Scheme'. The most well-known scheme is the http, but there are many others.

Uniform Resource Locator (URL) A URL is the address of a file accessible on the internet. An example of a URL is: http://www.usatoday.com/sports/sfront.htm, which describes a web page to be accessed with an HTTP (web browser) application that is located on a computer named www.usatoday.com. The specific file is in the directory named /sports and is named sfront.htm.

Uninterruptible power supply (UPS) UPS is a power supply that can continue to provide a regulated supply to equipment even after a mains power failure.

Unix A very popular operating system. Used mainly on larger multiuse systems.

Upload To transfer a copy of a file from a local computer to a remote computer.

USB storage devices Small storage devices accessed using a computer's USB ports, that allow the storage of large volumes of data files and which can be easily removed, transported and concealed. They are about the size of a car key or highlighter pen, and can even be worn around the neck on a lanyard. They now come in many forms and may look like something entirely different such as a watch or a Swiss Army knife.

Usenet This is like a collection of bulletin boards that is separate from but parallel to the internet and that carries newsgroups. There are an estimated 90,000 newsgroups on Usenet and each focuses on a single topic ranging from the bizarre to the mundane.

User name (User ID) The name that identifies you and that you use to 'sign on' with an ISP. In addition to your registered 'user name', you will also use a password.

USIM An enhancement of the Subscriber Identity Module (SIM) card designed to be used in third generation (3G) networks.

Video backer A program that allows computer data to be backed up to standard video. When viewed, the data is presented as a series of dots and dashes.

Virtual machine Software-based solutions that emulate computers. Virtual machine players, such as virtual box or VMWare player, are required to use a virtual machine.

Virtual Private Network (VPN) VPN usually refers to a network in which some of the parts are connected using the public internet, but the data sent across the internet is encrypted, so the entire network is 'virtually' private.

Virtual storage A 'third party' storage facility on the internet, enabling data to be stored and retrieved from any browser. Examples include Xdrive and Freeway.com.

Virus A computer virus is a computer program that can copy itself and infect a computer without permission (and often without knowledge) of the user. A virus can only spread from one computer to another when its host is taken to the uninfected computer, e.g. by a user sending it over a network or carrying it on a removable medium such as a floppy disk, CD or USB drive. Additionally, viruses can spread to other computers by infecting files on a network file system or a file system that is accessed by another computer. Some are harmless (messages on the screen, etc), whilst others are destructive (e.g. loss or corruption of information).

Appendix 1: Cyber Crime Glossary of Terms

Volatile data Data which can be lost or is temporary. For example, data stored in RAM is considered volatile as it is lost when a computer is turned off.

Wear-levelling The process of relocating altered files to extend the longevity of solid-state storage devices.

Web server A computer on the internet or intranet that serves as a storage area for a web page. When asked by a web browser, the server sends the page to the browser.

Website A related collection of HTML files that includes a beginning file called a home page.

Websitespoof Counterfeit site, which mimics an established one. When users submit information such as passwords and user names, the counterfeit site collects it.

White hackers A type of cyber hacker, also known as a 'security analyst', who use their knowledge for defensive purposes against cyber attacks.

Wide Area Network (WAN) WAN is a network, usually constructed with serial lines, which covers a large geographical area.

Windows Operating system marketed by Microsoft. In use on desktop PCs, the system automatically loads into the computer's memory in the act of switching the computer on. MSDOS, Windows, Windows 2.0, Windows 95, Windows 98, Office XP, Windows XP, Windows NT, Windows Vista and Windows Server are registered trademarks of Microsoft Corporation.

WindowsOT Operating system marketed by Microsoft primarily aimed at the business market. Multiple layers of security are available with this system.

Winzip The Windows version of a shareware program that lets you archive and compress files so that you can store or distribute them more efficiently.

Wireless network card An expansion card present in a computer that allows cordless connection between that computer and other devices on a computer network. This replaces the traditional network cables. The card communicates by radio signals to other devices present on the network.

Wiretapping Refers to sniffing and monitoring ongoing traffic in a communication channel.

Word processor Used for typing letters, reports and documents. Common word processing programs are Wordstar, WordPerfect and MSWord.

Working files Files created during examination for further examination or reference.

Worms Like a virus but capable of moving from computer to computer over a network without being carried by another program and without the need for any human interaction to do so.

Write-blocker A piece of hardware used to block alterations being made to a device. Write-blockers are often used during the imaging process as they allow the imaging software to read a device while protecting the data stored on it. Some operating systems, such as Linux-based ones, provide software write-blockers. Software write-blockers can be just as effective as hardware versions.

XRY A very popular forensic tool designed by Micro Systemation for extracting and decoding information from mobile phones.

Zero Day attack An attack used by hackers in order to exploit a system by an unidentified weakness and vulnerability in an application or a network system.

Zip A popular data compression format. Files that have been compressed with the ZIP format are called ZIP files and usually end with a .ZIP extension. There are other formats which form a similar function, including Rar, ALZip, Tar and Stuffit for the Mac OS.

Zip drive/disk A 3½-inch removable disk drive. The drive is bundled with software that can catalogue disks and lock files for security.

Zombie A program inserted into a vulnerable system to await further instructions; usually part of a DDoS attack.

Public Guidance to Prevent Online Fraud for Police Officers

Introduction

As a police officer your role in providing practical cyber crime preventative advice can have a significant impact on reducing the volume of cyber crime and cyber crime victims by providing simple prevention advice to support and reassure the public. Remember that cyber crime prevention can be straightforward—when armed with a little technical advice and common sense, many cyber crimes can be avoided. In general, online criminals are trying to make their money as quickly and easily as possible. The more difficult you can make their job, the more likely they are to leave the member of the public alone and move on to an easier target. You must do all you can to ensure that you are creating a robust and hostile environment for cybercriminals to operate. The guidance below provides basic information on how you can advise members of the public to help to protect themselves and prevent becoming a victim of online fraud.

Appendix 2: Public Guidance to Prevent Online Fraud

Advice	Explanation
Keep your computer current with the latest patches and updates	• One of the best ways to keep attackers away from your computer is to apply patches and other software fixes when they become available. By regularly updating your computer, you block attackers from being able to take advantage of software flaws (vulnerabilities) that they could otherwise use to break into your system. • While keeping your computer up to date will not protect you from all attacks, it makes it much more difficult for hackers to gain access to your system, blocks many basic and automated attacks completely and might be enough to discourage a less-determined attacker thereby encouraging them to look for a more vulnerable computer elsewhere. • More recent versions of Microsoft Windows and other popular software can be configured to download and apply updates automatically so that you do not have to remember to check for the latest software. Taking advantage of 'auto-update' features in your software is a great start towards keeping yourself safe online.
Make sure your computer is configured securely	• Keep in mind that a newly purchased computer may not have the right level of security for you. When you are installing your computer at home, pay attention not just to making your new system function but also focus on making it work securely. • Configuring popular internet applications such as your web browser and email software is one of the most important areas to focus on. For example, settings in your web browser such as Internet Explorer or Firefox will determine what happens when you visit websites on the internet—the strongest security settings will give you the most control over what happens online but may also frustrate some people with a large number of questions ('This may not be safe, are you sure you want to do this?') or the inability to do what they want to do. • Choosing the right level of security and privacy depends on the individual using the computer. Security and privacy settings can be properly configured without any sort of special expertise by simply using the 'Help' feature of your software or reading the vendor's website. If you are uncomfortable configuring it yourself, consult someone you know and trust for assistance or contact the vendor directly.

Advice	Explanation
Choose strong passwords and keep them safe	Passwords are a fact of life on the internet today—we use them for everything from ordering flowers and online banking to logging into our favourite airline website to see how many miles we have accumulated. The following tips can help to make your online experiences secure.
	• Selecting a password that cannot be easily guessed is the first step towards keeping passwords secure and away from the wrong hands. Strong passwords have eight characters or more and use a combination of letters, numbers and symbols (e.g. # $ %!?). Avoid using any of the following as your password: your login name, anything based on your personal information such as your last name and words that can be found in the dictionary. Try to select especially strong, unique passwords for protecting activities like online banking.
	• Keep your passwords in a safe place and try not to use the same password for every service you use online.
	• Change passwords on a regular basis, at least every 90 days. This can limit the damage caused by someone who has already gained access to your account. If you notice something suspicious with one of your online accounts, one of the first steps you can take is to change your password.
Protect your computer with security software	• Several types of security software are necessary for basic online security. Security software essentials include firewall and antivirus programs. A firewall is usually your computer's first line of defence as it controls who and what can communicate with your computer online. You could think of a firewall as a sort of 'police officer' that watches all the data attempting to flow in and out of your computer on the internet, allowing communications that it knows are safe and blocking 'bad' traffic, such as attacks, from ever reaching your computer.
	• The next line of defence is your antivirus software which monitors all online activities such as email messages and web browsing and protects an individual from viruses, worms, Trojan Horses and other types of malicious programs. More recent versions of antivirus programs, such as Norton AntiVirus, also protect from spyware and potentially unwanted programs such as adware. Having security software that gives you control over software you may not want and protects you from online threats is essential to staying safe on the internet. Your antivirus and anti-spyware software should be configured to update itself, and it should do so every time you connect to the internet.

Advice	Explanation

- Integrated security suites such as Norton Internet Security combine firewall, antivirus and anti-spyware with other features such as antispam. Also parental controls have become popular as they offer all the security software needed for online protection in a single package. Many people find using a security suite an attractive alternative to installing and configuring several different types of security software as well as keeping them all up to date.

Protect your personal information Exercise caution when sharing personal information such as your name, home address, phone number and email address online. To take advantage of many online services, you will inevitably have to provide personal information in order to handle billing and shipping of purchased goods. Since not divulging any personal information is rarely possible, the following list contains some advice for how to share personal information safely online.

- Keep an eye out for phony email messages. Things that indicate a message may be fraudulent are misspellings, poor grammar, odd phrasings, website addresses with strange extensions, website addresses that are entirely numbers where there are normally words and anything else out of the ordinary. Additionally, phishing messages will often tell you that you have to act quickly to keep your account open, update your security or urge you to provide information immediately or else something bad will happen. Don't take the bait!
- Don't respond to email messages that ask for personal information. Legitimate companies will not use email messages to ask for your personal information. When in doubt, contact the company by phone or by typing in the company web address into your web browser. Don't click on the links in these messages as they make take you to fraudulent, malicious websites.
- Steer clear of fraudulent websites used to steal personal information. When visiting a website, type the address (URL) directly into the web browser rather than following a link in an email or instant message. Fraudsters often forge these links to make them look convincing. A shopping, banking or any other website where sensitive information is used should have an 'S' after the letters 'http' (i.e. 'https://www.yourbank.com' not 'http://www.yourbank.com'). The 'S' stands for secure and should appear when you are in an area requesting you to login or provide other sensitive data. Another sign that you have a secure connection is the small lock icon in the bottom of your web browser (usually the right-hand corner).

Appendix 2: Public Guidance to Prevent Online Fraud

Advice	Explanation
	• Pay attention to privacy policies on websites and in software. It is important to understand how an organisation might collect and use your personal information before you share it with them. • Guard your email address. Spammers and phishers sometimes send millions of messages to email addresses that may or may not exist in the hope of finding a potential victim. Responding to these messages or even downloading images ensures that you will be added to their lists for more of the same messages in the future. Also be careful when posting your email address online in newsgroups, blogs or online communities.
Online offers that look too good to be true usually are	• The old saying 'there's no such thing as a free lunch' still rings true today. Supposedly 'free' software such as screensavers or smileys, secret investment tricks sure to make you untold fortunes and contests that you've surprisingly won without entering are the enticing hooks used by companies to grab your attention. • While you may not directly pay for the software or service with money, the free software or service you asked for may have been bundled with advertising software ('adware') that tracks your behaviour and displays unwanted advertisements. You may have to divulge personal information or purchase something else in order to claim your supposed winnings. If an offer looks so good that it's hard to believe, ask for someone else's opinion, read the fine print or, even better, simply ignore it.
Review bank and credit card statements regularly	• The impact of identity theft and online crimes can be greatly reduced if you can catch it shortly after your data is stolen or when the first use of your information is attempted. One of the easiest ways to get the tip-off that something has gone wrong is by reviewing the monthly statements provided by your bank and credit card companies for anything out of the ordinary. • Additionally, many banks and services use fraud prevention systems that call out unusual purchasing behaviour (i.e. if you live in Birmingham and all of a sudden start buying refrigerators in Budapest). In order to confirm these out-of-the-ordinary purchases, they might call you and ask you to confirm them. Don't take these calls lightly—this is your hint that something bad may have happened and you should consider pursuing some of the activities mentioned in the area covering how to respond if you have become a victim.

Cyber Crime Investigator's Guide to Network Forensics

The following guidance reflects the national police advice from the *Good Practice Guide for Digital Evidence*. It is vitally important that only someone who has been trained and is competent to do so should undertake any of the actions detailed below. In addition, it must be recognised by the cyber crime investigator that technology develops at a rapid pace and it remains their responsibility to ensure their investigative actions are based on current good practice.

1. Home and corporate network environments

Networks of computers are becoming more common in domestic environments and are well established in corporate settings. In the home, they are usually based around the broadband internet connection, which often also offers functionality to set up a small internal (and often wireless) network in the household. In corporate environments, more advanced network setups can be found, for which no generic description can be given.

The use of wireless networks in both the corporate and home environment is also increasing at a considerable rate. To the cyber crime forensic investigator, this presents a number of challenges and an increased number of potential artefacts to consider.

KEY POINT—CRIME SCENE COMPLEXITY

Owing to the potential complexity of 'technical' crime scenes, specialist advice should be sought when planning the digital evidence aspect of the forensic strategy.

1.1 Wireless devices

A whole range of wired and wireless devices may be encountered.

- Network devices which connect individual systems or provide network functionality: switches, hubs, routers, firewalls (or devices which combine all four).
- Devices to connect individual computers to the network, such as network cards (which can also be embedded in the computer).
- Devices to set up a wireless network: Wireless Access Points.
- Printers and digital cameras.
- Bluetooth (small-range wireless) devices—PDAs, mobile phones, dongles.
- Hard drives which can be connected to the network.

KEY POINT—CONTROLLING WIRELESS NETWORKS

Wireless networks cannot be controlled in the same way as a traditionally cabled solution and are potentially accessible by anyone within radio range. The implications of this should be carefully considered when planning a search or developing the wider investigative strategy. A device, such as a computer or a hard drive, may not be located on the premises where the search and seizure is conducted.

1.2 Home networks and data

If devices are networked, it may not be immediately obvious where the computer files and data, which are being sought, are kept. Data could be on any of them. Networks, both wired and wireless, also enable the users of the computers to share resources: such as printers, scanners and connections to the internet. It may well be the case that if one of the computers is connected to the internet, some or all of the others are also.

With the widespread use of broadband-type internet subscriptions such as ADSL and cable, the internet connection is nowadays likely to be of an 'always on'-type connection. This implies that even if no one is apparently working on a computer or using the internet, there may be data processing to and from computers or between the network and the internet.

If a wired network is present, there will usually be a small box (called a 'hub' or a 'switch') also present, connecting the computers together. Hubs, switches and routers look very much the same

---

as one another. The network cables are usually connected at the rear. The network may also be connected to another device (called a cable modem or an ADSL modem) providing access to the internet. Sometimes, the hub/switch/router mentioned before are combined with these modems in one device.

One wire from a modem will usually be connected to the telephone or television cable system and another will be connected either to one of the computers present or directly to the network hub, or the modem itself may be incorporated in the hub in a modem/router.

1.3 Operation planning in networked environments

When planning an operation involving a network, consider carefully the possibility of remote access, i.e. person(s) accessing a network with or without permission from outside the target premises. Investigators should consider the possibility of nefarious activity being carried out through the insecure network of an innocent party. The implications of such a scenario are that search warrants could be obtained on the basis of a resolved IP address, which actually relates to an innocent party. The implications are potentially unlawful searches, legal action taken against the relevant investigative agency and a waste of resources.

Consider also the possibility of a computer's access to remote online storage, which may physically reside in foreign jurisdiction. This can include web-based services for email, photo or document storage or other applications offered via the internet. There will be legal issues in relation to accessing any such material. Legal advice should be sought prior to any access or retrieval and often the provider of the particular service will have to be contacted to ensure that material is preserved while the relevant mutual legal assistance requests are being arranged.

1.4 Network detection

Network detecting and monitoring is a specialist area and should not be considered without expert advice. Recommendations for dealing with networks and wireless implementations involve the following steps.

- **STEP 1:** identify and check network devices to see how much network or internet activity is taking place. Consider using a wireless network detector to determine whether wireless is in operation and to locate wireless devices. Consideration should be given to mobile internet devices such as 3G or GPRS dongles or phones, which operate using the mobile phone network.

- **STEP 2:** as you do so, consider photographing the layout of the network and the location of the machines connected to it, so as to allow a possible future reconstruction.

- **STEP 3:** once satisfied that no data will be lost as a result, you may isolate the network from the internet. This is best done by identifying the connection to the telephone system or wireless communications point and unplugging it from the telephone point. Keep modems and routers running, as they may need to be interrogated to find out what is connected to them. Owing to their nature, it is particularly difficult to ascertain what is connected to a wireless network.

- **STEP 4:** trace each wire from the network device to discover the computer to which it is connected. This may not be possible in premises where cables may be buried in conduits or walls (advice in this case should be sought from the local IT administrator, if available, as to the setup of the system). Make a note of each connection. Note which computer is connected to which number 'port' on the network device (hub/switch/router or multi-function device). Label each connection in such a way that the system can be rebuilt exactly as it stands, should there be any future questions as to the layout. It is highly recommended that pictures be taken of the setup.

- **STEP 5:** consider making a connection to the access point/ router in order to establish the external IP address. Most modem networks use Network Address Translation (NAT) which means that they communicate with an IP address and never get assigned an external IP address.

KEY POINT—PHYSICAL CABLING

In a wireless environment, remember that no cables are used between a PC and other devices. However, there will still be some physical cabling to each device (which could include network cable to the wired network, power cables, etc), the configuration of which should be recorded. Note that cable/ADSL modems can have wireless capabilities built in.

- **STEP 6:** once satisfied that the evidential impact is acceptable, you may remove each connection in turn from the network device once it has been identified. This will isolate each computer in turn from the network. The same can be done with cabling into wireless devices.

- **STEP 7:** seize and bag all network hardware, modems, original boxes and CDs/floppy disks, etc (provided they are easily removable).

- **STEP 8:** subsequently treat each device as you would a stand-alone device.

- **STEP 9:** remember that the data which is sought may be on any one of the computers on the network. Officers should make a decision based on the reasonable assumption that relevant data may be stored on a device before seizing that device.

- **STEP 10:** bear in mind the possibility that the network may be a wireless network as well as a wired one, i.e. certain computers may be connected to the network via conventional network cabling. Others may be connected to that same network via the mains system, and others may be connected via a wireless link.

- **STEP 11:** also bear in mind that any mobile phones and PDAs may be wireless or Bluetooth-enabled and connected to a domestic network.

KEY POINT—REMOTE WIRELESS STORAGE

Concerns with remote wireless storage often focus around the inability to locate the device. In this instance, it would be impossible to prove that an offence had been committed. Artefacts on seized computers might provide evidence that a remote storage device has been used, however the analysis of such artefacts will take time and this cannot be done during the on-site seizure.

1.5 Corporate network environments

When dealing with computer systems in a corporate environment, the cyber crime forensic investigator faces a number of differing challenges. If the system administrator is not part of the investigation, then seek their assistance. The most significant is likely to be the inability to shut down server(s) due to company operational constraints. In such cases, it is common practice that a network-enabled 'forensic software' agent is installed, which will give the ability to image data across the network 'on-the-fly', or to a network share or a locally connected removable storage medium such as a USB hard drive.

Other devices could be encountered which may assist the investigation. For example, routers and firewalls can give an insight into network configuration through Access Control Lists (ACLs) or security rule sets. This may be achieved by viewing the configuration screens as an administrator of the device. This will require the user names and passwords obtained at the time of seizure or from the suspect during interview.

By accessing the devices, data may be added, violating Principle 1 of the ACPO *Good Practice Guide for Digital Evidence* but, if the logging mechanism is researched prior to investigation, the forensic footprints added during investigation may be taken into consideration and therefore Principle 2 can be complied with.

In the case of large company networks, consider gaining the advice and assistance of the network administrator/supplier team (assuming that they are not suspects).

2. Volatile Data Collection

In certain circumstances, it may be necessary or advisable for computer forensic investigators to gather evidence from a computer whilst it is running or in a 'live' state. This technique has become a common practice as, even though some changes to the original evidence will be made, this method often allows access to evidence which would have been unavailable if the power had been removed from a system. In order to capture volatile data on a device, the device **will** have to be accessed. Therefore changes **will** be caused by the examiner.

Special consideration should be given to Principle 2 of the guidelines, as conducting live forensics implies access to the original evidence. Any person doing this needs to be competent and fully aware of the impact their actions have and should be prepared to explain their reasons for taking this route.

2.1 Live forensics approach

By profiling the footprint of trusted forensic tools used to gather volatile data, the digital forensic examiner can understand the impact of using such tools and can explain any artefacts left by the tools.

In order to ensure that a consistent approach is used and the chance of errors is minimised, it is recommended to use a scripted approach using a number of basic and trusted tools. Regardless of the tools used, it is advisable to start with capturing the contents of RAM, the volatile memory.

If then other tools are used before the contents of the RAM are stored, it is very likely that running the forensic tool will overwrite parts of the RAM.

Other examples of information, which might be available in the dump of the RAM contents, can be retrieved using different tools:

- listings of running processes;
- logged on and registered users;
- network information including listening, open and closing network ports;
- APR (Address Resolution Protocol) cache;
- Registry information.

The tools used to capture this volatile information are generally run from removable media like a USB stick, DVD or CD-ROM or a floppy disk. A USB stick is generally most convenient, as the output of the tools can be written back to the stick. Writing tool output to the original drive should be avoided whenever possible, as this changes the contents of the hard drive and can destroy potential evidence. Again, Principle 2 does allow the investigator to do this, but a conscious decision will have to be made and the process written down.

When inserting USB devices, the examiner must ensure that they know the details of the serial numbers of the devices they are connecting so that they can be eliminated when analysing the data captured.

When in doubt as to whether or not to use live forensics, it is not always possible to know upfront which approach will yield the best results. Whichever method is chosen, remember to take meticulous notes—as dictated by Principle 3.

2.2 Summary of steps

A summary of the steps to be taken is shown below. Documentation of all actions, together with reasoning, should also apply when following such steps.

- **STEP 1:** perform a risk assessment of the situation. Is it evidentially required and safe to perform volatile data capture?
- **STEP 2:** if so, install volatile data capture device to a removable data carrier (e.g. a USB stick). Preferably, this has already been done prior to starting the operation.
- **STEP 3:** plug the data carrier into the machine and start the data collection script.

- **STEP 4:** once complete, stop the device (particularly important for USB devices, which if removed before proper shutdown can lose information).
- **STEP 5:** remove the device.
- **STEP 6:** verify the data output on a separate forensic investigation machine (not the suspect system).
- **STEP 7:** immediately follow the standard power-off procedure.

The capture and analysis of volatile data no doubt presents the investigator with technical challenges. However, as cases become more complex and connectivity between devices and public networks proliferate, with an increase in more advanced malware, which cannot always be retrieved using more traditional disk forensics, the above recommendations will need to be considered.

Cyber Crime Investigator's Guide to Crimes Involving Websites, Forums and Blogs

1. Crime involving websites

Where a crime involves evidence displayed on a website the most convenient methods of recovering the evidence may be by engaging the assistance of suitable trained staff to visit the website and take copies of the evidential content. In order to do this the officer taking the report of the matter needs to obtain the address of the website, for example, http://www.npcc.police.uk, or if it is a specific page within the website, http://www/npcc.police.uk/About/AboutNPCC.aspx.

When carrying out any evidence recovery it is essential that an audit trail of all activity carried out by the investigator is recorded in a log. The recommended method for copying a website is to visit the site and record the relevant pages using video capture software so that there is a visible representation of how they look when visited at the time. If video capture software is not available, then the pages can be saved as screenshots. It is advisable to follow this by capturing the webpages themselves either by using website copying software or saving the individual pages. Copying the pages themselves, as well as obtaining a visual record, means that the code from the webpages is also secured should that become relevant later.

This work should be conducted from a computer which has been specifically set up to be non-attributable on the internet. Failure to use an appropriate system may lead to the compromise of other police operations. Anyone visiting a website generally exposes a certain amount of information to the website, for example it is common on police systems to have a web browser which is branded with the force's name. This branding is exposed to a website being visited and so may be recorded in logs on the site along with other information amongst which will be the pages visited.

Appendix 4: Guide to Crimes Involving Websites Etc

If it appears likely that the evidence on the website might be lost by a delay in carrying out the above procedures, then the person reporting may be asked to make a copy of the evidence by whatever means they are capable of (either printing, screenshot or saving pages), alternatively this could be done by the person receiving the report. Before taking these steps, every effort should be made to secure the services of a competent person to carry out this work as failing to capture the information correctly could have a detrimental impact on the investigation.

Where there is difficulty in capturing the evidence by visiting the site, it might be possible to make an official request to the owner of the site by whatever legal procedures are required within the jurisdiction. The Communications Service Providers/Internet Service Providers Single Point of Contact (CSP/ISP SPOC) or Digital Forensic Unit (DFU) can usually advise on the appropriate procedures.

By making a request to the service provider hosting the site, it may be possible to recover evidence of who has created the webpage or posting. It is not unusual for details of the user, such as name, address, phone number, banking details, email address and alternative email address, to be recorded by a host.

If there is a requirement to identify who has committed some activity on a website, for example where a fraud has been committed by purchasing goods from a website or by posting a message on a website, the likelihood is that the suspect may be traceable from the logs on the site. When any user accesses the internet they are allocated a unique address known as an IP address and their ISP keeps logs of the times and dates and the identity of the user allocated any IP address.

When a user visits a site and conducts some activity, for example logs on, posts a message or makes a purchase, it is likely that the user's IP address has been logged by the website. It is often possible to obtain copies of logs from websites if there is a requirement to see who has been active on a website by making a request via the CSP/ISP SPOC.

If the evidence is no longer available to be retrieved by any of the above means, and where the use of resources can be justified by the seriousness of the case, it may be possible to recover evidence of the site contents from an end-user device that has been used to view the site by conducting a forensic examination of the device.

Where investigators wish to carry out open-source intelligence research on the internet, they should be trained to do so and conduct the research from a computer which cannot be attributed to the investigator's agency.

2. Covert interaction on the internet

In circumstances where investigators wish to communicate covertly with an online suspect, they **must** use the services of a nationally accredited and registered Covert Internet Investigator (CII). CIIs have received specialist training which addresses the technical and legal issues relating to undercover operations on the internet.

3. Crimes involving email communication

There are generally two methods of sending and receiving email, one by using a web browser and accessing email online, for example at the Hotmail, Windows Live, Yahoo or Google websites. In these circumstances, the mail is stored on the webmail server and is read through the user's browser. The other method is to access email using a program such as Outlook or Windows Mail to download mail to the user's computer. The program is used to view and store the emails locally.

Where the evidence in a case involves an email sent from a person who the police want to trace, the key evidence is usually found in what is known as the email's 'Full Internet Header'. Each email sent over the internet contains this header which is normally not visible to the user. It contains details of the route taken across the internet by the email and includes the IP address of the sender. Even where an email has been sent with a fictitious email address which has been registered with false details, it is often possible to identify the sender from the Full Internet Header.

In order to obtain the Full Internet Header the person taking the incident report needs to ascertain which of the two methods the recipient uses to access their email. Where it is a web-based identity, the name of the webmail host is needed (i.e. Hotmail, Yahoo, etc) or if by a program on the computer ascertain what program and version number of the program. The version number can usually be found in the program's Help on the menu bar under an item called 'About'.

Each webmail provider and email program treat the Full Internet Header differently and if the officer or user does not know how to display the header, the details of the webmail provider or program need to be passed to a specialist in the DFU or CSP/ISP SPOC who will be able to provide advice.

Once the header has been exposed, the relevant email should be printed together with the header, and may also be saved electronically. Depending upon the seriousness of the case and the volume of email evidence, advice may be sought from the DFU on the most appropriate method of securing and retaining the email evidence.

Once the header has been obtained, the force CSP/ISP SPOC will be able to use this to conduct enquiries to attempt to identify the sender from the originating IP address.

Where an email address of a suspect is known but there is no email available from which a full header can be obtained, it may be possible to identify the user of the email address and their location. Depending on the email service provider, various details of the user may be recorded together with the first registration IP address and a varying period of IP address login history. These details may be obtained by making an appropriate CSP/ISP SPOC request for the email address. In conducting such enquiries, it needs to be recognised that it is a trivial exercise to send an email with a false email address in the 'Form:' field of an email.

On some occasions, the investigating agency might access a user's email account with a written authority from the user in order to secure evidence. Where this is the case, if third party material is exposed as a consequence of viewing the user's emails, advice should be sought as to whether a Directed Surveillance Authority should be in place in addition to the user's authority. Even if the password and login details are available. For example, as a result of the forensic examination authority a formal authority is required to access the email account.

Where justified by the investigation, consideration may be given to accessing messages on an email provider's server by obtaining the appropriate Regulation of Investigatory Powers Act (RIPA) authority.

4. Crimes involving internet chat

Users can employ a number of different devices to engage in chat on the internet. There are three main ways to chat—using a website's chat facility, for example Facebook, using an instant messenger program like Windows Live Messenger or, much less commonly, using Internet Relay Chat (IRC).

Where an incident is reported which involves the use of chat, the person taking the report needs to ascertain what method of chat was being used, i.e. what is the name of the website hosting the chat and its full internet address, or what program is being used. The key evidence to be secured is:

• any information which may identify the suspect party; and

• the content of any chat.

If the chat is web-based, the details of the website, any chat room name and the user name of the suspect should be obtained together with the times and dates of any chat activity. If the chat facility is part of a social networking site, the user will most likely have a unique ID number as well as a user name. This is usually visible in the web browser's address bar when viewing a user's profile or when the mouse pointer is moved over the user name. The force CSP/ISP SPOC or DFU can provide help in finding this ID number. If the chat is by instant messenger program, then the user name of the suspect should be obtained together with the associated email address which is usually available from the contact list of the person reporting. Generally, a user's contact list can be accessed from any computer connected to the internet so if it is considered that the user's computer might be retained for a forensic then it should not itself be used to access the contact list.

There is usually an option for a user to save chat logs but more often than not the default setting is for logs not to be saved. If the user has saved chat logs that contain evidence, the logs should be saved to removable media for production as evidence; if no removable media is available they should be printed out. Users are able to engage in chat from many types of device in addition to computers. Where the circumstances of the case warrant it, an end-user device could be submitted for forensic examination in order to recover evidence of the suspect's contact details and chat content. Where a suspect's user details are obtained it may be possible to identify the suspect by making the appropriate CSP/ISP SPOC requests.

In the event that the chat has been conducted using IRC, the following details should be obtained:

• the IRC program used;
• the name of the IRC server;
• the channel; and
• any usernames.

Further advice should then be sought from the DFU.

5. Communications in the course of a transmission

Digital evidence in transit may be any form of communication using the internet or a telecommunications network such as email, chat, voice calls, text messages and voicemail. Where such evidence is sought, advice should be obtained from the force Covert Authorities Bureau.

Interview Guidelines for Suspects Involved in Computer-Related Crime

SECTION 1: Basic information about the computer and its use

- **What sort of computer do you own?** (Make, model, specification—what processor, size of hard drive, how much memory)
- **How long have you had it? Have you had it from new?**
- **When did you buy it, where from, how much did you pay?**
- **What operating system is on it?** (Ask what version, e.g. Windows 95, 98, ME, 2000, XP (Home or Pro), Vista (Home Basic, Home Premium, Business, Ultimate), Linux (many versions), Mac OS (system 1–7, OS 8, 9, X))
- **What software is on it?**
- **What software do you use regularly?**
- **Who installed that software?**
- **Where did you get the software from?** (Purchased at shop, borrowed from friend, copied at work, downloaded and purchased online, downloaded and cracked)
- **Who has access to the computer?** (Co-occupants and visitors to the address. If anyone, plenty of detail, e.g. names, times, dates, purpose, etc)
- **Do these people have different user accounts?**
- **How are these accounts accessed, usernames, passwords, who set this up?**
- **If usernames, do the users stick to their own usernames or do they log on using others' details.**
- **If the suspect has more than one computer, are your computers connected together in any way?** (Direct cable, networked)
- **Who set up the connectivity?**
- **Do you use a wireless router?**
- **If so, who set it up?**
- **How is the security configured?** (WEP, WPA)
- **What is the login name and password for the router setup?**
- **Have you configured the router in any particular way?** (Site blocking, firewall rules, special ports, DMZ, remote access)

SECTION 2: Data storage

- **If you save some files or data on your computer, where do you store it?** (Hard drive of the computer (may be more than one), what folders (e.g. My Documents, My Pictures, My Downloads), how do you organise what you save in folders, what folder names)
- **Do you use a USB drive (aka thumb drive, flash drive, memory stick)?** (If yes, is it password protected –details, do you run any programs from the USB drive—details and why)
- **Do you use any other external media?** (Floppy disks, CD, zip disks, jazz drive, external hard drive, Compact Flash, Smartmedia, USB drive, Microdrive)
- **If stored on CD, what software do you use to copy files on to CDs?** (A process often known as burning CDs)
- **Do you store any files remotely on the internet or some other remote computer?**

SECTION 3: Other devices connected to your computers

- **Do you have any hardware attached to or used with the computer?** (Printer, scanner, webcam, digital camera, video editing equipment)
- **Who set up each item?**
- **What do you use each item for and frequency?**
- **Where do you normally store data recorded by any of this equipment?** (CD, floppy, hard drive, remotely)
- **If stored on the hard drive, in what directories or folders do you store the files and what file names do you use?**

SECTION 4: Connecting to the internet

- **Do you have internet access?**
- **What do you use the internet for?**
- **How often do you use it?**
- **How do you get connected to the internet?** (Dial-up access via modem, cable/broadband, TV access, satellite, mobile, access at work or via work, direct dial up)
- **Who is the provider?** (AOL, BT Internet, Tiscali, Virgin, etc, may use more than one)
- **Do you pay for this and if so how?** (Free, direct debit, credit card, one-off payment)
- **What are your user names for logging on to the internet?**
- **What are your passwords?** (Consider asking for written consent for Hi-Tech Crime Unit to examine any online email accounts by logging on and using the user name and password)

Appendix 5: Interview Guidelines for Suspects

SECTION 5: Email

- **Do you have email accounts, if so what addresses?** (In the format somesortofname@company.domain, e.g. billysmith@hotmail.com, john@roman.co.uk, i_ate_your_cat@msn.com)
- **What software do you use to read your email?** (If web-based email, a web browser likely to be used: e.g. Internet Explorer or Firefox, otherwise Outlook, Outlook Express, Windows Mail, Eudora, Pegasus, Forte Agent, AOL, etc)
- **Does anyone else use the computer for email?** (If yes, full details of person(s) and answers to above questions)

SECTION 6: Online chat

- **Do you use the internet for chat or instant messaging?**
- **What software do you use?** (May be web-based so again using a browser, or specific software or instant messenger client, e.g. MSN Messenger, ICQ, MIRC, etc)
- **What chat rooms do you use?** (You will need to know who provides the service and the name of the chat room, MSN might be the service provider and the chat room might be 'teen pop idols', or they might use a particular chat server like DALnet, irc.dal.net, and join a channel like #fragglerock)
- **Do you engage in private chat, if so how do you arrange this?** (May be using contacts or buddy list and they will be notified when the contact is online, or may meet in public group and then go private or create their own group)
- **What is your passport or username and password for your instant messaging?** (Not uncommon for people to have several passports)
- **If using an instant messenger, what is your display name and personal message** (Do you change these, how often, why, what changes have you made)
- **What nicknames do you use in chat?**
- **Have you ever used a webcam whilst chatting?** (If yes, explain details)
- **Have you exchanged files with other people whilst chatting?** (Explain how this works, what happens when someone sends a file, do you get the option to reject the file, where do you store the files)

SECTION 7: Browsing the internet/surfing the web

- **What software do you use to web browse?** (Microsoft Internet Explorer and Mozilla Firefox are the main two but there are many others)
- **What sites do you visit regularly?**

- **How do you find or choose sites to look at?** (Search engines, junk mail ads, recommendations from chat, computer magazines, newspapers, porn mags)
- **Which search engines do you use?** (Lots! Google, Yahoo, MSN, AOL, Ask)
- **Do you save favourites?** (Links to sites that can be revisited at a later date)
- **If so, how are these organised?** (Some people do not organise and have one long list, others will break them down into numerous sub-categories)
- **Do you save copies of your favourites or have a copy accessible online?**
- **Do you use any toolbar add-ins or search tool assistants with your browser?** (A lot of search engines have toolbars, e.g. Google, MSN, Yahoo)
- **Does your browser have a pop-up blocker, or have you installed a pop-up blocker?**
- **Have you created any websites?** (Where is it hosted, what is the URL, is it paid or free, what is the content, how long has it been up, what software was used to create the site, what software was used to upload the site to the web server)
- **Passwords and usernames?** (For any sites that require user logon, or for any websites that will require username and password to upload files to a website)

SECTION 8: Downloading files

- **Do you save or download files or images from websites?**
- **Explain how do you do this?** (Step by step and where are the files stored)
- **Have you accessed any password-protected websites for downloading files?** (Details)
- **Do you use newsgroups?**
- **What for and which ones?** (There are tens of thousands with all manner of interests. The names can be explicit, like alt.binaries.underage.sex, or more subtle, like alt.fan.prettyboy, they can be used for discussion of topics of interest or for sharing images and other files and are a major source of indecent images)
- **How do you access the newsgroups?** (Can be by using a web browser, if so what site is used (free or paid for?). Alternatively, using which software—Outlook Express, Forte Free Agent, NewBinPro)
- **Do you use file-sharing programs, if so which ones?** (Morpheus, Kazaa, Bearshare, Grokster, Mirc File Server, these enable people to search for and share all manner of files, a major source of indecent images)
- **Passwords and usernames?**
- **What files have you downloaded using such file-sharing software?**

Appendix 5: Interview Guidelines for Suspects

- **What files have you made available on your computer for others to share?** (What folders are shared)
- **Have you used any remote control or remote access software to enable you to control and access your computer from another location?** (Using Windows Terminal Services, Remote Assistance or Remote Desktop, or software like Laplink or PC Anywhere, VNC, or web-based service like GoToMyPc or LogMeIn)

SECTION 9: Computer security

(Be aware that previously it was common to have stand-alone software applications to deal separately with various aspects of computer security—anti-virus, firewall, spyware checker, but now they often come in a 'security centre' package)

- **Is there an anti-virus program installed on the computer?** (If yes, when was it installed? What program is it?)
- **Is it always active, does it do scheduled scans, on-access scans and mail scans?**
- **Do you keep the virus identity files updated, if so how often?** (New viruses are created every day so the anti-virus software must have its files updated frequently to ensure that it can identify new viruses. Most software will do this automatically)
- **Have you had a virus on your computer?**
- **Details, when, what was it, how dealt with?**
- **Do you have any firewalls installed, either hardware or software?** (Intended to prevent hacking into your computer from the internet and stop malicious software on your computer providing open access to others via the internet)
- **Details, hardware make and model, software name and version, when installed?** (Zonealarm, McAfee, Norton, XP has built in firewall if switched on by user)
- **Do you have a malware or spyware checker?** (Windows Defender, SpyBot, Ad-Aware)
- **Do you use any software to wipe delete files or shred files?** (BCWipe, PGP and others can delete files and then write over the space they occupied so that the deleted files are unrecoverable)
- **Why do you use this software?**
- **Do you defrag your hard drive?**
- **If yes, what is the purpose of doing this?** (Another method of limiting the likelihood of recovering deleted files)
- **Do you use any form of encryption?**
- **If yes, what software do you use?** (BestCrypt, TrueCrypt, PGP, Private Folders, etc)

- **Why do you use encryption?**
- **What passwords, are they stored somewhere?** (May be written on paper or stored on a floppy or other media)
- **Do you use any software or methods to cover your tracks when using the internet?** (Lots on the market: Evidence Eliminator, Window Washer, System Cleaner, Window Cleaner)
- **If so, explain what they are and why you do it.**

SECTION 10: Standard excuses

- **The images were sent to me unsolicited:**
  Who sent them?
  When were they sent?
  How often has this happened?
  What did you do about it?
  Did you complain to the person who sent them, the ISP, the police, anyone else?
  What did you do to get rid of the images?
- **It is part of a research project:**
  How long have you been undertaking the project?
  What is the purpose of the project?
  Is it funded and if so by whom?
  Who else knows about it?
  What have you written up about it so far?
- **I was gathering information to report to the police:**
  Why?
  How long have you been gathering the information?
  Who have you told about it?
  Have you reported any of this to the police or other agency?

Presentation of Evidence for Documents and Exhibits in Forensic Computing

The following national police guidance derives from the *Good Practice Guide for Managers of e-Crime Investigation* published by 7Safe.

1. Introduction

Forensic computing requires a high standard of documentation and exhibit handling. The examiner is involved in a specialised and responsible field which requires considerable knowledge and impartiality. The following guidelines discuss the writing of notes, statements and reports together with the production of exhibits in forensic computing cases. They are incomplete but are part of a wider attempt at producing a national standard.

2. Notes

2.1 Audience and purpose

Notes are made for different reasons and for different people to read. The following are examples.

2.1.1 *Notes are made for the examiner themselves*

Notes are made to record the examiner's own actions in such a way that they can review and recall them. This may be useful when writing statements or reports, for refreshing memory when giving evidence and when talking to other interested parties about the technical details of the case.

2.1.2 *Notes are made for colleagues*

Notes are made to record the examiner's actions so that colleagues can review them. They might do this to establish details of an examination they did not undertake when answering questions from other experts or lawyers. Managers may be required to examine notes in a supervisory capacity. Another examiner may be required to continue an examination in the absence of the original examiner.

2.1.3 *Notes are made for independent experts*

Notes are made to record the examiner's actions so that a defence expert can review them. Reasons for doing this include: the recreation of steps in the examination in accordance with ACPO guidelines; to understand why the examiner reached certain conclusions; to identify errors that they may have made and to establish what they did or omitted to do during the examination or to assist in supporting their evidence.

2.2 Structure of notes

Notes should be kept on an individual case or examination basis. Each case or examination should have its own set of notes. Notes relating to a particular case should not be spread over a number of different notebooks containing notes relating to other cases.

Each page should contain the case name and reference number and the name of the person making the notes together with the dated signature of the person making them.

Each note should include the date and time that it was made.

Notes may be kept electronically. There are significant advantages to this in terms of readability and the ease with which diagrams, tables and pictures can be pasted into the notes. Electronic notes should be printed and signed after each logical break.

2.3 Dos and don'ts for making notes

Do ...

- refer to the existence of notes in any associated witness statement or report;
- disclose the existence of the notes as unused material rather than produce them as an exhibit;
- make notes at the time or immediately after any examination or part of an examination;
- include reasons for any conclusions reached, exhibits produced, damage noted, examiner's intentions and reasons for actions;
- include relevant photographs (e.g. of examined equipment);
- make notes sufficiently legible for all likely parties to read and understand;

- include a high level of technical and procedural detail;
- include tables, diagrams, screenshots and appendices.

Don't …

- use acronyms or abbreviations that others will not understand.

3. Witness statements

3.1 Audience and purpose

Witness statements are made for different reasons and for different people to read. The following are examples.

3.1.1 *Statements are made for the court*

A witness statement provides the basis for the original evidence that an examiner may give to a court. Under certain circumstances, all or part of the statement may be read to the court in the absence of the examiner themselves.

3.1.2 *Statements are made for lawyers, barristers and advocates*

A witness statement provides sufficient information for prosecution (e.g. CPS prosecutors) and defence lawyers to understand the nature and context of an examiner's findings in order to establish how they will assist with case strategy and the legal points to prove. The statement must therefore be readable for a non-technical person. It allows advocates on both sides to formulate a strategy for arguing the case and for the examiner's examination or cross-examination.

3.1.3 *Statements are made for the investigating officers*

A witness statement provides sufficient information about an examiner's findings to assist with the investigation. It may be used to determine case strategy or tactics and may be extensively referred to during case conferences, meetings and interviews with suspects or witnesses.

3.1.4 *Statements are made for independent experts*

A witness statement provides independent experts working for the prosecution or defence with a summary of the examiner's technical findings.

3.1.5 *Statements are made for the examiner themselves and their colleagues*

A witness statement provides the examiner with a summary of their evidence for fast future recall and for colleagues to answer simple questions in the absence of the examiner.

3.2 Structure of witness statements

Witness statements for forensic examiners should be written with a consistent layout. The following headings as subheadings are suggested.

Introduction

Examiner

- The examiner should introduce themselves, their rank and position.
- They should include a personal profile or personal portfolio of their qualifications/skills/experience and include this either in the statement or as an appendix at the author's preference.

Instructions

- When and who submitted the examination request and what work was requested; e.g. 'On [date], PC [name] submitted a request for examination ...'

Continuity

- The continuity of property on arrival should be dealt with; e.g. 'On [date], the following items were delivered by PC [name] to ...'. If necessary, statements from other people may be required to prove this.

Compliance

- A statement of compliance with ACPO guidelines indicates if mistakes have been made, together with reasons and implications. Reference to existence of examiner's notes.

Item 1

- *Method*: a short summary of what was done with what tools, e.g. 'imaged using ...'.
- *Results*: what items were found—include tables, diagrams, etc.
- *Technical explanations*: technical details of matters raised by results; e.g. explanation of newsgroups. Refer to glossary if appropriate.
- *Context and discussion*: the context of the findings and technical points in relation to what was being asked of the examiner. A discussion of any points which may have multiple explanations.

Item 2

- *Method*: as above continuing for each item or group of items submitted. Try to use logical groups. Examples might be to group all hard disks in one computer in a section or to group a box of floppy disks in one section.
- *Summary*: a summary of the findings. Many readers will jump straight to this point in a long statement.
- *Conclusions*: not always required, but in some cases the examiner may need to draw conclusions. These should always be strongly reinforced by factual argument in the main body of the statement and may cause the court to attribute expert status on the examiner.

Appendices

- Personal profile/portfolio if not in main body of statement; include experience and qualifications.
- List of exhibits; include the ID reference, description, reference of exhibit they originated from.
- Selected glossary.
- References.

3.3 Dos and don'ts for making statements

Do ...

- use appropriate headings and sub-headings;
- number each heading and sub-heading using a decimal system;
- keep technical explanations simple;
- include appendices where appropriate: these should be included in the statement page count;
- include a personal profile/portfolio;
- include a glossary of specified terms that you understand;
- provide a summary of findings and any conclusions at the end of the statement;
- include references to the sources of any external information used (e.g. manuals, online technical factsheets);
- give clear explanations of where and why evidence or data has been extracted or altered for presentation purposes (e.g. pictures reduced to thumbnails).

Don't ...

- include anything in the statement or glossary that is not understood sufficiently to explain under cross-examination;

- use abbreviations or initials without using the term in full on its first occurrence. For example, 'I found in RAM (Random Access Memory), the following ...'.
- refer to pictures as 'images' as this causes confusion with forensic images. Use 'pictures' or 'photographs' instead.

4. Expert reports

4.1 Audience and purpose

In general terms, an expert report is likely to contain a higher level of detail than a witness statement. It should be considered as a response to another expert's report dealing with technical matters raised by that expert. Courts usually expect to see reports from expert witnesses.

Reports, therefore, share similar audiences to statements but are less likely to be as easily understood. Similarly, in most cases, reports share the same purposes as statements but reports made for other experts have a slightly different focus.

4.1.1 *Reports are made for independent experts*

Reports are written for independent experts to read and understand the technical details of an examination. They may be written because the technical detail is so central to an examination that it needs to be explained in a highly complex fashion. They may be written in response to a technical report by an independent expert either agreeing with or opposing the views in that report.

4.2 Structure of reports

In general, reports should follow the same structure as witness statements. Reports in civil cases must conform to the Civil Procedure Rules 1988.

4.3 Dos and don'ts for making reports

Do ...

- attach a report to a short witness statement as an appendix or even an exhibit;
- put a sufficient level of technical detail in the report to argue or establish any facts that are in dispute;
- agree with other experts where appropriate.

Don't …

- produce reports unnecessarily; in many cases a witness statement will suffice;
- assume that just because a report is produced as an exhibit the jury will see it. They won't.

5. Exhibits

5.1 Audience and purpose

Exhibits are real evidence. This is different to original evidence which comes from the testimony of witnesses. Examples of real evidence in computer cases are the computers themselves, print-outs of files present on computer media, tables of file attributes—file names, dates and times. Exhibits should be produced and referenced in a statement or report. The primary reason for producing exhibits is for the court but they additionally serve a useful purpose for other parties.

5.1.1 *Exhibits are produced for the court*

An exhibit is the real evidence that will be considered by the court. For example, in a Crown Court the jury may be allowed to examine printed file listings. Exhibits such as diagrams made by the examiner, which by their nature reflect the work of the examiner, may be shown to the court if it is considered that they act as useful tools for the jury. It is, however, vital to understand that the real evidence is just that alone and cannot contain comments or additions representing the explanations by or opinion of the examiner or anyone else. These explanations will have to come from oral evidence. Items containing such amendments should not be shown to a jury.

5.1.2 *Exhibits are useful for lawyers, barristers and advocates*

Exhibits are useful both to assist lawyers in understanding the evidence and to assist advocates in understanding and explaining facts to the court.

5.1.3 *Exhibits are useful for the investigating officers*

Exhibits may assist the investigating officers both to understand important technical points and to assist them during an interview.

5.2 Exhibit references

Exhibit references serve the purpose of uniquely referencing an item (exhibit) referred to in a statement.

There are numerous local methods of referencing exhibits. In general, complex systems should be avoided in preference to simply understood references together with a table of exhibits added as an appendix to a statement or report (see **3.2** above). In this way an interested party can quickly see what an exhibit is, and where it came from.

5.3 Dos and don'ts for exhibits

Do ...

- reference the exhibit in brackets after it is mentioned in a statement or report. For example, 'I made an image (ABC/1) of the first hard drive present in the computer ...';
- remember what is being exhibited. Is it data or hardware;
- produce tables of file attributes for all computer files referred to or produced as an exhibit.

Don't ...

- use over complex exhibit references;
- add comments or explanations to exhibits;
- make unnecessary copies of unlawful images.

Bibliography

Akhgar, B, Bosco, F and Staniforth, A, *Cyber Crime and Cyber Terrorism Investigator's Handbook* (London: Elsevier, 2014).

Ashour, O, 'Online De-Radicalization? Countering Violent Extremist Narratives: Message, Messenger and Media Strategy' (2010) 4(6) Perspectives on Terrorism 15–20.

Awan, I and Blakemore, B, *Policing Cyber Hate, Cyber Threats and Cyber Terrorism* (Farnham: Ashgate, 2012).

Awan, I and Blakemore, B, *Extremism, Counter-Terrorism and Policing* (Farnham: Ashgate, 2013).

Bakker, E, *Jihadi Terrorists in Europe, their Characteristics and the Circumstances in which they Joined the Jihad: An Exploratory Study* (The Hague: Netherlands Institute of International Relations, 2006).

Brown, SD, *Combating International Crime: The Longer Arm of the Law* (Abingdon: Routledge-Cavendish, 2008).

Chen, H, Chung, W, Qin, J, Reid, E, Sageman, M and Weimann, G, 'Uncovering the Dark Web: A Case Study of Jihad on the Web' (2008) 59(8) Journal of the American Society for Information Science and Technology 1347–1359.

Chen, H, Thoms, S and Fu, T, *Cyber Extremism in Web 2.0: An Exploratory Study of International Jihadist Groups.* Conference on Intelligence and Security Informatics (ISI) (Taipei: IEEE, 2008), pp 98–103.

Christmann, K, 'Preventing Religious Radicalisation and Violent Extremism: A Systematic Review of the Research Evidence', Youth Justice Board for England and Wales (2012).

Coll, S and Glasser, SB, 'Terrorists Turn to the Web as Base of Operations', *Washington Post*, 7 August 2005.

Cook, T and Tattersall, A, *Blackstone's Senior Investigating Officer's Handbook* 3rd edn (Oxford: Oxford University Press, 2014).

Cook, T, Hibbitt, S and Hill, M, *Blackstone's Crime Investigator's Handbook* (Oxford: Oxford University Press, 2013).

Gercke, M, *Understanding Cybercrime: A Guide for Developing Countries* (Geneva: International Telecommunication Union, 2011).

Gerstenfeld, PB, Grant, DR and Chiang, C, 'Hate Online: A Content Analysis of Extremist Internet Sites' (2003) 3(1) Analysis of Social Issues and Public Policy 29–44.

Livingstone, S and Bober, M, 'Regulating the Internet at Home: Contrasting the Perspectives of Children and Parents' in

Bibliography

D Buckingham and R Willett (eds), *Digital Generations: Children, Young People and New Media* (Mahwah, NJ: Lawrence Erlbaum, 2004), pp 93–113.

Jugendschutz.net, 'Right-Wing Extremism Online—Targeting Teenagers with Stylish Websites' (2009), available at http://www.jugendschutz.net/fileadmin/download/pdf/report_cyberhate_2008.pdf.

Masferrer, A and Walker, C, *Counter-Terrorism, Human Rights and the Rule of Law* (Cheltenham: Edward Elgar Publishing, 2013).

McCauley, C and Moskalenko, S, 'Mechanisms of Political Radicalization: Pathways Toward Terrorism' (2008) 20(3) Terrorism and Political Violence 415–433.

Qin, J, Zhoub, Y, Reidc, E, Lai, G and Chenc, H, 'Analyzing Terror Campaigns on the Internet: Technical Sophistication, Content Richness, and Web Interactivity' (2007) 65 International Journal of Human-Computer Studies 1–84.

Reid, E, Qin, J, Zhou, Y, Lai, G, Sageman, M, Weimann, G and Chen, H, 'Collecting and Analyzing the Presence of Terrorists on the Web: A Case Study of Jihad Websites' (2005) 3495 Intelligence and Security Informatics 402–411.

Reiner, R, *The Politics of the Police* 4th edn (Oxford: Oxford University Press, 2010).

Sageman, M, *Leaderless Jihad: Terror Networks in the Twenty-First Century* (Philadelphia: University of Pennsylvania Press, 2008).

Schmid, AP, *The Routledge Handbook of Terrorism Research* (Abingdon: Routledge, 2011).

Silke, A, *Terrorists, Victims and Society—Psychological Perspectives on Terrorism and its Consequences* (Chichester: Wiley, 2006).

Stelfox, P, *Criminal Investigation: An Introduction to Principles and Practice* (Cullompton: Willan Publishing, 2009).

Tabatabaei, F, Akhgar, B, Nasserzadeh, SMR and Yates, S, 'Semulating Online Customer Satisfaction using Fuzzy Cognitive Mapping' (2012) Information Technology: New Generations (ITNG) 540–547.

Tabatabayi, R, Nasserzadeh, SMR, Yates, S, Akhgar, B, Lockely, E and Fortune, D, 'From Local to Global: Community-Based Policing and National Security' in B Akhgar and S Yates, *Strategic Intelligence Management: National Security Imperatives and Information and Communications Technologies* (London: Elsevier, 2013), pp 85–92.

Thompson, R, 'Radicalization and the Use of Social Media' (2011) 4(4) Journal of Strategic Security 167–190.

Walker, C, *Blackstone's Guide to the Anti-Terrorism Legislation* 2nd edn (Oxford: Oxford University Press, 2011).

Wall, DS, *Cybercrime: The Transformation of Crime in the Information Age* (Cambridge: Polity Press, 2007).

Wojcieszak, ME, 'Computer-Mediated False Consensus: Radical Online Groups, Social Networks and News Media' (2011) 14 Mass Communication and Society 527–546.

Yang, CC, Liu, N and Sageman, M, 'Analyzing the Terrorist Social Networks with Visualization Tools' (2006) 3975 Intelligence and Security Informatics 331–342.

Bibliography

Index

Index

Index

Index

Index

Index

Index

Index